THE ANA B'KOACH

ANA, B'KOACH, GEDULAT, YEMINKA, TATIR, TSERURA, KABEL, RINAT, AMKHA, SAGVEINU, TAHAREINU, NORA, NA, GIBOR, DORSHEI, YEHUDKA, KEVAVAT, SHAMREM, BARKHEM, TAHAREM, RAHMEI, TZIDKATKHA, TAMID, GAMLEM, HASIN, KADOSH, BEROV, TUVKHA, NAHEL, ADETEKHA, YAHID, GE'EH, L'AMKHA, P'NEI, ZOKREI, KEDUSHATEKHA, SHAVETEINU, KABEL, U'SHMA, TZAK'ATEINU, YODE'A TA'ALUMOT

Written in ancient Aramaic, the Ana B'Koach is one of the most powerful prayers in existence. It may be used to protect the user and his or her loved ones, to sustain them in time of need, to heal them in illness and to comfort them in grief. Ancient legend states that the Ana B'Koach was created before the world was born at a time when chaos did not yet exist.

ISBN # 0-9708190-0-5
Dr. Mitchell Gibson
2600 East Southern
Suite C-2
Tempe, Az 85282

Table of Contents

About the Author 3

Overview 4

A Very Special Person 6

Medical School 12

What is PSI? 17

The Biology of PSI 21

Astrology: A Basic Course 27

New Advances in Astrology 35

The Astrological Signs of General Psychic Ability 41

Psychic Healers 67

The Astrological Markers of Mystical Ability 101

Mediumship 117

Time, Space and the Paranormal 138

A General Theory of Astrology and the Paranormal 163

Applications 166

Calculating Modern Astrology Charts 189

Bibliography and Resources 198

Index 219

ABOUT THE AUTHOR

Dr. Mitchell E. Gibson is one of the most well known and highly respected medical doctors in the state of Arizona. He has been the mental health consultant for the largest television station (NBC-Affiliate KPNX-TV12 Phoenix) for the past eight years. Dr. Gibson has also been consulted by every major television, radio, and newspaper service in Arizona for his expertise in the fields of mental health and human behavior. He has also spoken at a number of regional and national professional conventions. He is a diplomat of the American Boardof Psychiatry and Neurology, The American College of Forensic Medicine, and the American Board of Forensic Examiners. Dr. Gibson is a former Chief of Staff at the East Valley Camelback Hospital and he was Chief Resident in Psychiatry at the Albert Einstein Medical Center in Philadelphia. He has also served as Chairman of the Joint Chiefs of Staff Services Committee for the Camelback Hospital System. Dr. Gibson is a graduate of the University of North Carolina at Chapel Hill School of Medicine.

Dr. Gibson has been named to the "Top Doctors" list in Phoenix Magazine three times and twice to the Woodward and White "Best Doctors listing. Dr. Gibson was named to the position of "Honorary Chairman" for the state of Arizona by the National Republican Health-Care Reform Committee for his work on health-care reform. In addition to his expertise in medicine, Gibson is a research member of the American Federation of Astrologers and a contributing author for American Astrology magazine and Today's Astrologer. He recently received the Dr. F. Sims Pounds Jr. Award for "Best Lecturer" in Astrology at the 2000 International Astrological Convention in Las Vegas. The award was presented by the American Federation of Astrologers. He is the author of the groundbreaking book ***"Signs of Mental Illness"*** which is now in its second printing. Dr. Gibson is currently completing the first software package based on his work in astrology that will be entitled ***Signs: The Spiritual Sky.*** In addition to his other accomplishments, Dr. Gibson is an accomplished contemporary artist and has shown works in New York, Los Angeles, Paris, Philadelphia, Scottsdale, San Francisco, and numerous other cities around the globe. He recently received the Jury Prize for Creativity in the competition at the Museum of Fine Art in Paris, and his art work is published in the ***Encyclopedia of Living Artists and New Art International.***

Dr. Gibson has consulted for feature articles for Upscale, Ebony, Essence, the Arizona Republic, Phoenix Gazette, Arizona Informant, Arizona Business Journal, The Mountain Astrologer, The Astrological Reporter, American Astrologer, and a number of other business and trade journals. He was also the host of a regional weekly radio program entitled "The Male Perspective" on KFNX 1100AM Phoenix.

OVERVIEW

My name is Dr. Mitchell Gibson and I am a board-certified psychiatrist and professional astrologer. I recently (Sept./98) published a book with Llewellyn Publications entitled ***"Signs of Mental Illness".*** The book details my research that examines the question; Can the occurrence of mental illness be predicted using astrological birth data? The research indicated that there are indeed readily identifiable astrological markers which may be used to predict the occurrence of a major mental illness.

"Signs of Mental Illness" is now in its second printing since its October release. The reviews of the book have been exceptional and it has been called ground-breaking (Horoscope 3/99) and a quantum leap in the sciences of astrology and medicine (American Astrology 1/99). **Signs II: An Astrological Study of Psychic and Spiritual Ability,** is the second installment in a six book series that I am in the process of completing. Signs II explores an original technique which I have pioneered that allows anyone to accurately predict the presence of psychic or spiritual potential in the natal chart of any individual. By applying the ground-breaking techniques which I discovered in ***"Signs of Mental Illness,"*** I have unveiled a system that allows me to utilize never before seen astrological markers which great psychic or spiritual potential. This system can be applied to individual natal charts as well as the chart of any date which one might wish to study. The second installment of ***Signs*** is based on research which I completed over a two year period which compared the natal charts of 130 famous psychic and spiritual leaders with those of a group of normal (non-psychic) people.

This remarkable research shows that individuals gifted with enhanced paranormal abilities may be identified on the basis of their birth data alone! Citing dozens of famous cases such as Edgar Cayce, Nostradamus, Rasputin, Padre Pio, Joan of Arc, Sai Baba, Olga Worrall, and a host of other gifted human beings, Signs *II* repeatedly and convincingly demonstrates that not all birthdays are created equal. If as person happens to be born in a place and time which possesses high latent spiritual potential, then that person is much more likely to develop and manifest high spiritual potential. My research also shows that natal charts that depict a heightened level of spiritual capacity are also more likely to be associated with spontaneous paranormal phenomena than charts with low spiritual ability! Interest in the paranormal and astrology is at an all-time high.

Hollywood has recently added to this fascination by releasing a spate of movies that are based on the occult and paranormal themes. "The Sixth Sense", a supernatural thriller about a young boy who sees ghosts, was the number one movie on screens across America for more than five weeks. Its run at the number one spot was ended by yet another movie concerning the supernatural, "Stigmata," which chronicled the life of a woman who displayed the mystical markings associated with the crucifixion of Christ. With the advent of the millennium rapidly approaching, the public's fascination with all things metaphysical is likely to rise exponentially!

I believe that the synthesis of astrology and the paranormal which is embodied in ***"Signs"*** is a winning combination. A book written by a medical doctor who is also an astrologer which seeks to answer the question, How psychic am I? is likely to be a phenomenon. The techniques that I describe in Signs II also enable the reader to predict future events related to their own lives.

Astrology is one of the oldest sciences known to mankind. Every major newspaper carries an astrology section and millions of people follow their horoscopes on a daily basis. Research has shown that more people know their sun sign than know their own blood type. Today, presidents of countries, Fortune 500 executives, movie stars, health professionals, and millions of individuals from many walks of life regularly consult astrologers in order to gain greater insight into their lives.

The "Signs Project" represents a critical next step in the ongoing alternative health and science revolution. All too often, the merit of an alternative treatment or diagnostic technique rests heavily on anecdotal data or simply word of mouth. A research tool which accurately identifies the paranormal potential of an event or person would be an enormous benefit in identifying healers, psychics, saints, mediums, and future spiritual events that could ostensibly provide tremendous advancement to our understanding of this most mysterious aspect of reality.

Dr. Mitchell E. Gibson MD PC

A VERY SPECIAL PERSON

During the first week of August 1994, I met a very special person. One of my very best friends had asked me to visit him in his new home in Poona, India. He had moved there some six years earlier after retiring and he loved the country in a way that he could not easily explain. I had met Paul Tesla in New Jersey in 1988 after he had given a seminar on forensic palmistry. He had created a system that allowed him to read aptitudes, vocational and marriage patterns, psychological profiles and physical characteristics from the palm of an individual's hand. In 1972, a mathematical psychologist by the name of Dr. Tapas Sen conducted a double blind test in which he evaluated the method that Paul used in his work. Paul's methods were found to be more than 97% accurate in reading dated events from the hands of carefully selected test subjects. Paul Tesla was indeed a very unusual man.

Paul attended Julliard and had studied classical music. He chose to support himself however by working as a palm reader. His services had been utilized by police and detective agencies all over the United States on some of the most high profile crimes of the last 25 years. In using his own special admixture of astrology and palmistry, Paul could take the birthdate and fingerprints of a suspect and accurately map out exceedingly intricate details of his lifestyle, psychological profile, and probable whereabouts. He had helped to solve an impressive number of cases before retiring to India. He had worked almost exclusively with the Barstow Florida Police Department for several years as a special consultant.

During one of his frequent visits to the southern region of India, Paul contracted a severe case of bacterial meningitis. He was hospitalized for several weeks and received intravenous antibiotics and fluids that should have subdued the infection. The therapy did not work and his condition continued to worsen. One night, his temperature spiked to 106 degrees and after running a series of desperate tests, his doctors discovered that he had developed a brain abscess. They decided that he required aggressive surgical treatment if he were going to live through the week. Paul's physical condition had deteriorated quite badly over the course of his two-week struggle with the infection and his doctors did not give him much hope of living through his operation. The surgery was scheduled for the following morning and Paul was left with the ominous prospect of surgery that might potentially save his life or kill him. He heard that there was a "holy woman" who made regular rounds in the hospital. She prayed for those patients who requested her services. Paul asked his nurses that the Lady be called in to pray for him. He waited for several anxious hours far into the night for her arrival and when he awoke, the early morning rays of the sun were beginning to trickle into his room. He noticed that he felt much better and that his headache and fever was gone! His nurses explained to him that as he slept, the Lady had come to pray for him and that she had laid her hands on his forehead for about ten minutes. To the amazement of his doctors, nurses, and support staff, all traces of his brain abscess and meningitis had disappeared! They had rarely seen a recovery even remotely similar to this, with the possible exception of those patients whom the Lady had prayed for. After running several more tests to check his condition, his doctors decided to let him go home that day. They did not understand how, but he had been completely cured. Paul was ecstatic and he could not wait to free him from the confines of the room that had been his world for the past three weeks. He also could not help but notice the curious current that ran through his body like a stream of living electricity. He felt stronger and more vigorous than he had in years. He could only embrace one thought as he gathered himself in preparation for his return home, he desperately to meet the Lady who had so generously brought this miraculous blessing to him.

Paul learned that she lived in an ashram located a few miles from the hospital. As soon as his discharge papers had been completed, he hailed one of the many rickshaw taxis that roamed the streets nearby. When he finally arrived at the ashram, he announced to two of the disciples met him at the main entrance that he had come to speak with the Lady who had healed him at the hospital. The disciples smiled knowingly and ushered him quietly into the main prayer room. That was Paul's first waking meeting with the Lady. He has lived at her ashram ever since.

The Lady, better known as Sri Matajhi Indira Devi, was born to a very wealthy family in Southern India. Beautiful, cultured, and well-educated, she quickly became one of the most desirable women in India. She married a handsome and successful executive who was later to become India's ambassador to England. Their marriage was happy and she raised three healthy children in a life of luxury and comfort. Then the visions started. Terrifyingly beautiful in their intricacy and intensity, these mystical excursions would last for hours. Indira initially tried to explain away her experiences as the product of fatigue or as flights of fancy. Her family however noticed that after these "excursions" she would become radiant with an almost supernaturally brilliant light that surrounded her and the room. She also began to speak of a being, "Mirabei" who would appear to her during these visions and dictate exquisitely beautiful songs about God and the mystical world. Her husband sought the counsel of a variety of physicians who could find no physical explanation for the experiences and invariably they would prescribe sedatives, dietary changes, and massage therapy for what they diagnosed as exhaustion. However, Indira was not exhausted by her experiences in fact, she was elated and invigorated.

On October 8, 1946, she was to preside over an annual social gathering at a college. That night, a local holy man was scheduled to attend as a guest of honor. Indira said to him upon their first meeting, "I am in darkness and I need guidance." Sri Dilip Kumar Roy answered and said in reply, "I am a seeker, I have not reached the goal. I am myself a disciple of Sri Aurobindo and the Mother. How can I guide you?" Indira then replied with a statement that was to change her life forever. "If I am half as sincere as you are, I cannot go wrong; and as for realization, will it be blasphemy if I say that I have a secret conviction that even God is not static but is leaping from one perfection to another? We shall grow together. You by leaps and bounds floating from peak to peak, and I trudging behind." Shortly after this meeting three years later in February 1949, Indira gave up her servants and her luxurious wealth and moved into the ashram. Her family predicted that she would last perhaps a few weeks without her servants and chefs. She has lived there for 49 years.

I met "The Lady" on August 2, 1994 in Poona. She sat in a room surrounded by scientists, community leaders, spiritual seekers, doctors, businessmen, and scores of townspeople. She looked to be approximately seventy years old but her energy and presence may have masked a much older spirit. She sat in the lotus position resplendent upon a mass of gold and turquoise colored pillows. Her dress consisted of a simple blue and white sarong tied at the waist and neck. She was surrounded by three handmaidens, all in their early twenties, who waited upon her every move and gesture. The room contained a curious admixture Christian and Hindu religious artifacts. Paul later explained to me that Indira respected the teachings of Jesus and all of the world's great religious leaders. He also explained that most of the statues and crosses had materialized in place out of nowhere. He had witnessed this phenomenon on several occasions. I later learned that this was not an uncommon miracle in this part of the world.

Indira sat quietly as a steady stream of aspirants passed before her, knelt down, and asked for her blessing. Paul, who had agreed to act as my tour guide and interpreter, further explained that this time was very special because Indira, who was known by her disciples affectionately as "Ma", had set aside only one hour per day to share this blessing time or "darshan" with the crowd. This day was doubly special he added because Ma had entered into "Samadhi" while she was performing darshan. "Samadhi", Paul explained, was a very rare spiritual state that Ma entered which allowed her to see and commune with God and yet maintain contact with others. I sensed a very palpable feeling that pervaded the room which was not easily described. I had never felt it before except perhaps for a few fleeting minutes in some of my deeper meditations. The feeling was one of strong reverence, humility, love, beauty, and majesty all combined into the presence of a single person. When Ma was in Samadhi, no one stood. I too felt an overwhelming urge to kneel with the throng and pray. I prayed before her in that room for almost two hours. During this prayer, I felt more peace and tranquility than I had felt at any time in my life. Ma promised that I could have a brief private audience with her before my visit was completed. She knew that I had traveled all the way from the US to see her and she said that she had a special gift for me.

On Thursday August 5, I met with Ma in her study. She told me many things about my life that she said I would need to know and gave me some profound guidance about my future. Everything that she said would happen in my future happened in exactly the way she described. She also said that I should write about our meeting one day and it would help me understand the full ramifications of what was about to transpire. She then instructed me to kneel before her and to close my eyes. I felt her grasp my forehead and the top of my head with both of her hands. I then heard he begin to pray softly. She began to sing a beautiful song which filled the room with the same energy and power that I had felt when she was performing darshan. Her touch was wonderful and loving and I assumed that she was offering me a blessing. Then suddenly, the energy in her hands shifted and I felt a powerful surge of extremely strong and potent energy begin to course through my brain. Initially, I felt a great stab of pain as the energy filled my skull but over the course of a few minutes it subsided and settled into a dull but steady throbbing sensation. The memory of the event is still very clear in my mind. The energy felt like a cross between a strong current of electricity and a warm stream of water. At first, the energy was confined to my skull but as time progressed, it traveled to my chest, torso, and lower body in succession. I felt light-headed but heavy at the same time. After about ten minutes, (I lost all track of time), Ma removed her hands and kissed my forehead. She said that I would need that "gift" later in life but it would take time for me to fully understand it. This was the single most moving experience of my life. Weeks later my system was still buzzing with this current.

Paul once told me that Ma had blessed a child who had been hit by a rickshaw in front of the ashram several years ago. The child had suffered multiple injuries from her accident including a fractured pelvis, a skull fracture, cracked ribs, a punctured lung, and a ruptured spleen. Her doctors brought her to Ma and left her. They fully expected that she Ma would see to it that she would be sent home to die quietly with her family. Ma placed her hands on the child's forehead and prayed. On the morning after she had been blessed the child awoke, got up, and ran outside to play. She had miraculously recovered from all her injuries! The doctors repeated her X-rays and found no evidence of any of her previous injuries. The child has been well since that time with no follow-up medical treatment. I had been wearing a silver cross at the time of my audience with Ma. When I returned to the states, I meditated and prayed everyday while I wore it. It was my most prized possession. A few months later, my office manager, told me that her sister had been diagnosed with terminal liver cancer and had been given a few months to live. The tumor had metastasized to her bones, lungs, and brain. The family had picked out her burial plot and everyone gathered to be with her during her final days. Sharon, office manager and right arm, was totally distraught with grief. I couldn't bear to see her suffer that way but I also knew that there was nothing that I could do considering the situation. Sharon made arrangements to take a leave of absence so that she could be with her family. One day before she left, she broke down in my office and started to cry. I too experienced her grief because she had told me a great deal about her relationship with her sister and about how difficult it would be for her to see her go through this hardship. Suddenly, I felt a strong urge to give her the cross. I had never parted with it since I left India but now, I wanted her to have it. I hoped that it would help to ease her suffering, if even for a while.

Sharon left for Kentucky the next day and she was gone for the better part of six months. I received a phone call one day and the receptionist said that it was Sharon. I assumed that she had called to tell me of her sister's passing and I readied myself to give my condolences. I was totally surprised when I picked up the line and I heard Sharon laughing and in good spirits. The story she told me shocked me to the core. Her sister was alive and well and was planning to go back to work the following month! Furthermore, her doctors could find no trace of the cancer, which only a few months before had caused her family to plan her funeral and last rites. Sharon explained that soon after she had arrived back home, she saw her sister and was overwhelmed by the amount of weight that she had lost. She then gave her sister the cross that I had given to her. She felt that her sister needed the cross more than she did. Within two weeks, her sister's energy began to return and her hair began to grow. Two months later, she had regained almost all the weight she had lost during her struggles with chemotherapy and radiation treatments. During this time, she wore the cross constantly. Sharon wanted to thank me for giving her the cross and she felt that it had saved her sister's life. I quickly told her that I had nothing to do with the power of the cross and that whatever miracle she felt that it had performed upon her sister was solely attributable to Sri Matajhi Indira Devi. Sharon did not care who the power had come from. She was merely thankful that her sister was alive and well and healthier than she had seen her in years. The cross is now hanging on her sister's wall. She calls it her key to a new lease on life.

I don't profess to understand how any of the events that I have described up to this point may be explained. Indeed, Paul's healing, the recovery of the child, and the miraculous delivery of my office manager's sister from the clutches of terminal cancer are all events that are clearly beyond the power of conventional medical science. It may be that part of the energy that Ma poured into me was absorbed by my cross and later absorbed by Sharon's sister. This may have subsequently resulted in a remission of her cancerous tumors. However, medical science does not recognize such occurrences as legitimate proof of curative treatment. Was this energy transferred to me so that I could then act as a living messenger for the treatment and cure of this woman via the cross? I am the last person in the world who would ever profess to be a saint or holy person. My medical school and residency exploits alone during my nights on call would dispel any such thoughts in a reasonable person. Since this episode, I have grappled with this and numerous other such events repeatedly in attempt to make sense of the phenomenon. After much deliberation, I readily admit that I cannot force rational thinking or wisdom upon this phenomenon. I do know that these events have profoundly influenced how I practice medicine and they have changed how I view the world. I now believe in the existence of psychic and spiritual abilities and in their effect upon the human spirit.

Psychic and spiritual abilities have been part of the human experience since the beginning of recorded history. Sri Matajhi Indira Devi and Paul Gabriel Tesla represent two examples of the extraordinary heights to which human psychic and spiritual abilities may be developed. In Paul's case, the abilities, which he displays probably, spring from his exceptional psychic development and in Ma's case the abilities are definitely attributable to the energy manifestations of a very highly evolved spirit. In writing this second installment of the "Signs" series, I asked myself two questions: Is it possible to foresee the development of an individual's psychic and spiritual potential from birth? If one can foresee the development of such abilities, then is it also possible to foretell which form these abilities are likely to take? To date, no one has attempted to look at this question from an astrological perspective. Quite simply, I wanted to know if I could look at a person's birth chart and quickly make an accurate assessment of their inherent psychic and spiritual abilities. Also, I wanted to know if I could calculate with reasonable accuracy the latent psychic and spiritual potential any particular date might hold. After completing the research, I feel that I have accomplished this task and much more.

In this book, the reader will find data on some of the greatest spiritual giants of all time. Edgar Cayce, Nostradamus, Sai Baba, Olga Worrall, Gerard Croiset, P.B. Randolph, Cagliostro, Arigo, and Eileen Garrett are only a few of the more than 120 assorted psychics, spiritual healers, mediums, and mystics that I have included in my database. To my amazement, I discovered that not only were there repetitive astrological configurations, which are closely correlated with the birth dates of those born with exceptional paranormal ability, but the dates upon which extraordinary events take place also tend to have these same rare configurations! Upon finishing this book, the reader will be able to ascertain with accuracy their respective latent psychic and spiritual abilities as denoted by the presence or absence of specific astrological signs. It is with great pleasure that I present "Signs: An Astrological Study of Psychic and Spiritual Abilities".

Dr. Mitchell E. Gibson
Phoenix, Arizona

*MEDICAL SCHOOL**

The University of North Carolina is one of the most prestigious medical schools in the United States. I began my medical education there in the summer of 1981. Without really realizing it, I had also initiated what was to become the most important educational and emotional journey of my life. I soon became acquainted with the deep and insidious indoctrination techniques that all new doctors endure before they are allowed to take the sacred oaths that allow entrance into the halls of medical antiquity. The journey is made easier by making friends and I was fortunate enough to make several friends quickly. Dusec James was probably the most unforgettable of all my new acquaintances. Dusec had come to America from Nigeria after earning a full soccer scholarship to Notre Dame. He worked two part time jobs while also taking a heavy pre-med curriculum at Notre Dame in order to help bring the remainder of his family to the United States. Dusec graduated at the top of his class in the premedical program at Notre Dame University. He was a tall, ruggedly built black man who had an easy smile and a great laugh. He also loved playing practical jokes and quite often, the victim didn't know that they had been had until long after Dusec had slipped away to some secluded corner and waited for the punch line to fall.

Once, he called me at home early on a Sunday morning and told me that he had come by to see if I wanted to go running with him. He didn't see my car in the lot so he assumed that I wasn't home. To my knowledge my car should have been in the parking lot where I left it. I dashed outside as soon as possible and ran to the spot where I had left my car. My heartbeat quickened, my face became pale and ashen, and my throat instantly became parched. My car was gone! Who would steal a 1968 Plymouth Satellite?....insurance was not going to give me enough to replace it......all of my Micro-biology notes were in there.....Jeanne's phone number (that hot babe that I had met at Fevers last nite) was on the dash.....and worst of all....now I had to take the bus to school! I must have looked around the neighborhood for over two hours before I finally gave up and sat down to call the police. Just then, there was a knock at my door and when I answered it there was Dusec standing in the hall grinning.

"Looking for something Mitch?" "Dusec, somebody stole my car!"; I shouted, I was closer to tears than I was willing to admit. "Really?" he replied calmly, still grinning. "Just what is so funny?" I snapped. "I just thought you might want to see how clean I got that dirty engine of yours. Took me two hours at the 7-11." Before I could smack the hell out of him he ran off for his Pinto which was parked and waiting downstairs.

The engine was still running. I was so mad that I could have strangled him if I could have caught him. He avoided me in class for a week after that. From time to time he would rub it in and shout over the din of the cafeteria noise, "Hey Mitch, need a ride home?"

He thought that it was very funny but then, that was Dusec.

During our first year at Carolina, Dusec was elected president of the freshman class. He knew everybody and his sense of humor got him elected as much as his standing in the class. He was also one of the top students in the school. Unfortunately, Dusec was to teach me one of the most painful lessons of my medical career.

Dr. Richard Dunheim was the chairman of the Biochemistry Department at Carolina. He had been tenured for more than 20 years and his tests were legendary for their ridiculous ambiguity. If you didn't pass Biochemistry, moving on to the second year was next to impossible. Dunheim knew that and he took great pains to torture and ridicule potentially weak students at every turn. The worst "sin" a first year student could commit against this "Professor" was to question him openly on one of his numerous ambiguous and esoteric questions. Dunheim was a 5'8", 250 pound 65 year old German immigrant who had survived the rigors of Dachau. He always wore short sleeved shirts so that everyone could see that he still bore the infamous numbers that had been burned into his flesh. The man needed some serious counseling but he preferred to nurture a nasty temperament and a constant menacing smirk that he wore even while lecturing. Where did they find these people? I sweated his final exam more than any of the others that year. It was challenging, abstruse, and it bore little if any resemblance to the lecture material he had inflicted upon us. Thank God for the old tests! Dusec did well on all of the tests as usual but he took exception to one of the questions on Dunheim's final. I asked him to drop it and come to the finals party on Franklin Street that the First years gave at the end of each term. He insisted on having the last word on that one question. He had always thought that Dunheim was an asshole and what he really wanted was to give him a piece of his mind; especially now that he had passed his class and was safely on his way to the second year. The event that transpired after that still outrages me to this day.

Dusec went to Dunheim's office and found him reading a biochemistry journal. He asked if he could speak to him about the final and Dunheim nodded yes and ushered him in. Dusec then explained his concerns about the final and expressed his confusion about a certain question. Dunheim blew a fuse and a shouting match quickly ensued. He asked security to escort Dusec out of the building and accused him of being disrespectful and belligerent. Dusec left without creating an incident. One week later, Dusec was asked to appear in front of the academic board and explain his actions. He knew that he had passed all of his classes, we had all received our grades and he had finished near the top of the class. Dunheim expressed concern that Dusec's actions were indicative of an unstable temperament and that the board should recommend he repeat the first year. Dusec was not allowed to defend himself and he was given a failing grade for the entire first year. Even his appeal was denied and he was forced to repeat the first year. Dunheim made sure that Dusec never passed first year biochemistry and after repeating the first year twice, Dusec was forced to drop out of Carolina.

I have never fully recovered from the rage and humiliation we went through in trying to get Dusec reinstated. Some of Carolina's medical school professors had been on the faculty since the time when the school's official policy was not to admit blacks and minorities. Some of these professors still took great pride in ridiculing and degrading black students. Half of all black students who started medical school in my class never finished. Dusec was one of them. He gradually became more and more bitter after this incident and his famous smile faded into memory. As I continued my medical education, we slowly lost touch with each other as we now moved in different circles. A few years ago I heard that he was a computer salesman at CompUSA in Raleigh. Dusec would have been a good doctor today if he had not broken the first rule of medicine: Never openly challenge the prevailing medical establishment! I promised myself then that I would never allow my thinking to be shaped by minds as narrow and myopic and Dunheim's. Little did I know that the road to completing the medical education is lined with such minds. I still miss my friend. Perhaps most of all, I miss the wonderful spirit that had created a man capable of such a wonderful smile.

During my third year I completed a number of clinical rotations in all of the basic medical specialties. Initially, I wanted to become a neurosurgeon. M.A.S.H. reruns had done quite a number on my head and the idea of becoming a rich and famous surgeon appealed to me. I quickly learned during my first rotation on neurosurgery that Alan Alda would never make it as a surgeon and that television doctors are the stuff of fantasy. I learned two valuable lessons that would stay with me for the rest of my life while I studied surgery.

The first of these lessons was perhaps the most painful and enlightening. One cold December morning during my vascular surgery rotation, I was asked to help the nurses bring a patient into the clinic who was having trouble getting out of her car. Mrs. Hattie Pearl Davis, (not her real name), was a beautiful 64 year old black lady who suffered from severe diabetes mellitus. Mrs. Davis was 5'2" and weighed approximately 280 pounds. Her presence and warmth made you want to sit at her feet and let her read you a bedtime story. She wore a flowing aquamarine pastel colored sun dress with a large wide-brimmed sun hat adorning her head. She looked as though she were on her way to a Sunday morning church service at Bethel Baptist. The patients that came to the outpatient clinic at Carolina were largely indigent and they viewed the services that the doctors performed for them with reverence and respect. In their minds, the doctors and the students were on the same societal level as a judge or a priest. Whatever a doctor said and did was sacrosanct and many of the patients wore their Sunday best to the appointments. Unfortunately, Mrs. Davis had a habit of not taking her insulin on a regular basis and as a result, she had developed serious microcirculatory problems in her lower extremities. Her legs were swollen and filled with fluid and she was being evaluated for surgery to alleviate the problem. Walking was a major chore for her and five nurses and two medical students, myself included, were required to lift her out of the car. I wondered how she ever got in there in the first place.

Dr. Fred Carlson was the vascular-surgeon who had been assigned to her case. Dr. Carlson was one of the old guard at Carolina. He had been there since the 1968 when minorities were not allowed. He was particularly bitter about the schools decision to admit blacks and rumor had it that he had been active in the KKK in his younger days. He looked a great deal like an aging Clark Gable and he knew it, though age had caused his back to stoop slightly and had taken the handsome portions of his hair. His surgical practice was immense and his primary residence was a 275 acre palatial estate. Carlson was outspoken, arrogant, and exceptionally brilliant.

Mrs. Davis waited in the examination room while the surgical team made its way through the menagerie of boils, wounds, infections, and assorted post-surgical amputations that were the mainstay of a vascular surgeon's life. Dr. Carlson loved this stuff but already I was beginning to have second thoughts about cutting on people for a living. When we finally got to Mrs. Davis' room she sat up on the examination table and beamed a bright happy grin at the team. I took one look at her leg and I knew that the smile was purely for our benefit. The swelling and varicosities that marred her legs had to create excruciating pain. I hoped that we could help her.

Dr. Carlson talked with her for a few minutes and took a brief history. He had already read the chart and I had presented the case to him in the hall before we entered the room. He knelt down, examining her right leg first and then the left. Mrs. Davis was quiet during the inspection. Dr. Carlson stood up, looked her in the eye and told her that he would have to remove both of her legs. He then turned and walked out of the room; no explanation, no sympathy, not even a simple discussion of the alternatives to surgical amputation! Since she was my patient, I wanted to know how and why he had come to that conclusion.

"Mrs. Davis seems very frightened Dr. Carlson. Would physical therapy and weight reduction help in this case?" Dr. Carlson stopped and turned around while examining the next chart.

"Mitch, it would be too much trouble to get that lady to lose weight and physical therapy would be a waste of time."

"But couldn't we try it and if it doesn't work then we could do surgery?"

Carlson looked at me with a wide unblinking stare as though he were trying to divine the depths of my soul and I wondered if I had broken the first axiom that Dusec had taught me. He kept his stare for a full minute and the whole team stood petrified in anticipation at what he would say next. Then he smiled, took one step toward me, and said in one smooth unbroken sentence:

"Mitch, we don't think like that here and you are going to assist me in the operation." Then he walked away without even looking at me.

I had seldom disliked a person as much as I did Dr. Carlson at that moment. Telling Mrs. Davis that we would have to remove her legs and then helping Dr. Carlson perform the surgery was the hardest thing that I ever did in medical school. That beautiful lady would never walk again only because one person wanted to make a buck. I realized that Carlson (I couldn't bring myself to call him Doctor after that) had financed his palatial estate through thousands of surgeries just like hers. That was when I learned the second lesson. Modern medicine is a business and doctors are the gatekeepers. Mrs. Davis' surgery would help to line not only Carlson's pockets but also those of the drug company that provided her pain medicines and anti-inflammatory pills, the wheel-chair company, the nurses, the surgical teams, surgical equipment companies, the internists, and the psychiatrist who would eventually have to help her with the pain of losing her legs. I saw this scenario replayed a thousand times while I completed my medical training and each time was no more palatable than the last. I vowed to myself that I would one day try to find a healthier, less mercenary way to relate to the people who came to me for care. I knew that to a certain extent that the system was what it was and that one person could only do so much. But if I did not at least try, I felt that I was in danger of losing whatever soul I had left in exchange for a palatial estate in Kannapolis. The medicine that I hoped to create was as much for my soul as for those of my patients.

I asked the nurses if I could push Mrs. Davis out to the van that was to take her home. We had to arrange for a driver to take her car back home. As we made our way to the entrance of the hospital where the van awaited, I had to let her know how I truly felt about what had happened to her.

"Mrs. Davis, I am sorry we had to operate on you. I didn't want to do this. I thought there was another way." I felt partly like a coward and partly like the guy that buries the corpses in trenches after a massacre. Helpless didn't begin to fathom the depth of the emotion.

"I know child. You just a baby trying to learn this work. Dr. Carlson is a good man and he did what he thought was best. The Lord did his work through him. I be just fine, but you pray for me you hear."

I looked at her and gave her a big hug. I didn't want her to see how upset I really was but I couldn't help myself. I knew that what had happened to her was totally unnecessary but it had happened anyway; and she had accepted it with grace and a smile. She had even managed to find the space within herself with all of her own pain and loss to feel sympathy for me! I was totally humbled by her spirit. For a little while, as I stood there hugging her and fighting back the emotions that threatened to overwhelm me, I forgot Carlson, medical school, and all of my selfish ego-driven pain. Since that moment, I have prayed for all of my patients after I have begun treating them. I still wonder what happened to Mrs. Davis and if she ever got the hang of getting around in that chair.

Mrs. Davis taught me something very valuable that morning. She showed me that the soul of a person is much more important than anything we could remove from their body. Her spirit was never touched by our cutting. She also reminded me that I still had a soul and that if I wanted to keep it, I should think long and hard about the type of doctor that I wanted to become. After completing my vascular surgery rotation, I gave up the idea of becoming a surgeon and I began to look for another specialty.

---

* The names, circumstances and exact identities of the parties involved in the above vignettes have been changed to protect their privacy.

WHAT IS PSI?

Psychic and spiritual abilities have been part of the human experience since the beginning of recorded history. Mankind has long sought to understand this ***enigmatic and esoteric aspects of human nature.*** In a September 21, 1993 Time magazine article, the following statement appeared: "The past few years have been an age of miracles. Unimaginable events have succeeded one another as if the Creator had whistled up a new world".....

The last ten years have indeed brought upon the world an onslaught of incredible and inexplicable experiences which have continued to defy the laws of science and nature. While traditional scientists rush in to quickly debunk and deride these signs of a new world, the masses of humanity continue to report them at an alarming pace. Psychic and spiritual experiences seem to be increasing and even Hollywood has been affected by the public's growing hunger for all things spiritual. Dozens of movies and television shows have been devoted to angels, ghosts, witches, near-death experiences and a host of other related phenomena. What then is the focus of this extraordinary ion of the population, in our highly rational society accept the reality of psychic and spiritual (psi) phenomena, as opposed to rejecting it?

In the mid-1970's, Dr. John Palmer mailed out a 46 item questionnaire to 300 university students and 700 adult residents of Charlottesville, Virginia, and asked respondents about the frequency and characteristics of their psychic experiences. Responses were obtained from about half the resident population, and 90% of the students. In general, it was clear that there were two distinct groups; people either tended to report no psi experiences or else many of them. Overall, more than half of the respondents claimed to have had at least one ESP experience, either in the waking state or through dreams. Psi experiences were more frequently reported from people who recorded and analyzed their own dreams. Insofar as Charlottesville is fairly representative of the American population (as asserted by marketing survey groups), it seems safe to say that spontaneous psi experiences would be claimed by about half the adult U.S. population.[1] In Europe, a similar survey was undertaken about the same time by Dr. Erlendur Haraldsson and his associates. This was a national survey based on a survey quite similar to Palmer's, and involving over 1100 randomly selected people in Iceland. Around 80% of the people responded to the questionnaire, and psychic experiences were reported by 64% of the respondents- suggesting that two out of three people in Iceland believe to have had at least one such experience. As in Palmer's study, higher percentages were reported by people who studied their own dream life. In addition, it was found that experiences were reported somewhat more frequently by women than men (70% vs. 50%).[2]

A final survey worth noting deal with a particular population: scientists. In the early 70's, a skeptic conducted a survey to determine what the scientific community thought of parapsychology and it's subject matter- psi. His subject population was readers of the New Scientist, an interdisciplinary science magazine whose readership consists mostly of working scientists and technologists. The results based on an impressive 1500 responses were quite unexpected: 88% of the respondents thought that parapsychology is a legitimate scientific discipline, and a full 67% considered the existence of ESP either a "likely possibility" or an "established fact".[3]

Businessmen are beginning to appreciate the potential utility of psi; given the increasingly chaotic and unpredictable scene of ever-changing markets, even a little precognition or clairvoyance could make a big difference. In their study of CEO's of large corporations, Dean and Mihalasky found that a third of them believed firmly in psi; according to the survey, the basis of their was constant- and successful- use of intuition or ESP in their business decisions. The researchers also ran CEO's through actual precognition tests. CEO's who had a record of doubling their company's earnings over a period of five years had by far the highest psi scores. In fact, almost everyone who had substantially improved their company's earnings had positive test results. The researchers concluded that psi testing of executive decision-makers or problem solvers might help companies select individuals who are likely to have the best intuitions.[4] Perhaps our best and most successful companies are run by psychics who are unaware of the full scope of their potential!

These surveys suggest that psi is a phenomenon that is experienced by one-half to two-thirds of the general population and is perhaps accepted by scientists and businessmen as a valid and useful discipline. Granted, there are many skeptical people among the general and scientific populations, these surveys point to an inescapable reality: the phenomenon of psi is real and it is accepted by millions ofpeople all over the world. If we then examine psi phenomena further, we discover that not only is it real, but it's practitioners perform a host of vital functions in our society.

Ontario Hydro, the world's third largest water company, disclosed that they regularly employ dowsers in conjunction with their engineering techniques. Dowsing is a psychic technique utilized in locating, (among other things), underground water, minerals, and metals. Often huge problems arise from uncharted cables and pipelines, as during the construction of the Pickering nuclear plant in Ontario, when Catepillar operators were almost electrocuted by striking 4,000 volt power lines which they were unable to locate precisely. After delays entailing considerable costs, the chief engineer at Hydro called in a dowser who traced out the cable path with a rod, enabling them to excavate it.[5]

The waterless city of Elsinore had been paying Los Angeles large sums to bring water from there. All the federal and state experts had concurred that there was simply no water in that sector. A well-known dowser named Verne Cameron who lived in the city, insisted that he had located an aquifer under the dried-up lake bed.

After being refused a more ample supply of water, the city finally decided to test Cameron's claim, and struck one of the largest wells in Southern California, exactly where he had predicted.[6]

Henry Gross, one of America's best known dowsers, was at a reception in the state of Maine, when a dinner conversation about drought-stricken Bermuda led him to try to locate water there with his map. Three out of the four locations he proposed were revealed exact; wells were found in that area for the first time in over 300 years!

The use of psychics for detective work is one of the most widespread forms of psi applications. Gerard Croiset, the famous Dutch psychic, owes much of his reputation to the many cases in which he collaborated with police to locate missing persons. In France, Raymond Reant has been involved in a number of attempts to locate missing persons. In one case that he helped to solve successfully of a teenage runaway in Paris, Reant had followed the girls movements so closely with his psychic vision that after she was found she exclaimed that her father must have had her followed by a detective![7]

While camping with his wife in the countryside, Mr. Drummond, an elderly man, took off for a walk, and didn't return. Very worried, his wife asked the local sheriff for help. In all, three hundred persons volunteered to join the search, but after two weeks not the slightest trace had been found. Six months after the incident, Mrs. Drummond sought Kathlyn Rhea, a psychic famous for her police work. She recorded a 40 minute cassette of her impressions, which stated that Mr. Drummond had lost all sense of direction and had walked towards the East. She described a gravel road near a cabin in a grove of trees. Then, she continued, Mr. Drummond had suddenly had an attack and fallen down under one of the large thorn-bushes of that region. She claimed that the body was still there, and was surprisingly intact.

Mrs. Drummond brought the cassette to the sheriff, who decided to try to locate the place with the help of his deputy, before organizing a new search party. Indeed, Kathyln Rhea's descriptions were so accurate that they had no trouble finding the body. In the deputy's opinion Rhea's impressions had been almost completely correct.[8]

Arthur Young, inventor of the helicopter rotor, was trying to come to terms with helicopter accident which had killed both the pilot and co-pilot. Driven by guilt, he had searched in vain for some technical fault. Eventually, he brought a piece of the helicopter blade to the famous medium Eileen Garrett, who handled it while attempting a psychometric vision of the pilot himself, who at the time had been on the verge of a nervous breakdown. She added that he had just decided on some radical life changes, to go to a monastery. Young did not wish to interrogate the mourning family, but a year later he went to see the head of the agency which had hired the pilot. This man admitted that the pilot had indeed been on the verge of a nervous breakdown and was about to enter a monastery![9]

Clairvoyance is a psychic ability that allows the practitioner to view events, people, and objects through space and time. The modern term which is used to describe clairvoyance is remote viewing. Major Ed Dames, U.S. Army (Ret.), is the world's foremost instructor of remote viewing. As Operations and Training Officer for the military's psychic intelligence unit, Major Dames was intimately involved in the development and use of his remarkable gift which he used to help to support critical classified military operations. The successes his unit compiled were stunning. In one search problem that involved a U.S. helicopter that had gone down, for some reason, in a remote corner of Peru, a remote viewing squad was called to find the craft. A Pentagon satellite had picked up what seemed to be the copter's locator beacon, but the signal had died before anyone could triangulate in on it. Ken Bell, the remote viewer assigned to the case closed his eyes and followed his mind's eye to the location of the crash high in the Andes. He found the pilot, and the copilot, and then he began sobbing uncontrollably.

His commander soon understood what was happening. Bell was tightly wound at the best of times, but now under trance conditions, with many of the normal inhibitory mechanisms of consciousness inoperative, he had become explosively sensitive to emotions evoked by the target. The helicopter's pilot and copilot were not only dead; they were broken and roasted. The horror of the scene had risen up and washed over him like a wave. His commander had to stop the session. Bell was later to find out that his terrifying vision was completely accurate! [10]

In 1989, Dames founded PSI TECH, Incorporated, and began applying what were originally TOP SECRET techniques to the civilian sector. For $4500, trainees are required to come to Los Angeles for 10 consecutive days where they learn remote viewing. Most of his clients are businessmen and he has been very successful.

Thousands of books have been written about the powers and abilities of these individuals. Suffice it to say, their talents are indeed quite useful in the modern world. How then, can we use astrology to screen individuals for these abilities? In this book, I compared the birth charts of over 120 very talented psychics and spiritual leaders to a control group of people who have not demonstrated any appreciable psychic or spiritual talent above that of the normal population. To date, there have been no similar attempts made utilizing astrology to complete this type of research. I used the same modern astrology techniques which I summarized in my study of mental illness. The results I believe are remarkable and now for the first time, we may have a set of useful astrological markers which identify latent psi talent in the birth chart or within a particular transit period. I chose four major groupings of psi phenomena that will comprise the research base for this study: general psychic ability, mediumship, psychic healing, and mystical ability. In the following chapters, I will further define each of these abilities.

---

[1] Psi-Explorer: Exploring Spontaneous Psi, Surveys; p.1, Mario Vargolis Ph.D. UGM-IGK MULTIMEDIA PRODUCTIONS, 1996.

[2] Ibid.; p.2

[3] Ibid., p.2

[4] Dean, D., Mihalasky, J., Ostrander, S. & Schroeder,L. (1974). Executive ESP. Englewood Cliffs, NJ: Prentice Hall

[5] Psi Explorer; Dowsing: p.1

[6] Ibid.; Dowsing, p.1

[7] Ibid.; Psi Detectives.p.2

[8] Ibid.; Psi Detectives.p.2

[9] Ibid.; Psi Detectives.p.1

[10] Remote Viewers, Jim Schnabel ;p.40-41, Feb.1997, Dell.

THE BIOLOGY OF PSI

In the everyday world, the five senses reign, but their ability to perceive reality is sharply limited. We perceive only a tiny bit of the totality of the possibility of experience through our sight, hearing, smell, taste, and touch. Scientists however are beginning to believe that nature did not intend for mankind to enter into the realms of probability with such a limited armament of sensory tools. All over the world, from time immemorial, some people have been gifted with what is known as second sight, the third eye, and the sixth sense powers of the mind that seem to bypass the usual sensory channels and transcend mundane reality. Shamans have communed with their gods, saints have seen their visions, and oracles have foretold the death of kings. And from time to time, ordinary people have felt a moment's slippage into the inexplicable and the uncanny.[1]

The ability to see things far from the physical body would have been of great use to our hunter-gatherer ancestors. Hunters who found game by natural selection would have been more likely to breed. This would mean that any genetic material they carried that posited psychic material would have also been selected. Throughout our hunter-gatherer past, "psi genes" would have gradually increased as those carrying the genes would be more likely to survive. With the onset of agriculture, this selective pressure would have ceased to be so important. This would mean that highly developed cultures, such as our own , would have lost the psi genes while hunter gatherer cultures such as the aborigines of Australia or the Kalahari bushmen would still have psi abilities at large in the population. Only cultures that have not persecuted paranormal ability would have kept a high level of psi genes. Research has shown that there are primary and secondary psi genes. The secondary psi genes are those that facilitate biophysical integration within the organism and which code for richer and higher function neural networks to interface with the biophysical energy. Primary psi genes are those that give enhanced psychic capability by the specific nature of the proteins they code for which act as biophysical batteries and other more obscure phenomena that are involved with biophysical processing, storage, and utilization. The high basal stress levels of western man release a torrent of neurohormonal and electrical stimuli that appear to switch off the psi genes. Instead this overstimulation switches on the oncogenes that cancer.[2]

The Russians have been world experts on psychic phenomena since the 1950s. Research in this area has concentrated on military uses of biophysical field effects, telekinesis, and the search for psi genes. This had led to their uncovering of a vast body of knowledge regarding the biological basis of psi. It is well known that the physical body is surrounded by a mantle of electromagnetic energy. Our eyes pick up this photonic emission; though 90% of this information is filtered out in the thalamus. The remainder is fitted into a visual mental model that we see as reality.

Since our neurons are affected by electromagnetic fields, the EM [3]mantle around our bodies and anything that affects it, will affect brain function. The mechanism for this is that ELF (extremely low frequency) modulated microwaves can effect calcium efflux in the neurons, which affects short and long term potentiation of the neurons with a concomitant effect on memory.[4] Since the body has an intrinsic EM mantle, could this EM field be projected outside the body? Could information gathered by roving biophysical EM field effects be the basis for psi? These EM fields could be picking up information, then transferring it to the brain by the above mechanism. This theory seems rational and sound enough to perhaps explain the phenomenon; however, it is not the whole picture.

Highly trained psi operators can travel backward and forward in time, enter facilities protected by metal Faraday-like cages and US facilities armed with EM flytrap field generators. All of these phenomena indicate something not limited by Einstein's Special Relativity theory and Maxwell's EM field equations is acting as the carrier of psi. To understand what is really going on beyond the EM spectrum, we need to reexamine physics. In the early part of this century, Einstein formulated his General Theory of Relativity. It linked the curvature of space-time with gravity. In formulating the field equations to link curvature of space-time with gravity, Einstein found that the Energy-Momentum tensor (the sum total of mass-energy), did not equate to the Ricci tensor (a curvature function). To balance his equation, Einstein had to subtract the Ricci tensor R, a sort of one term summary of curvature, which varies from point to point. It would seem to indicate that reality is not singular but a duality. The Einstein tensor only balances when one subtracts the mathematical summation of the curvature of this other reality from the curvature of physical space. Does reality have a dual nature which Einstein alluded to in his pioneering work and which psi-operators tap into during their excursions? Is our knowledge of reality hampered by our blindness to this second reality? Italian astronomers Luigi Stella and Mario Vietri were the first to prove that space itself is indeed distorted around neutron stars. When one combines the revolutionary breakthrough in thought that Einstein presented to the world with his Relativity theory with the confirmation that space is indeed "flexible", the probability of the dual nature of reality takes on a whole new light. Astrology may be one way to predict and measure some of the temporal and subjective qualities of this parallel reality.

This parallel reality is often alluded to in dreams and psychic experiences and is at times glimpsed in daydreaming states. Australian aborigines have a whole body of knowledge about this parallel reality which they call "dreamtime". Dreamtime may not be electromagnetic in nature, but may be composed of a whole new set of field effects not ordinarily seen in our dimension. Most people in the modern world continue to report the vast majority of their psi experiences during the dream state as we have seen in numerous research studies. Do we glimpse this dreamtime during our sleep states and carry the memory forward to the present time as a psi experience? Does this perhaps explain why deep trance states are conducive to psi phenomena? Central to the psi experience is the phenomenon of being able to be aware of two places at one time. Physical perception and psi can be practiced at the same time. This means that during the psi experience, our brains and our biophysical field effects can be aware separately from one another. Dr. Gerald Edelman, a leading neurophysiologist, has formulated the theory of Neural Darwinism. This postulates that neurons compete with each other by natural selection, and in the process, neuronal group selection forms neural networks which have the capability of primary consciousness. As the process is repeated, successively higher levels of consciousness are developed which ultimately leads to sapience.[5] Thus, the brain can think independently without biophysical field effects, but these effects when modulated by neuronal potentiation events, can interact in a synergistic manner.

Biophysical field effects may mediate a form of Higher-Order Consciousness. It is known by morphogenetic developmental researchers that the human genome does not contain enough information to turn the blastocyst into an embryo. Morphogenetic field effects are needed to switch on specific gene groupings dependent on their position in the blastocyst. These biophysical morphogenetic fields switch on specific genes and turn off other genes all based on their location in space-time. In this way biophysical fields control gene expression! Like the neurons affected by neural Darwinism, morphogenetic fields could evolve through primary consciousness to High-Order Consciousness. If all living things are controlled by biophysical fields, could these fields then in turn communicate with each other and subsequently create even more complex High-Order fields? Could they continue to evolve and perhaps develop a form of Superior Intelligence that coordinates all life under its domain? If that indeed were to happen, tapping into the database of information contained within this Superior Intelligence would allow psi operators access to knowledge regarding all life forms, time, and space!

How then can this High-Order Consciousness be accessed directly? In other words, how can psi abilities be activated within the brain? Research and anecdotal subjective experiences have given us clues as to some of the processes that may trigger this phenomenon:

1. Traumatic experiences
2. Direct transmission
3. Spiritual training
4. Magnetic induction
5. Drugs/hallucinogens
6. Near death experiences
7. Lucid dream work
8. Deep hypnosis/trance work
9. Genetic inheritance
10. Astrological influences

Traumatic experiences have long been associated with the development of abilities. These experiences typically involve a blow to the head, gunshot wound, falls, life-threatening accidents or injuries, or catastrophic events that heighten the survival instinct to critical levels. War veterans have recounted stories for years about psi experiences during the heat of battle that have saved their lives. The novel "***Dream Baby***", by Bruce McAllister, is an ingenious examination of the CIA's experiments with combat-induced, extra-sensory perception in Vietnam.[6] The World Wars in Europe would have acted on any males in combat as a considerable selective pressure to choose for individuals carrying psi genes, as they would be more likely to survive. Traumatic injury is a dangerous and unreliable method by which to induce psi experiences. However, many of today's most talented psychics state that their abilities were turned on only after a traumatic shock.

Psi induction by direct transmission postulates that psychic and spiritual abilities may be directly "downloaded" into the biophysical field of one individual from that of another whose field contains specific information relative to those abilities. Spiritual masters and teachers are said to possess this ability and generally transmit certain portions of their power to their followers after a period of initiation. The Master Jesus was said to have transmitted the "power of the Spirit" via a method which Gnostic writers have called the paradosis. This technique involved a very special recitation of words and phrases combined with a specific touch that allowed an exchange of energy between the Master and the apostle. In this way, His energy was successively transmitted to each of the apostles who were in turn able to perform "miracles" immediately after the transfer. The prophet Mohammed was said to be able to imbue his faithful with a portion of the "Power" simply via a touch. One modern day Sufi Master whose ritual transmission of power to his followers has drawn much media attention is associated with the Tariqa Caznazaniyyah in Jordan. Following a two minute ritual which combines a touch with the recitation of a special series of prayers, the new disciple is said to become immediately invulnerable to physical injury. Documented scientific studies have shown that these new initiates, some of whom include children, are indeed able to withstand piercing injury with knives, swords, axes, poison, electrical shock, and a host of potentially fatal traumas.

The Master is also able to allow certain distinguished followers (caliphs) to act as batteries for His power. Legend states that the Archangel Gabriel carried this power from God himself to the original Master of the Order (Oman) who successively transmitted it to His followers. Is this an example of Superior Intelligence propagating itself in the manner that we posited earlier? History is replete with legends describing powerful masters who could bestow upon their faithful certain powers following acts of courage or allegiance. It would appear that the ancients may well have known something of High-Order biophysical effects which modern man is only now appreciating. Legend also states that there exists a Spiritual Directorate that controls the flow and dispersal of spiritual power in this world. This group of High Initiates has supposedly used this power to control and guide the evolution of mankind for centuries. From time to time, the members of this group will choose individuals from the population at large and transmit to them the power and authority to teach and disseminate the higher teachings. This process is examined in an intriguing book entitled ***"People of the Secret"*** by Ernest Scott.[7]

Spiritual training is perhaps the most popular and widespread method of triggering psi. A very large number of spiritual groups, covens, cults, and magical orders claim to have special training techniques that develop latent psi talent in the aspirant. Each of these groups has their own special set of admission criteria and generally require that their members take a vow of secrecy upon entering into training. The effectiveness of this training varies from group to group.

Magnetic induction as a method of developing latent psi potential is a relatively new phenomenon. Biophysicists from all over the world assert that electromagnetic pulsating fields lower than 10hz are highly health giving, especially if directed to the brain. Exposure to electromagnetic fields of 2hz or lower frequencies allows for better functioning of the

DNA-RNA in the cerebral endocrine system. Paranormal faculties have been consistently demonstrated in people who have been exposed to low intensity (<200gauss) 1-3hz fluctuating magnetic fields. Precognition, clairvoyance, psychokinesis, clairaudience, astral travel, and psychometry are only a few of the abilities which have been artificially induced in volunteers who have been treated with these special waveforms. Yogis and spiritual masters have been measured to have ambient brain frequencies which radiate in the range of 1-3 Hz. The average person (without psi talent) radiates normal brain frequencies of 14-20 Hz.[8]

Drugs and hallucinations are famous for inducing psi. LSD, PCP, amphetamines, mescaline, peyote, cocaine, and a host of other drugs have been used for thousands of years for this purpose. This is perhaps the most dangerous and controversial method of psi induction known to man.

Near-death experiences have caused the development of psi in many people. Many people report developing the ability to read auras and thoughts after this experience. A number of individuals also report a loss of the fear of death and a greater sense of connectiveness to the universe after an NDE. The effect is permanent and appears to be widely reported.

Lucid dreaming also induces psi talent in its practitioners. Lucid dreams occur when a person experiences waking consciousness within the dream state. This ability can be learned and it is highly developed among certain Tibetan adepts and practitioners of certain mystical faiths. The development of psi is a by-product of extended periods of lucidity during the dream state according to these adepts.

Hypnotists claim the ability to induce psi in certain very suggestible people during deep trance work. Research suggests that spontaneous telepathy can be demonstrated in up to 5% of subjects who enter the deep trance state. Indeed, certain subjects have even demonstrated a vast array of psychic abilities during deep trance work that they cannot duplicate during the waking state. When the brain frequencies of these subjects are measured, they are consistently within the 1-3 Hz range while they are performing psi phenomenon!

The occurrence of psi genes is higher in some families than in the general population. These families tend to have specific psi talents that are passed through their genetic material at a much higher rate than chance would allow. The Russians, Chinese, and Italians have made extensive use of this fact in their research on psi and have developed screening programs that isolate potentially useful gene pools for further experimentation. Individuals born with these special psi genes tend to demonstrate a high potential for psi ability without training or induction procedures.

Astrological influences also affect the development and expression of psi abilities. In my last book, ***"Signs of Mental Illness"***[9], I detailed my research into the astrological influences upon the development of mental illness. Using the same research techniques, I have discovered a number of accurate astrological markers that may be demonstrated within the birth chart. I compared the birth data for more than 130 gifted psychics, mystics, mediums, and healers to those of individuals who have not displayed significant psi talent. I then isolated those astrological markers within the psi group that were different from those in the control group. The results were astonishing. Not only are there readily identifiable astrological markers for psi in the birth chart, but these same markers occur at a much higher frequency in the charts of dates upon which remarkable psi events took place than would be expected by chance! Many of these markers are only visible using multiple planet aspects and declinations. In the next chapter, I will briefly summarize these new techniques which play such a prominent role in this research.

A thorough understanding of the biology of psi is dependent on knowledge of biophysical reality. Electromagnetic fields and morphogenetics play a large role in the research and experimental work which surrounds psi research. The average person associates psi with charlatans, hustlers, and otherwise unsavory elements within society who seek to mislead and abuse the unsuspecting masses. Fortunately, the world of psi is far more intricate and involved than the general populace would ever begin to suspect.

---

[1] Psychic Powers, Time Life Books; p.1- George Constable; editor 1987.

[2] "Remote Viewing: The Story of the Real X-Files; Turan Rifat, July 1996. Internet Website

[3] abbreviation for "electromagnetic"

[4] Electronics World and Wireless World: The healing face of electromagnetic fields; 1993

[5] Gerald Edelman, Bright Air, Brilliant Fire; New York Basic; 1992.

[6] Dream Baby; Bruce Mcallister, Tom Doherty Associates Books-TOR, first edition 1989.

[7] The People of the Secret: Ernest Scott, Octagon Press; London, 1983.

[8] Mind Expanding Machine: Can the Graham Potentializer Do for the Brain What Nautilus Does for the Body?, Michael Hutchinson, New Age Journal; July/Aug 87.

[9] Signs of Mental Illness; Mitchell E. Gibson MD; Llewellyn Publications, 1998.

ASTROLOGY: A BASIC COURSE

Many of the people reading this book will not have a working knowledge of astrology and it's basic principles. In this chapter I will provide a brief introduction to astrology and it's core principles in the hope that this will make the main body of the research more easily comprehensible to the uninitiated. The following discussion is not intended to turn the untrained reader into a professional astrologer, but I hope that it will expand their vocabulary to a suitable working level in this fascinating field.

THE BIRTH CHART

A Birth Chart is a map of the heavens as a newborn hild would see it at the moment of his birth. In this work, we will not consider the stars and their movements, but we will be chiefly concerned with the motions of the ten moving planets. If a person were to look up at the time of their birth they would see the planets and the Sun displayed in a circular band. On a birth chart, the earth is represented by a small circle in the center of the chart. Around the Earth the 12 equal sign of the Zodiac form an encircling band along the ecliptic, each sign occupying a fixed 30 degree field. Against these fields of the ecliptic move the main forces of astrology-the planets. They pass, at differing speeds, out one sign of the Zodiac and into the next in a never-ending circuit. As the planets move, so the angles they form with Earth can be measured for any given moment. In astrology the moment of birth is taken as the decisive time in the subject's life, and the degree calculations which appear on the birth chart record exactly how the planets appeared in the heavens at that moment.[1] For the purposes of this study, I have used a standardized birth time as the exact time of birth was not available for many of the patients. In addition to traditional ecliptic (longitudinal) astrological data, this study makes use of the declinational (latitude) related data. In essence, this allows the astrologer to plot the position of the planets along an additional axis of reference. Figure (1) shows my birth chart mapped along the traditional circular axis. This is the format the vast majority of today's astrologer utilize in presenting birth data to clients. Figure (2) depicts my birth mapped along the declinational and longitudinal axes. I have discovered that most of the significant planetary relationships which are not at all discernible on the circular (longitudinal) chart are readily seen in the second format. I will expand upon the myriads uses and applications of this new format in the following chapter on new advances in astrology.

The astrologer assumes that the Earth is a fixed point, and that all other cosmic bodies revolve round it once a day. He then applies this 24-hour system to the birth chart. The main circle of the chart is divided into 12 equal segments; one segment, or house, equals two out of the total 24. Outside this circle, the 12 equal signs of the Zodiac are plotted for the moment of birth. Figure (3) represents the glyphs or symbols of the signs used by astrologers.

The inner circle of the birth chart is divided into 12 sections known as houses. These are a distinct astrological category and relate to everyday activities, the first house to physical appearance and temperament, the first house to physical appearance and temperament, the second to possessions etc. For the purposes of this study, I did not use data related to houses or the position of the planets within a particular house. I have found the there is a vast treasure trove of untapped data within the declinational chart that may change the way we look at birth data all together. However, all of this data relates primarily to the planets. The planets are not thought to directly influence the individual but rather they are believed to act as guideposts within the unconscious for our actions along the road of life. One of my teachers once told me that one should not look upon astrological guidance as a *fait accompli* to unbridled fatalism. Rather, he believed that the stars provide the core blueprints for our choices and account for no more than 80% influence over our entire destiny. Free will and determined effort provide the remainder of the guidance for the individual though a lack of concerted and focused effort could ostensibly increase the unconscious guiding principle contained within the stars. I have found this to be an invaluable rule of thumb in the interpretation of an individual's chart. I believe that the harder a person works at unfolding the higher possibilities of their lives the greater the chance that they will overcome the hardships inherent within the karmic boundaries mapped out in the birth chart. I have also found that an intimate knowledge of the latent strengths and weaknesses inherent within one's birth chart can and does significantly improve one's chances of realizing their highest destiny. Guidance by a highly trained and experienced astrologer can help one avoid obvious pitfalls and to take advantage of a myriad of opportunities which present themselves within the course of everyday life.

The Zodiac and it's associated myths are of essential value in astrology. They represent the position and movements of the planets along the ecliptic as seen from Earth and greatly influence astrological interpretation and prediction. Each moving planet was given a special relationship with a fixed sign of the Zodiac. The Sun and Moon ruled one sign each, and the other planets two signs each. Each planet and sign are associated with positive and negative traits which help shape the course of a particular reading. A planet in exaltation is well-placed and should positively influence a person's life. A planet in detriment is ill-placed and loses some of its power. A planet increases in power when it is in its home ruling sign.

THE PLANETS

THE SUN

The Sun is the star around which Earth and the rest of the planets orbit. It is the most prominent heavenly body in solar system and is often associated with ruling deities and kings. In Western astrology, the Sun is associated with Jupiter and Apollo. In Mesopotamian astrology, the sun-god was Shamash (Utu), who represented the life-giving rays of the Sun. He was an all-seeing god who was also the god of justice who protected the good and destroyed evil. The Sun is said to rule the sign Leo, a relationship indicating a similarity between the characteristics of the Sun and the traits of Leo. Leo is the sign of the king, the central personality of a country and the person responsible for over-seeing the kingdom, coordinating its activities, and administering justice. In the birth chart, the Sun is the basic self and its position within a particular sign colors the entire orientation of the personality. The aspects made by the Sun to other planets tend to be more significant than that of the planets.

The Sun is associated with vitality and its placement can be an important indicator of physical vitality. The Sun also represents ambition, urge for power, leadership, creative-ness, constructiveness, self-reliance, organization and administration, masculinity, indi-viduality and the ability to carry out heart-felt desires. Negative solar traits include arro-gance, extravagance, a domineering nature, and a strong desire to control others. The Sun is exalted in Aries, is in detriment in Aquarius, falls in Libra.[2]

THE MOON

Second to the Sun, the Moon is the most important body in the birth chart. It is the only one of the planetary moons regarded as having any astrological influence. The word lunar derives from the name of the Greek goddess Luna who was identified with the moon. The correlation between month has influenced cultures all over the world to asso-ciate the Moon with women and fertility. Only one culture seems to be an exception to this general rule. The Mesopotamian Moon deity was the male divinity Nanna (Sin or considered to be superior to him.

The Moon completes an orbit of Earth ever 27.32 days. The Moon rules Cancer; is exalted Taurus, detriment in associated with women and childbirth. It also represents the principle of creativity, in the sense of giving birth to ideas. With respect to the goddess Artemis as a huntress, the Moon and Cancer and not so much associated with the passion of the hunt as they are with nourishment, which is the purpose of behind the hunt. The Moon's placement in a birth chart can show where and how we nurture as well as where and how we seek nurturance. The Moon is responsive and adaptable.

Positive Lunar traits include passivity, tenacity, imagination, sensitivity, receptivity, a good memory, and a maternal nature. Negative Lunar traits include weak reasoning power, gullibility, narrow-mindedness, unreliability, and changeability. The Moon also represents the subconscious mind, embodying the unconscious patterns of our past. The Moon's placement within a chart shows us an area of life where we create as well as experience change.[3]

The Moon is the fastest moving body in the birth chart. It moves through the entire Zodiac over the period of one month and moves through an entire house in a little over 2 days. The position of the Moon is therefore extremely changeable and can vary widely over the course of any given day. In comparison, the other major astrological bodies move much more slowly and their positions will change by very small amount over the course of any given day or hour.

MERCURY

Mercury is the nearest planet to the Sun and is always found within 28 degrees of it. In the birth chart Mercury appears either in the same sign as the Sun, in the next sign ahead of it, or in the previous sign. Mercury was named after the Roman god who carried messages between the gods and humanity. Mercury was also associated with the Mesopotamian deity Nabu, the divine scribe who presided over learning, writing, and science.

Mercury has a short orbital period of only 88 days. Because it's orbit lies between Earth and the Sun, it does not appear ever to be very far from the Sun Mercury is associated with travel and communication. Like it's mythological namesakes, Mercury is associated with writing, teaching, and learning. Mercury represents the mind, particularly that part of the mind, which interfaces with the outer world-perception reason, and communication. In other words, Mercury represents the conscious aspects of the mind. The placement of Mercury in a person's chart has a powerful effect on the quality and character of their mind. I have also discovered that the placement of Mercury also influences to a large degree the presence or absence of a large number of intellectual gifts or deficits. Positive Mercury traits include good reasoning abilities, perceptivity, versatility, coordination, and communicativeness. Negative Mercury traits include cynicism biting sarcasm, uncontrolled nervous energy, inconsistency, a hypercritical nature, and lacking a sense of purpose. Mercury rules Gemini and Virgo; is exalted in Virgo; detriment in Sagittarius; and falls in Pisces.[4]

VENUS

Venus is always close to the Sun as seen from the Earth and never travels more than 48 degrees from it along the ecliptic. Venus either occupies the same sign in a Birth chart as the Sun, or falls within two signs to either side of it. Venus was named after the Roman goddess of fertility and beauty and is associated with love, harmony, and beauty. The planet Venus has an orbital period of 244 days. Venus is traditionally thought to represent the center of one's feelings and interpersonal relationships. It's placement in a natal chart shows much about how one relates and what one loves. Venus is considered to be a benefic planet; i.e., a planet that is traditionally as having a positive influence on a person. It's positive influence is second only to Jupiter in power according to classical astrologers. Positive Venusian traits include cooperation, harmony, adept in love and the social arts, appreciation of beauty, and a kind of friendly manner. Negative Venusian traits include laziness, indecisiveness, excessively romantic, weak willed, careless, impractical, and dependence on others. Venus rules Taurus and Libra; is exalted in Pisces, detriment in Aries; and falls in Virgo.[5]

MARS

Mars, named after the Roman god of war, is the next planet from the Sun after the Earth. The Roman Mars was a mature god and was originally invoked to protect crops. He had an affair with the goddess Venus and was not well by the other deities in the pantheon.

Mars has an orbital period of 686.98 days. According to tradition, Mars ruled both Scorpio and Aries. Sometime after Pluto was discovered, the rulership of Scorpio was reassigned to Pluto, leaving Aries with Mars. Mars is associated with aggression, emotional passion, and conflict. Mars is also associated with spontaneity, impulsiveness, and ambition. Mars represents outgoing, aggressive energy, the active and outgoing part of oneself. Mars shows where one is likely to experience conflict.

Positive Martian traits include a strong sex drive, a defender of the weak, a strong leader, energy, passion, initiative, independence, and enterprise. Negative Martian traits include aggressiveness, selfishness, rudeness, indifference to detail, and boisterousness. Mars is considered to be a major malefic i.e.; a planet that rules the minor mishaps in one's life. It is second only to Saturn in it's negative effect on the birth chart. Mars also rules violence, bloodshed, knives, guns, murder, arson, and strife. Mars is exalted in Capricorn; detriment in Libra; and falls in Cancer.[6]

JUPITER

Jupiter was named after the ruler of the Roman Pantheon of deities and is the largest planet in the solar system. In mythology, Jupiter was associated with storms, victory, and justice. Jupiter has an orbital period of 11.86 years and stays in each sign of the zodiac about one year. Jupiter ruled both Pisces and Sagittarius at one time but after the discovery of Neptune, rulership of Pisces was given to Neptune.

Jupiter's astrological influences have more to do with its physical size and position in the solar system than any other trait. Its primary characteristics of Jupiter are expansiveness and good fortune. Jupiter is also related to religion, philosophy, wealth, and success. The area in which Jupiter is placed in a birth chart shows good luck and multiplicity. Jupiter is called the Greater Benefic and is the most positive planetary influence in the chart. Jupiter represents the expansive, generous, optimistic, and positive side of the self and where it is likely to manifest. Negative Jupiter traits include blind optimism, extravagance, conceit, self-indulgence, and unbalanced beliefs. Positive Jupiter traits include generosity, loyalty, joviality, luck, progressiveness, justice, and opportunism. Jupiter is exalted in Cancer; detriment in Gemini; and falls in Capricorn.[7]

SATURN

Saturn was named after the mythological king of Italy Saturnus and is the farthest planet from the Sun that can be seen with the unaided eye. As the most distant and slowest-moving planet known to the ancients, it was attributed with age and wisdom. Saturnus was a god of agriculture who founded civilization and social order. Saturn takes 26-46 years to complete an orbit of the Sun. Traditionally, Saturn was said to rule both Aquarius and Capricorn. However after the discovery of Uranus, Saturn was assigned exclusively to Capricorn. Saturn is exalted in Libra; detriment in Cancer; and falls in Aries.

In ancient times Saturn was considered to be the outermost planet in the universe. Therefore, it came to be associated with limitation. Saturn is also associated with time, age, and social order. It is an embodiment of the principle of stability and the opposite of upheaval. Saturn is also associated with the harvest, big business, and with the principle of contraction. Saturn is also related to the process of bringing what is vague and unformed into manifestation. Saturn has been given the title of Greater Malefic and traditionally carries the most negative influence in the birth chart. Positive Saturnian traits include caution, patience, ambition, reliability, thrift, self-discipline, good endurance, and responsibility. Negative Saturn associations include selfishness, a dogmatic nature, a life of sorrow and ill-health, cruelty, and tyrannical nature.[8]

URANUS

Uranus is the first of the Modern Planets. It was discovered in the 1781 by William Herschel and the capitol "H" in the glyph commermorates his pioneering work. Uranus is a giant planet, 29,300 miles in diameter. It has an unusual axial inclination, more than a right angle, and is correlated with an eccentric and unusual nature. Uranus is the only planet to be named after a Greek rather than a Roman god. This is because the Greek god Chronos, whom the Romans identified with Saturn, was the son of the oldest god, Uranus[9]. Astronomers felt at the time that they had discovered the ancestor of all the planets. This was of course not the case.

Uranus was god of the sky. He was a tyrant who imprisoned his offspring, he was castrated by his son Chronos. Modern astrologers believe that the more appropriate mythological association was this planet is Prometheus, the Greek creator and defender of humanity who stole fire from heaven and gave it to mankind. Prometheus was also a trickster and a rebel. Uranus takes 84.01 years to orbit the Sun and therefore stays in each sign of the zodiac for seven years. Uranus rules Aquarius and is associated with humanity, ideals, eccentriciy, and rebelliousness. It is different from all other planets in that it rolls around the Sun on it's side and the moons of Uranus were named after Shakespearean characters rather than traditional mythological figures.

Uranus rules sudden, unexpected change, astrology, science, elecricity, magic and occultism. Uranus represents the creative, innovative, freedom-seeking part of the self. It's placement in the chart shows much about how a person expressses his/her creative genius.

Positive Uranian traits include, kindness, independence, originality, genius, verstility, curiosity, and strong-willed nature. Negative Uranian traits include eccentricity, perversity, rebelliousness, crankiness, and extreme abnormality. Uranus is exalted in Scorpio: detriment in Scorpio, and falls in Taurus[10].

NEPTUNE

Neptune was named after the Roman god of the sea and orbits between Uranus and Pluto. Neptune is also associated with fresh water and the Greek god Poseidon. The glyph for Neptune is the trident which was also a symbol associated with these two deities.

Neptune completes an orbit around the Sun ever 164.79 years, meaning that it stays almost 14 years in each sign of the zodiac. Neptune rules Pisces, is exalted in Leo; detriment in Virgo; and fall in Aquarius. Neptune represents the subtle, intangible side of human existence. It also represents the unconscious mind at the individual level (personal unconscious). Neptune is also a mystical and spiritual planet. The negative expressions of this planet are escapism, self-deception, confusion, and vagueness. Neptune represents the human imagination and areas in life where it is easiest for us to delude ourselves. Positive Neptune traits include idealism, imagination, sensitivity, creativity, and inspiration. Negative Neptune traits include carelessness, self-deception, worrying, deceit, unworldliness, and disorganization[11] .

PLUTO

Pluto was named after the Roman god of the underworld and death. It is the farthest planet from the Sun. It was not discovered until 1930. Pluto completes an orbit of the Sun every 247.69 years and therefore spends more than 20.6 years in each sign. Pluto is said to rule Scorpio and it's exaltation, detriment, and fall have not been determined. Pluto represents the human collective unconcious, life and death matters, and the will to control and dominate. It also represents basic life drives i.e.; sex, aggression, and the creative and regenerative forces of the body. Pluto is also associated with eruptions, volcanoes and earthquakes, big business, and enforced change. Positive Pluto traits include a flair for big business, financial security, an analytical nature, and regeneration. Negative Pluto traits include an unhealthy unconscious, sadism, curelty, bestiality, and criminal tendencies[12] .

THE ASPECTS

Planets are in aspect when there certain specific angular distances between them as they are placed along the ecliptic. The relationship between them reveals the areas of personality where the native's characteristics can attain full and positive expression, and other areas in which there may be some experience of psychological stress and strain. The major aspects are the conjunction (0 degrees), sextile (60 degrees), square (90 degrees), trine (120 degrees), and opposition (180 degrees). Astrologers allow for varying degrees of tolerance in identifying these aspects. Squares and oppositions are regarded as hard aspects and usually represent challenges to be faced and overcome. Sextiles and trines are regarded as soft aspects and usually represent an easy and harmonious combination of forces. The conjunction is indicative of a powerful blending of forces and can be easy or challenging depending on the planets involved. Why are some aspects harmonious and some produce conflict is a question that has never been answered?! Most astrologers do not use the minor aspects and stick primarily to the major aspects. Minor aspects include the semisextile (30 degrees), the decile (36 degrees), the semiquare (45 degrees), the quintile (72 degrees), the sesquisquare (135 degrees), the quincunx (150 degrees and probably the most commonly used of the minor aspects), and the biquintile (144 degrees). The major hard aspects come from dividing the horoscope circle into halves, and quarters, soft aspects from dividing it into thirds and sixths.

Most readers will be much more familiar with the Sun sign aspect of their particular astrological chart than any other part. However for the purposes of this study, I will not include the Sun sign as a major point of reference. For further information on the Sun sign, the reader is referred to one the hundreds of texts written specifically on this subject.

NEW ADVANCES IN ASTROLOGY

Astrology is one of the oldest arts known to man and it has been responsible for influencing human history more than almost any other single discipline. Amazingly, the actual practice of astrology has remained largely unchanged for more than 2000 years. Computers have allowed birth charts to be created by almost anyone with even rudimentary computer knowledge and skill. However, the actual mechanics of chart preparation and examination have remained unchanged.

In the book "Astrology Really Works", the Magi Society expounded upon several new techniques and terms which have been instrumental in expanding the vistas of astrological research. They were the first researchers to begin use of declinations and multiple planet aspects. Their work has sports, and a small grouping of world events. To date, they have not done any definitive work on mental illness or psychic abilities. Therefore, this new, and untouched remains a totally uncharted area even for those who are involved in the "new research".

Almost all astrologers use the longitudinal coordinates for the birth chart as the sole measure of planetary movement. There are however equally valid and immensely useful latitudinal (declinational) data for all the planets and stars which to date has remained part of a vast uncharted territory for astrological research. There are two coordinates on any map used for the location of positions, horizontal and vertical. This same principle applies to the stars in the sky. The horizontal coordinates are called the longitudes and the vertical coordinates are called the declinations. Longitudes refer to the sign or part of the sky in which a particular planet or star resides at any given time i.e.; Leo, Aries etc.. The signs refer to the horizontal motions which the planets during their trek through the sky. All of the objects in the sky move vertically as well and this vertical movement has powerful astrological significance.

The Sun reaches its maximum height in the sky during the summer solstice. It reaches its lowest height in the sky during the winter solstice. This difference in apparent height is caused by the 23.5 degree axis tilt assumed by the Earth as it revolves around the Sun. The midpoint of this 47 degree shift in the Sun's apparent of motion is called celestial equator. The declinations of all the planets is measured as either north or south of this celestial equator. On December 21, the Sun is in 23.4 degrees south declination. At the same time, it is in 0 degrees Capricorn. Astronomical texts always carry the vertical and horizontal coordinates for the planets and stars.

Astrologers have always maintained that we are influenced by the movements of the planets. It is curious that fully one-half of these movements have been ignored by astrology for 2000 years. I have found that there is a vast treasure trove of knowledge and untapped data waiting to be mined and analyzed by the evolving research oriented astrological community. The public at large also deserves to be made privy to the fascinating information hidden in this largely unknown sector of their birth charts.

NEW TERMS

There are a number of new terms and definitions which I am going to introduce which are crucial to understanding the use of declinations. Most of the significant astrological correlation that I have found in the birth charts of clients with spiritual ability have been discovered in the declinations. I will now outline the major terms and definitions which will act as guideposts during our journey into this uncharted territory. Some of these terms were first used by the Magi Society in their excellent book "Astrology Really Works". This book was the first title to seriously explore the various uses of declinations in modern charts. However, many of the terms listed and discussed below are new and are the result of new research findings during the course of my work.

1. elevation: a word used to describe a special planetary interaction which affects the basic expression of a planet's energies. Elevations may be positive or negative depending on the planet's position in the sky or upon the planey(s) it interacts with.

2. parallel: a term used to describe a latitudinal planetary interaction in which two celestial bodies are positioned within an orb of two degrees and thirty four minutes on the same side of the celestial equator.

   Example: Mars +17 degrees 21 minutes
   Jupiter +17 degrees 39 minutes

3. contraparalles: a term used to describe a latitudinal planetary interaction in which two celestial bodies are positioned within an orb of two degrees and thirty four minutes on opposite sides of the celestial equator.

   Example: Mars +17degrees 21 minutes
   Jupiter +17degrees 39 minutes

4. triangle elevation: a term used to describe a latitudinal planetary interaction wherein three celestial bodies are parallel or contraparallel to each other (or any combination thereof) at the same time.

   Example: Mars +17 degrees 21 minutes
   Jupiter +17degrees 39 minutes
   Uranus –18 degrees 2 minutes

All planets within a triangle elevation must be either parallel or contraparallel to all other planets within the triangle. Triangle elevations are fairly common.

5. quad elevation: a term used to describe a latitudinal planetary interaction wherein four celestial bodies are parallel or contraparllel to each other (or any combination thereof) at the same time.

   Example: Mars +17 degrees 21 minutes
   Jupiter +17 degrees 39 minutes
   Uranus-18 degrees 2 minutes
   Neptune +18 degrees 12 minutes

All planets within a quad elevation must be parallel or contrapallel to all other planets within the quad. Quad elevations are uncommon.

6. plenary elevation: a term used to describe a latitudinal planetary interaction wherein five celestial bodies are parallel or contraparallel to each other (or any combination thereof) at the same time.

   Example: Mars +17 degrees 2 minutes
   Jupiter +17 degrees 39 minutes
   Uranus –18 degrees 2 minutes
   Neptune –18 degrees 20 minutes
   Venus +17 degrees 10 minutes

All planets within a plenary elevation must be parallel or contraparallel to all other planets within the elevation. Plenary elevations are rare.

7. band elevation: a term used to describe a latitudinal planetary interaction wherein six celestial bodies are parallel or contraparallel to each other (or any combination thereof) at the same time.

   Example: Mars +17 degrees 2 minutes
   Jupiter +18 degrees 2 minutes
   Uranus –18 degrees 2 minutes
   Neptune –18 degrees 10 minutes
   Mercury +17 degrees 30 minutes
   Venus +17 degrees 10 minutes

All planets within a band elevation must be parallel or contraparallel to all other planets within the elevation. Band elevations are extremely rare.

8. elevation by high declination: a term used to describe the latitudinal position of a celestial body when it is found between 21 degrees and 23 degrees and thirty minutes on either side of the celestial equator. The term is often referred to in its abbreviated form: HIDEK.

   Example: Jupiter +22 degrees 12 minutes

9. elevation by extreme declination: a term used to describe the latitudinal position of a celestial body when it is found above 23 degrees thirty minutes on either side of the celestial equator. The term is often referred to in its abbreviated for EXDEK.

    Example: Moon-25 degrees 16 minutes

10. elevation by proximity: a term used to describe the latitudinal position of two celestial bodies when they are found within 30 minutes of each other in a parallel or contraparallel relationship.

    Example: Jupiter +17 degrees 21 minutes
    Venus –17 degrees 10 minutes

11. planetary eclipse: a term used to describe an event which occurs when two planets are simultaneously in conjunction and parallel to each other. Planetary eclipses are fairly common occurrences.

12. binary eclipse: a term used to describe an event which occurs when three planets are simultaneously in conjunction and parallel to each other. Binary planetary eclipses are very uncommon occurrences

13. Plenary eclipse: a term used to describe an event which occurs when four or more planets are simultaneously in conjunction and parallel to each other. Plenary eclipses are exceptionally rare occurrences.

14. degree of elevation: a term used to describe the number of elevations (positive or negative) which a particular planet may have in a chart. When Mercury has a fourth degree negative in a chart it means that within that particular chart, Mercury has four negative elevations. The greater the number of elevations (positive or negative) that a planet has within a chart, the greater its influence upon the native.

15. grand elevation: a term used to describe a special occurrence which happens when a planet has six or more be either positive or negative. (The sum of the positive and negative elevations of a planet within a chart does not indicate the presence of grand elevation.) If Venus has 8 positive elevations within a chart, that particular chart is said to have a grand elevation of Venus. The presence of a grand elevation of a planet within a chart indicates and area of great influence and activity. Most charts have 1-3 grand elevations though it is not uncommon for a chart to possess seven or eight grand elevations. Multiple grand elevations indicate a greater than normal amount of longitudinal and declinational interactivity among the planets within a chart. This enhanced number of planetary interactions can result in greater positive or negative stress upon the native depending upon the type of elevations involved. A grand elevation is considered to by "high order" when a planet displays 9 or more positive or negative elevations.

16. planetary index: a number which equals the sum of the positive and negative elevations of a particular planet multiplied by 100. A planetary index may be positive or negative and it is used as measure of the relative activity of a planet in a chart.

17. general planetary index: a number which equals the sum of all the positive and negative elevations within a chart. A high general activity index means that a chart has a high degree of interactivity among the planets. The general activity index of a group of charts may be calculated by averaging the individual general activity indices of each chart within the group.

18. P/N ratio: a fraction which equals the total number of positive elevations within a chart of group of charts divided by the total number of negative elevations. A high P/N ration denotes a high number of positive elevations relative to the number of negative elevations. The P/N ratio is a relative measure of the amount of constructive versus destructive energy latent within a chart and may be a positive or negative number.

19. temporal environment index- a number which refers to the positive (constructive) or negative(destructive) energy surrounding the time of the casting of a chart or the start of a particular event. A positive temporal environment is very helpful for the completion of constructive events and for fostering harmonious actions. A negative temporal environment is useful for destructive purposes and it is not recommended for the initiation of constructive activities. Activities started within a positive temporal environment tend to last longer and remain more harmonious than similar events which are initiated within a negative temporal environment. Individuals born within a negative temporal environment tend to have a greater amount of disharmony and chaos within their lives than normal people born in a positive temporal environment. The temporal environment index is calculated as follows:
    TE index = general activity index x P/N (100)

    Example: 34.69 x +0.833 (100) = +2809.72

20. cardinal elevation: a planetary elevation which occurs as a marker aspect for more than one mental illness or spiritual ability.

21. karmic index: a number which refers to a relative measure of the positive and negative growth potential within a birth chart. The positive karmic index is calculated as follows: (SUN INDEX + JUPITER INDEX + VENUS INDEX) X P/N. The negative karmic index is calculated as follows: (SATURN INDEX + MARS INDEX) DIVIDED BY P/N.

22. complexity index: a number which refers to the sum of the triangles, quads, eclipses, plenary, band, and proximity elevations within a chat.

These terms form the core of the new paradigm in astrology. The following chapters will focus on how these new concepts may be utilized to examine the birth chart in an all new system. This system is designed to provide the tools with which the modern astrologer may now delve even more deeply into the mysteries of the sky.

1 “The Compleat Astrologer”;p. 78-81,;McGraw Hill Book Company, New York; 111971, Michael Beasley.

2 Ibid;,p.86.

3 Ibid;p.88.

4 Ibid;,p.90

5 Ibid;,p.92

6 Ibid;,p.94

7 Ibid;,p96.

8 Ibid;,p.98

9 The Roman Saturn’s father was not named in existing myths.

10 Ibid;, p. 101.

11 Ibid;, p. 102.

12 Ibid;, p. 103.

THE ASTROLOGICAL SIGNS OF GENERAL PSYCHIC ABILITY

A psychic may be defined as a sensitive person who is susceptible to the subtle influences of the intangible body or soul. Sergeant Cox in his book "Mechanism of Man" wrote that the soul is composed of attenuated matter, and has the same form as the physical body, which it permeates in every part. From the soul radiates the psychic force, by means of which all manner of psychic phenomena emerge. Through this agency, man becomes endowed with telekinetic, clairvoyant, and clairaudient powers. When he uses these abilities, man is able to overcome the very forces of nature and exert a profound influence on his surroundings. Psychic abilities are regarded as productions of the psychic body, which is an intermediary between the physical body and the soul. The psychic body forms an envelope around the soul itself and encloses it completely at the point of physical death. In time, the psychic body decays and leaves the soul free to incarnate and take on a new body.

Some individuals are able to control their psychic bodies to extraordinary degrees. Thus far in this book, we have seen a staggering number of examples of the various forms that the psychic force assume in its manipulation of reality. Does astrology influence the nativity and development of the psychic form as well? Mankind has been aided by the abilities of gifted psychic savants for centuries. Every morning on his way to work, J.P. Morgan, the great financier-industrialist, purportedly visited an astrologer named Evangeline Adams. When asked; Is it true that millionaires consult astrologers, Morgan replied; "No, Billionaires do." This bold statement reflects the fact that Morgan relied greatly on the guidance he received from gifted individuals. Evangeline Adams was well known to be one of the greatest psychic astrologers of her time. She has the singular distinction of having successfully defended her astrological gifts in a court of law after she had been accused of practicing charlatanism. Perhaps Morgan knew something that the courts came to understand and accept; psychic and spiritual gifts are part of the human condition and to some extent, they can be used to benefit mankind. If it were possible to identify at the time of birth those persons who were likely to display a high level of psychic proficiency, mankind's lot in life would be improved immeasurably. This chapter focuses on the identification of the astrological signs for general psychic ability. My goal in completing this aspect of the research was to create a working model that would allow astrologers to rate the psychic potential of any given chart. In accomplishing this task, I examined the charts of more than 31 famous psychics and gifted spiritual leaders. I then compared them to a group of 30 age-matched control charts of individuals who have not displayed heightened psychic or spiritual ability. The astrological aspects that occurred with at least a 50% increase in frequency in the psychic group when compared to the control group were designated "Marker Aspects" for psychic ability. Those marker aspects for psychic ability which were at least 300% more common in the charts of psychics than the controls were designated as "Delphi Markers" for psychic's ability. Ordinary marker aspects for psychic ability were assigned a point value of 10 points and Delphi markers for psychic ability were assigned a point value of 25 points. The point total for each chart was then The resulting score was called the "General Psychic Potential Index"

The control group revealed an average general psychic index of 50.83 points. The psychic group revealed an average psychic potential index of 148.7 points. The research showed that there is a discernible group of astrological marker aspects for psychic ability that occurs at a significantly increased frequency among psychics when compared to the normal population. The marker aspects for general psychic potential are listed on the next page.

Birth / Event Data

____
Place of birth/event (city, state, county)

____
Date of birth/event

____
Time of birth/event (exact time, i.e. birth certificate)

Client Data

____
First and last name

____
Mailing address

____
City, state, country, zip code

____
Telephone no. and fax no.

____
E-mail address

GENERAL PSYCHIC POTENTIAL – MARKER ASPECTS

(All aspects score 10 points each, unless otherwise indicated)

CONJUNCTIONS

_____ Saturn - Mars
_____ Jupiter - Saturn
_____ Moon -Venus
_____ Saturn - Uranus
_____ Jupiter - Moon
_____ Jupiter - Uranus
_____ Sun - Mars
_____ Uranus - Mars

TRINES

_____ Neptune – Mars
_____ Venus – Jupiter
_____ Mercury - Mars
_____ Jupiter – Uranus (25 pts)

SEXTILES

_____ Saturn – Mercury
_____ Pluto – Uranus (25 pts)
_____ Sun – Uranus (25 pts)
_____ Mercury – Mars (25 pts)
_____ Jupiter – Mercury (25 pts)
_____ Saturn – Pluto (25 pts)
_____ Saturn – Sun (25 pts)
_____ Saturn – Neptune
_____ Sun – Mars
_____ Uranus – Moon (25 pts)
_____ Venus – Pluto (25 pts)
_____ Mercury – Venus (25 pts)
_____ Neptune – Moon (25 pts)
_____ Moon – Mars
_____ Jupiter – Moon

SQUARES

_____ Pluto – Moon
_____ Sun – Jupiter
_____ Uranus – Pluto
_____ Jupiter – Moon
_____ Jupiter – Uranus
_____ Venus – Jupiter
_____ Saturn – Moon
_____ Jupiter – Saturn
_____ Jupiter – Neptune

OPPOSITIONS

_____ Pluto – Mars
_____ Saturn – Moon
_____ Venus – Saturn
_____ Saturn – Neptune

PARALLELS

_____ Moon – Venus
_____ Pluto – Moon (25 pts)
_____ Sun – Moon
_____ Mercury – Mars
_____ Pluto – Mars
_____ Jupiter – Moon
_____ Saturn - Neptune
_____ Venus – Neptune (25 pts)
_____ Pluto – Uranus
_____ Moon – Mercury
_____ Jupiter – Mars (25 pts)
_____ Sun – Mercury
_____ Mercury – Venus (25 pts)
_____ Jupiter – Saturn

CONTRAPARALLELS

_____ Jupiter – Saturn (25 pts)
_____ Moon – Mercury (25 pts)
_____ Pluto – Moon (25 pts)
_____ Jupiter – Mercury
_____ Jupiter – Neptune
_____ Jupiter – Moon
_____ Sun – Jupiter (25 pts)
_____ Sun – Moon (25 pts)
_____ Uranus – Neptune (25 pts)
_____ Pluto – Mars (25 pts)

HIDEK

_____ Mercury
_____ Mars

EXDEK

_____ Venus
_____ Mars
_____ Uranus
_____ Pluto

PROXIMITY ELEVATIONS

_____ Pluto – Mars (parallel)
_____ Sun – Pluto (contraparallel)

ECLIPSES

_____ Saturn – Mercury
_____ Jupiter – Uranus
_____ Any Mars Eclipse

GRAND ELEVATIONS

_____ + Mercury
_____ - Sun
_____ - Uranus
_____ - Neptune
_____ + Moon

GRAND TOTAL		SCALE
_____	Below Average	0 - 30
_____	Average	31 - 60
_____	Above Average	61 - 100
_____	Superior	101 - 140
_____	Outstanding	141 - 180
_____	Delphi Class	181+

The following psychics were included in this study: BIRTH DATA FOR ALL PSYCHICS WAS TAKEN FROM THE HUNTER DATABASE.

JOHANN VOGHT
2/13/1813
AUGSBURG, GERMANY
12:24 PM LMT
ZONE 00:00 010E53 48N2300

URI GELLER
12/20/1946
TEL AVIV, ISRAEL
02:00 AM EET
ZONE -02:00
034E46 32N04

PATRICIA HOUGH
SEPTEMBER 15, 1936
LANSING, MI
7:41 PM EST
84W33 42N44

LUCILLE VAN TASSEL
3/16/1924
TACOMA, WA
1:00 AM PST
ZONE +8:00
122W 26'35"
47N15'11"

DANIEL LOGAN
4/24/1936
NEW YORK, NY
9:30 AM EST
ZONE +5:00
74W00
40N43'00"

JEAN MACARTHUR
3/9/1931
CHICAGO, IL
8:00 AM CST
ZONE +6:00
87W39
41N51

BARBARA STABINER
2/28/1937
BROOKLYN, NY
7:00AM EST
78W44
42N25

IRWIN GRIEF
5/29/1930
BROOKLYN, NY
4:15 AM EST
ZONE +5:00
73W56
40N38

ROBERTA JACOBSON
MARCH 16, 1948
CHICAGO, IL
8:46 AM CST
ZONE +6:00
87W39
41N51

ELEANOR ZUGAN
LOZNA, ROMANIA
1:50 PM LMT
ZONE 00:00
26E36
47N50

PETER HURKOS
1911
ROTTERDAM NETHERLANDS
6:00AM LMT
ZONE +00:00
004E28
51N55

NOSTRADAMUS
12/14/1503
SAINT REMY, FRANCE
6:00AM LMT
ZONE 00:00
002E05
48N42

FRED KIMBALL
11/12/1904
PROVIDENCE, RI
3:35 AM EST
ZONE +5:00
71W24 41N49

RONALD LEE WARMOUTH
4/3/1942
NEWARK, MO
5:25 AM CST
91W58
40N00

MARILYN JOYCE
5/11/1950
PETERBOROUGH, ENG
1:05AM GMD
000W15
52N35

KELLY QUINN
3/10/1942
BROOKLYN, NY
8:30AM EWT
ZONE +4:00
78W44'55"
42N25'59"

JUDITH RICHARDSON
3/10/1944
PHILADELPHIA, PA
6:42AM EWT
ZONE +4:00
75W09
39N57

LINDA GOLDNER
11/10/1942
LOS ANGELES, CA
1:49 AM PWT
ZONE +7:00
118W15
34N03

PAUL SOLOMON
7/7/1939
ROGERS, AR
7:00AM
ZONE +6:00
94W07 36N20

CHARUBEL
11/9/1826
WALES, ENG
7:00AM
ZONE +00:00
003W03
52N33

KENNY KINGSTON
2/15/1927
BUFFALO, NY
6:15 AM EST
ZONE +5:00
78W53'
42N53

JOAN FORREST
10/16/1921
GLASGOW, SCOTLAND
ZONE +00:00
004W15
55N53

MARC REYMONT
6/7/1941
NEW YORK, NY
8:35 PM EDT
ZONE +4:00
74WOO
40N42'51"

LAURA MARTIN-SMITH
8/7/1888
SPRINGFIELD, MA
3:55PM EST
ZONE +5:00
72W35'25"
42N06'05"

CARALYN
12/08/1954
ALPENA, MI
8:35 AM EST
ZONE +5:00 83W26 45N04

JEAN DIXON
1/05/1904
MEDFORD, WI
2:00AM CST
ZONE +6:00
90W20
45N08

ALAN VAUGHAN
12/28/1936
AKRON, OH
8:09 AM EST
ZONE +5:00
81W31
41N04

WILLIAM WINGFIELD
4/10/1934
SHARON, PA
7:20PM EST
ZONE +5:00
80W31
41N14

ERIC HANUSSEN
6/2/1889
LITOMERICE, BOHEMIA
4:00AM LMT
ZONE +00:00
14E09
50N35

KARL ERNST VON KRAFFT
5/10/1900
COMMUGNY, SWITZERLAND
12:45 PM LMT
ZONE +00:00
006E30
46N32

There have been thousands of examples of gifted psychic individuals over the centuries but perhaps the most famous of these was ironically a trained physician and healer. Many of these are certainly worthy of inclusion in our study, but for the sake of brevity, we will examine only a few in this work. The first profile we will examine for our study of psychic markers is that of the Prince of Prophets, Michelle de Nostredame.

NOSTRADAMUS

Nostradamus was born in the town of Saint-Remy in Provence on December 14, 1503. His father practiced there as a notary, and came of a Jewish family that had been converted to Christianity. He was fortunate in having a devoted maternal grandfather in Jean de Saint-Remy, a physician and astrologer, who took his education under his personal charge, teaching him Greek, Latin, Hebrew, mathematics, the Arts, herbology, and medicine. He also taught the boy how to use the astrolabe, and fostered in him an enthusiasm for studying the stars and their courses. In those days, astrology and astronomy were on opposite sides of the same coin, and magic was still at the helm of medical science. He taught the young Nostradamus not only the particular efficacy of each herb but also how important it was to gather them under the right aspects, and how the lives of human beings themselves were supposed to be influenced by the conjunction of heavenly bodies.

Jean de Saint-Remy passed away when Michel was still very young. The child's on his father's side, who was a grain-dealer, then continued his education until he was sent to the university of Avignon, where from the first he proved to be their brightest student. According to Chavigny, he taught his fellow students the movements of the planets, claiming that the earth was round and revolved annually around the sun, which, when it appeared to set, lit up the other side of the globe. These views were of course espoused one hundred years later by Galileo.

Michel's father decided that he should follow his grand father's profession, and for that purpose transferred him to the university of Montpellier which was renowned for its school of medicine, where anatomy was first studied by dissecting corpses, owing to the Duke of Anjou having granted them privilege of receiving once a year an executed malefactor's body. Michel had qualified easily for admittance but shortly after his matriculation, the plague brought him into combat. It was unfortunately the most virulent type of the illness called le charbon, and black pustules formed on the bodies of those infected. Michel fought tirelessly to save lives with skill and courage. Michel came up with a powder that purified the air and soon news of his success spread, and many towns begged for his help.

Michel's travels took him to Toulouse, Narbonne and Bordeaux. Then, when the epidemic had died out, he went back to Montpelier to take his doctorate. But, having done so, he was expected to teach, and then found himself increasingly in conflict with orthodox tenets and methods of treatment, so in 1531 he left, and for two years led the life of an itinerant physician in Languedoc and Provence, ministering to all classes, including many notable in their castles and country houses. Among these was the Princess of Navarre. On a visit to Agen in the Garonne, he became friendly with Julius Caesar Scaliger, who after Erasmus was regarded as the foremost European scholar of the period, and as a result he settled there in 1533 and soon married. When his wife and two children died in another outbreak of the plague, he was brokenhearted and left to try to forget his sorrows.

For the next eight years, he spent wandering France, Italy and Sicily. It was during these travels that his gift of second sight began to develop in earnest. On one famous occasion when in the March of Ancona, he passed on a road some friars. Among them was a youth of humble birth, Felice Peretti, who had been a swineherd until he joined a mendicant order. On seeing the young man, Michel dismounted from his mule and knelt before him. The astonished monks asked why he did this. "Because I must kneel before His Holiness", he replied. The were more astonished than ever at such an unlikely prophecy. However years later, after Nostradamus himself had died, the former swineherd (the Cardinal Montalto) became Pope Sixtus V.

In 1547 he decided to settle in windswept Salon de Craux, midway between Avignon and Marseilles, where he married a wealthy and well-connected widow and went to live in a narrow impasse off the place de la Poissonerie, not far from the boulevard now named after him. The house can still be seen today, overshadowed by the gloomy thirteenth-century chateau de l'Emperi, with its dungeon and dark history, that is perched on the summit of a rocky hill, where in 1966 the first world conference of astrologers was held in commemoration of the 400th anniversary of his death. On that occasion, a statue of him was unveiled. At the very top of the house, reached by a spiral stone staircase, is the room where he read and wrote undisturbed and studied the stars.

The pension from Aix-en-Provence, together with his wife's money, now gave him the financial security to enable him to devote much of his time to esoteric pursuits, though he still spent some time working as a physician. During his travels, he came across a rare book, De Mysteriis Egyptorum, and guided by its contents he set about developing his occult powers. It was in the quiet seclusion of his study he began to record his famous prophecies, the Centuries, on which he spent some four years. Nostadamus' famous quatrains have become synonymous with prophecy and the study of astrology. His predictions about World War I and II, Hitler, the French revolution, the advent of the Atomic bomb, King Henri of France, and a host of other equally magnificent prophecies are now legendary in their own right. Entire books have been written about his prophecies and we will not recount them in this work. I am much more intrigued by the possibility that this great and brilliant prophet was marked from birth as a great psychic.

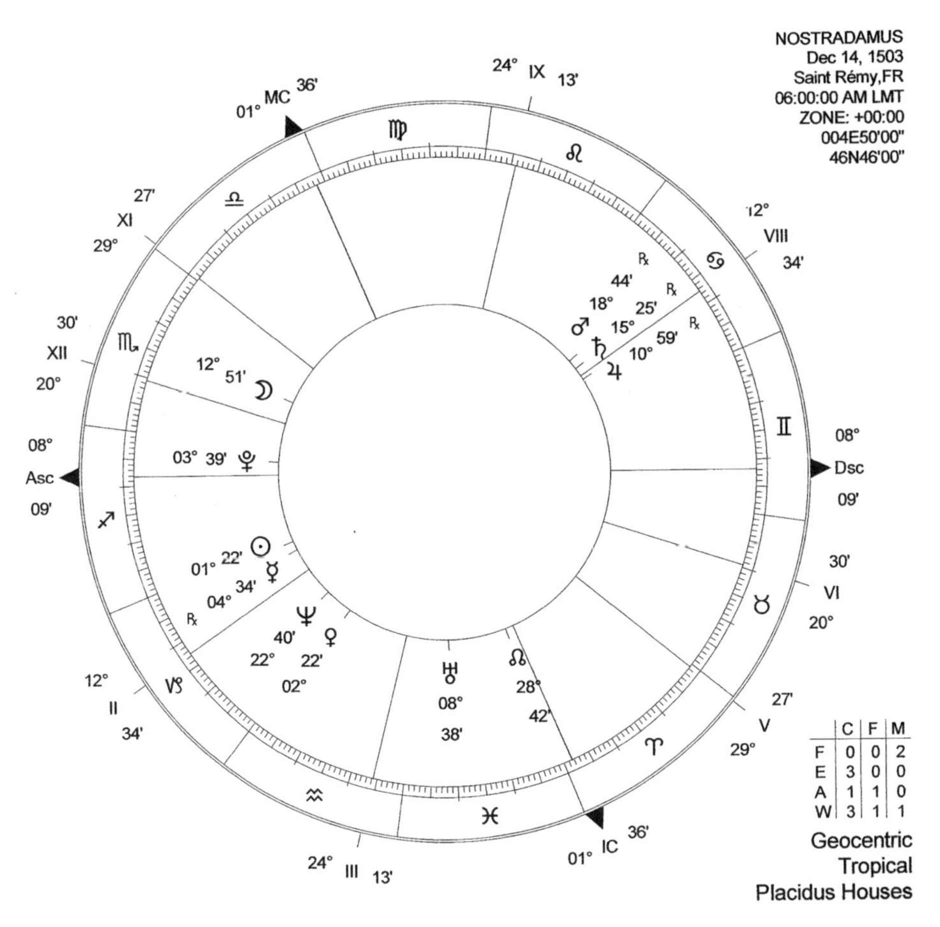

Planetary Hour: Moon (☽)
11th Hour of Mercury-Night
☉/☽ MidPt: 247°06'
Asc/Mc MidPt: 214°52'

RAMC: 181°28'
ST: 12h05m51s
LMT: 06:00:00

Pl	Geo Lon	℞	Decl.	G.Lat
☽	12°♏51'		- 19° 03'	- 03° 29'
☉	01°♑22'		- 23° 30'	+00' 00"
☿	04°♑34'	℞	- 21° 18'	+02° 08'
♀	02°♒22'		- 19° 00'	+00° 42'
♂	18°♋44'	℞	+25° 50'	+03° 40'
♃	10°♋59'	℞	+23° 09'	+00° 06'
♄	15°♋25'	℞	+22° 21'	- 00° 16'
♅	08°♓38'		- 09° 03'	- 00° 45'
♆	22°♑40'		- 21° 12'	+00° 24'
♇	03°♐39'		- 10° 01'	+11° 06'
☊	28°♓42'		- 00° 31'	+00' 00"
Mc	01°♎36'		- 00° 38'	+00' 00"
Asc	08°♐09'		- 21° 44'	+00' 00"

Birth / Event Data

Nostradamus

Place of birth/event (city, state, county)

12-14-1503 6:00AM

Date of birth/event

Saint Remy FR

Time of birth/event (exact time, i.e. birth certificate)

Client Data

First and last name

Mailing address

City, state, country, zip code

Telephone no. and fax no.

E-mail address

GENERAL PSYCHIC POTENTIAL – MARKER ASPECTS

(All aspects score 10 points each, unless otherwise indicated)

CONJUNCTIONS

- ✓ Saturn - Mars
- ✓ Jupiter - Saturn
- ___ Moon -Venus
- ___ Saturn - Uranus
- ___ Jupiter - Moon
- ___ Jupiter - Uranus
- ___ Sun - Mars
- ___ Uranus - Mars

TRINES

- ___ Neptune – Mars
- ___ Venus – Jupiter
- ___ Mercury - Mars
- ✓ Jupiter – Uranus (25 pts)

SEXTILES

- ___ Saturn – Mercury
- ___ Pluto – Uranus (25 pts)
- ___ Sun – Uranus (25 pts)
- ___ Mercury – Mars (25 pts)
- ___ Jupiter – Mercury (25 pts)
- ___ Saturn – Pluto (25 pts)
- ___ Saturn – Sun (25 pts)
- ___ Saturn – Neptune
- ___ Sun – Mars
- ___ Uranus – Moon (25 pts)
- ✓ Venus – Pluto (25 pts)
- ___ Mercury – Venus (25 pts)
- ___ Neptune – Moon (25 pts)
- ___ Moon – Mars
- ___ Jupiter – Moon

SQUARES

- ___ Pluto – Moon
- ___ Sun – Jupiter
- ✓ Uranus – Pluto
- ___ Jupiter – Moon
- ___ Jupiter – Uranus
- ___ Venus – Jupiter
- ___ Saturn – Moon
- ___ Jupiter – Saturn
- ___ Jupiter – Neptune

OPPOSITIONS

- ___ Pluto – Mars
- ___ Saturn – Moon
- ___ Venus – Saturn
- ___ Saturn – Neptune

PARALLELS

- ✓ Moon – Venus
- ___ Pluto – Moon (25 pts)
- ___ Sun – Moon
- ___ Mercury – Mars
- ___ Pluto – Mars
- ___ Jupiter – Moon
- ___ Saturn - Neptune
- ✓ Venus – Neptune (25 pts)
- ✓ Pluto – Uranus
- ✓ Moon – Mercury
- ✓ Jupiter – Mars (25 pts)
- ✓ Sun – Mercury
- ✓ Mercury – Venus (25 pts)
- ___ Jupiter – Saturn

CONTRAPARALLELS

- ✓ Jupiter – Saturn (25 pts)
- ___ Moon – Mercury (25 pts)
- ___ Pluto – Moon (25 pts)
- ✓ Jupiter – Mercury
- ✓ Jupiter – Neptune
- ___ Jupiter – Moon
- ___ Sun – Jupiter (25 pts)
- ___ Sun – Moon (25 pts)
- ___ Uranus – Neptune (25 pts)
- ___ Pluto – Mars (25 pts)

HIDEK

- ✓ Mercury
- ___ Mars

EXDEK

- ___ Venus
- ✓ Mars
- ___ Uranus
- ___ Pluto

PROXIMITY ELEVATIONS

- ___ Pluto – Mars (parallel)
- ___ Sun – Pluto (contraparallel)

ECLIPSES

- ___ Saturn – Mercury
- ___ Jupiter – Uranus
- ___ Any Mars Eclipse

GRAND ELEVATIONS

- ___ + Mercury
- ✓ - Sun
- ___ - Uranus
- ✓ - Neptune
- ___ + Moon

GRAND TOTAL		**SCALE**
___	Below Average	0 - 30
___	Average	31 - 60
___	Above Average	61 - 100
___	Superior	101 - 140
___	Outstanding	141 - 180
280	Delphi Class	181+

When we examine his chart and look for marker aspects we find that he has a rating of 280! This number places him well into the Delphi range of ability according to the results of our study. He has six Delphi aspects and a host of other marker aspects that would readily identify him as a world-class psychic by sheer right of his natal chart. Nostradamus marker aspects for psychic ability are listed on the next page. He has six grand elevations in his chart and two different eclipse patterns. Nostradamus also has three of the top ten markers for psychic ability: Jupiter/Uranus trine, Jupiter/Mars parallel, and the Mercury/Venus parallel. Overall, his chart indicates that he would have likely discovered the gifts within his being at some point during his life. Did he study the occult at the home of Julius Caesar Scaliger as some accounts of his life suggest? Did he receive instruction in the mystic arts during his many travels to the East? Did his grandfather impart to him some secret of the Ages prior to his passing? We can only speculate on the answer to these questions, but it is quite clear that Nostradamus did spend some time developing his healing and scrying gifts during his travels. I believe that it is not enough to simply be born with a gifted chart. Some impetus or force is necessary to bring the gifts to the fore. In his case, grief, intellect, and esoteric instruction seem to have combined to give him the necessary initiation into the Art. Many people wonder why they do not develop psychic or spiritual ability even if they have a high potential score or if they have read many books and meditated. Focused, disciplined study is required to bring out the gift to its fullest potential in all but the most gifted savants. The student would do well to take full note of the life of Michelle de Nostradame. To whom much is given, much is required. We will examine more of Nostradamus' prophecies in a later chapter.

URI GELLER

Uri Geller was born December 20, 1946 in Tel Aviv. His parents are of Hungarian and Austrian descent and he distantly related on his mother's side to Sigmund Freud. At the age of four, he had a mysterious encounter with a sphere of light while in a garden near his home. He became aware of his unusual powers when he was five. One day, during a meal, his spoon curled up in his hand and broke, although he had placed no pressure on it. He continued to develop these powers by demonstrating them to his friend. His mother thought that he had inherited them from Sigmund Freud.

When he was eleven, he went to live in Cyprus, where he lived until he was seventeen. He then returned to Israel, served as a paratrooper in the Israeli army and fought in the Six-Day War of 1967 during which he was wounded in action. From 1968 to 1969 Uri worked as a model and he was photographed for many magazine advertisements.

In 1969, he began to demonstrate his powers of telepathy and psychokinesis to small audiences. By the end of 1971, he had become a household name throughout Israel thanks to his numerous stage appearances. He was given an endorsement by Prime Minister Golda Meir who once said on a national program what she predicted for the future of Israel, she replied, "Don't ask me- ask Uri Geller!"

Much of the press that Geller has received in the US has been tainted by his now famous fights with the magician Randi. However, Geller has accomplished some rather amazing feats that the American press tends to dismiss and refuses to report. I will not bow to that horrible convention. In Germany, witnessed by reporters and photographers, he stopped a cable car in mid-air using only the power of his mind. He then did the same to an escalator in a major department store. That same year at the invitation of astronaut Captain Edgar Mitchell of the Apollo 14 mission, inventor and author Andrija Puharich MD, Professor Gerald Feinberg of the Columbia University physics department, Ronald Hawke from the Lawrence Livermore National Laboratory, Ron Robertson of the Atomic Energy Commission, and NASA's Wernher von Braun he took part in a series of now famous experiments that verified his power. The results of these experiments were published in a book called the Geller Papers published by Houghton Mifflin and edited by Newsweek science writer Charles Panati.

Tests at the Stanford Research Institute in California where carefully witnessed Geller Effects included the creation of a loss and gain of mass in a gram weight on a high precision balance. He also called out the eight out of ten die-throws against odds of a million to one. He also guessed the location of some hidden targets at the odds of a trillion to one. These controlled experiments were published as a scientific paper in the prestigious British journal Nature.

Experiments at Birkbeck College, University of London, with a team of research physicists headed by Professor J.B. Hasted, and eminent theoretical physicist Professor David Bohm, who has worked with Albert Einstein studied the abilities that Geller produces. In these experiments, Geller caused a Geiger counter to register 500 times its normal count, deformed a molybdenum crystal 1cm in diameter and caused part of another crystal inside a pill capsule to dematerialize! Witnesses at the Birkbeck experiments included Arthur Koestler, Arthur Clarke, and Arthur Ellison.

The general public is not aware of many of the fantastic exploits of this great psychic. Much of his activity is obscured by obsessive coverage of skeptical press related diatribe. However, Geller with his friend Meir Gitlis, has developed a number of inventions that are already in production around the world. He has invented a machine that tells a fake banknote from a genuine one; a machine that does the same for diamonds; a gas leak detector, and a number of security devices including sensors for defense installations. Another of his inventions is the Gold-Meter, a compact electronic device for examining solid and other precious metals by an electro-chemical process controlled by a micro computer. He has also invented a device for use with cellular telephones that may be used as a shield to prevent the harmful long-term effects of exposure to the short waves penetrating the brain.

With this introduction, what does the birth chart of Uri Geller tell us about his psychic ability? Not surprisingly, his general psychic potential score is 180. This score places him at the highest category of psychic potential in our survey! Coincidence, I think not. Geller's marker aspects are listed on the next page. He has two delphi aspects and over 13 additional marker aspects for psychic ability. Overall, his chart is quite a gifted and fortunate one. How were his abilities triggered? From the charts we have seen in previous biographies, a trigger is usually present at the advent of most psychic's initiation. Did the glowing sphere that he encountered as a child activate this phenomenal man's potential? Before his encounter with the orb, there are no known accounts of Geller's psychic ability. This is not to say that the ability was not present, rather, it ostensibly lay dormant until the proper trigger could activate it. Geller himself is rather reserved and pensive about his gift. He recognizes that his skeptics would rather that he admit to trickery and go away quietly into that good night. Rather, he now busies himself by finding oil and diamond mines for major corporations. In the process, he has made himself millions of dollars. Perhaps, success is the best revenge!

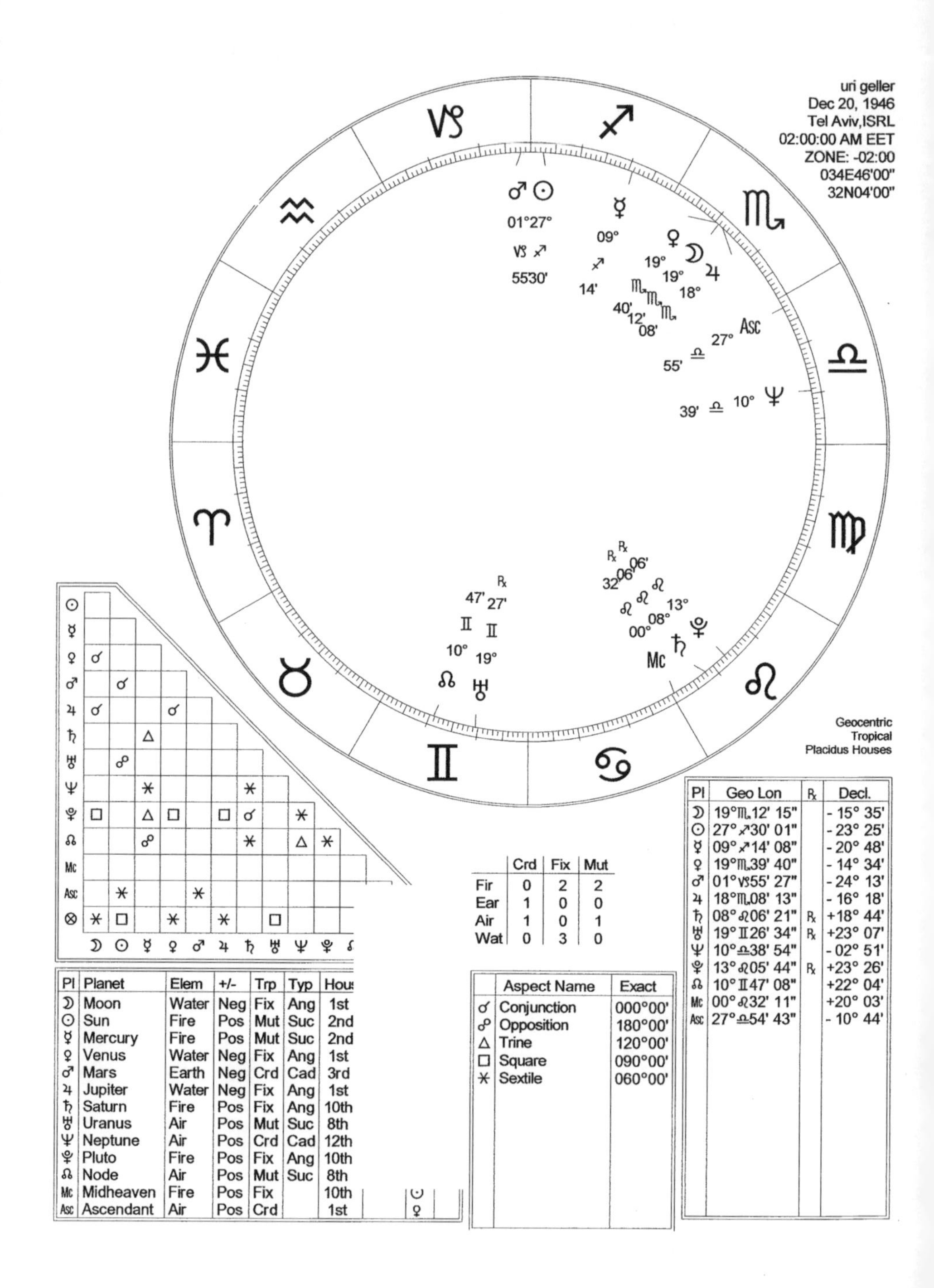

	☽	☉	☿	♀	♂	♃	♄	♅	♆	♇	☊
☉											
☿											
♀	☌										
♂		☌									
♃	☌			☌							
♄			△								
♅		☍									
♆			⚹				⚹				
♇	□		△	□		□	☌		⚹		
☊			☍				⚹		△	⚹	
Mc											
Asc		⚹			⚹						
⊗	⚹	□		⚹		⚹		□			

	Crd	Fix	Mut
Fir	0	2	2
Ear	1	0	0
Air	1	0	1
Wat	0	3	0

Pl	Geo Lon	℞	Decl.
☽	19°♏12' 15"		- 15° 35'
☉	27°♐30' 01"		- 23° 25'
☿	09°♐14' 08"		- 20° 48'
♀	19°♏39' 40"		- 14° 34'
♂	01°♑55' 27"		- 24° 13'
♃	18°♏08' 13"		- 16° 18'
♄	08°♌06' 21"	℞	+18° 44'
♅	19°♊26' 34"	℞	+23° 07'
♆	10°♎38' 54"		- 02° 51'
♇	13°♌05' 44"	℞	+23° 26'
☊	10°♊47' 08"		+22° 04'
Mc	00°♌32' 11"		+20° 03'
Asc	27°♎54' 43"		- 10° 44'

Pl	Planet	Elem	+/-	Trp	Typ	Hous
☽	Moon	Water	Neg	Fix	Ang	1st
☉	Sun	Fire	Pos	Mut	Suc	2nd
☿	Mercury	Fire	Pos	Mut	Suc	2nd
♀	Venus	Water	Neg	Fix	Ang	1st
♂	Mars	Earth	Neg	Crd	Cad	3rd
♃	Jupiter	Water	Neg	Fix	Ang	1st
♄	Saturn	Fire	Pos	Fix	Ang	10th
♅	Uranus	Air	Pos	Mut	Suc	8th
♆	Neptune	Air	Pos	Crd	Cad	12th
♇	Pluto	Fire	Pos	Fix	Ang	10th
☊	Node	Air	Pos	Mut	Suc	8th
Mc	Midheaven	Fire	Pos	Fix		10th
Asc	Ascendant	Air	Pos	Crd		1st

	Aspect Name	Exact
☌	Conjunction	000°00'
☍	Opposition	180°00'
△	Trine	120°00'
□	Square	090°00'
⚹	Sextile	060°00'

Birth / Event Data

Uri Geller
Place of birth/event (city, state, county)

12-20-1946
Date of birth/event

2:00 AM EET 34E46 32N04
Time of birth/event (exact time, i.e. birth certificate)

Client Data

Uri Geller
First and last name

Sonning Berkshire RG4 64R
Mailing address

England
City, state, country, zip code

Fax 01189 655 435
Telephone no. and fax no.

www.uri-geller.com
E-mail address

GENERAL PSYCHIC POTENTIAL – MARKER ASPECTS

(All aspects score 10 points each, unless otherwise indicated)

CONJUNCTIONS

- ___ Saturn - Mars
- ___ Jupiter - Saturn
- X Moon -Venus
- ___ Saturn - Uranus
- X Jupiter - Moon
- ___ Jupiter - Uranus
- X Sun - Mars
- ___ Uranus - Mars

TRINES

- ___ Neptune – Mars
- ___ Venus – Jupiter
- ___ Mercury - Mars
- ___ Jupiter – Uranus (25 pts)

SEXTILES

- ___ Saturn – Mercury
- ___ Pluto – Uranus (25 pts)
- ___ Sun – Uranus (25 pts)
- ___ Mercury – Mars (25 pts)
- ___ Jupiter – Mercury (25 pts)
- ___ Saturn – Pluto (25 pts)
- ___ Saturn – Sun (25 pts)
- X Saturn – Neptune
- ___ Sun – Mars
- ___ Uranus – Moon (25 pts)
- ___ Venus – Pluto (25 pts)
- ___ Mercury – Venus (25 pts)
- ___ Neptune – Moon (25 pts)
- ___ Moon – Mars
- ___ Jupiter – Moon
- ___ Jupiter – Moon
- ___ Jupiter – Uranus
- ___ Venus – Jupiter
- ___ Saturn – Moon
- ___ Jupiter – Saturn
- ___ Jupiter – Neptune

SQUARES

- X Pluto – Moon
- ___ Sun – Jupiter
- ___ Uranus – Pluto

OPPOSITIONS

- ___ Pluto – Mars
- ___ Saturn – Moon
- ___ Venus – Saturn
- ___ Saturn – Neptune

PARALLELS

- X Moon – Venus
- ___ Pluto – Moon (25 pts)
- ___ Sun – Moon
- ___ Mercury – Mars
- ___ Pluto – Mars
- X Jupiter – Moon
- ___ Saturn - Neptune
- ___ Venus – Neptune (25 pts)
- X Pluto – Uranus
- ___ Moon – Mercury
- ___ Jupiter – Mars (25 pts)
- ___ Sun – Mercury
- ___ Mercury – Venus (25 pts)
- ___ Jupiter – Saturn

CONTRAPARALLELS

- X Jupiter – Saturn (25 pts)
- ___ Moon – Mercury (25 pts)
- ___ Pluto – Moon (25 pts)
- ___ Jupiter – Mercury
- ___ Jupiter – Neptune
- ___ Jupiter – Moon
- ___ Sun – Jupiter (25 pts)
- ___ Sun – Moon (25 pts)
- ___ Uranus – Neptune (25 pts)
- X Pluto – Mars (25 pts)

HIDEK

- ___ Mercury
- ___ Mars

EXDEK

- ___ Venus
- X Mars
- ___ Uranus
- ___ Pluto

PROXIMITY ELEVATIONS

- ___ Pluto – Mars (parallel)
- X Sun – Pluto (contraparallel)

ECLIPSES

- ___ Saturn – Mercury
- ___ Jupiter – Uranus
- X Any Mars Eclipse

GRAND ELEVATIONS

- ___ + Mercury
- X - Sun
- X - Uranus
- ___ - Neptune
- ___ + Moon

	GRAND TOTAL	SCALE
___	Below Average	0 - 30
___	Average	31 - 60
___	Above Average	61 - 100
___	Superior	101 - 140
180	Outstanding	141 - 180
___	Delphi Class	181+

JEAN DIXON

Jean Dixon was born in Medford Wisconsin on January 5,1904. She was one of the most prominent astrologers and psychics of the 20th century. She is perhaps most famous for her prediction of the assassination of President John F. Kennedy. She said that the 1960 election would be won by a Democrat who would be assassinated or die in office. Dixon states that she saw the event unfold before her while she prayed in the very church that Kennedy was laid to rest! She was a devout Catholic and she went to Mass every Sunday. We will cover this vision in detail in a later chapter.

Dixon is perhaps a good example of a psychic who repeatedly outstripped her power. She was remarkably accurate in her political revelations but her visions on the 1958 advent of World War III, a cancer cure that would materialize in 1967, and her prediction that the Soviet Union would absorb the Western Hemisphere by 1990 were well off the mark. This inconsistency is a trademark for Ms. Dixon. When we examine her birth chart, we find that she falls squarely in the outstanding category with a score of 165. However, we do not find any evidence of training or a distinct trigger that would further enhance or develop her abilities. Is it possible that her ability, though prominent and considerable, would have been further enhanced by serious training and discipline? Given her outstanding rating, this work may well have strengthened Ms. Dixon's legacy as a world-class psychic. Jean Dixon's chart is listed on the next page.

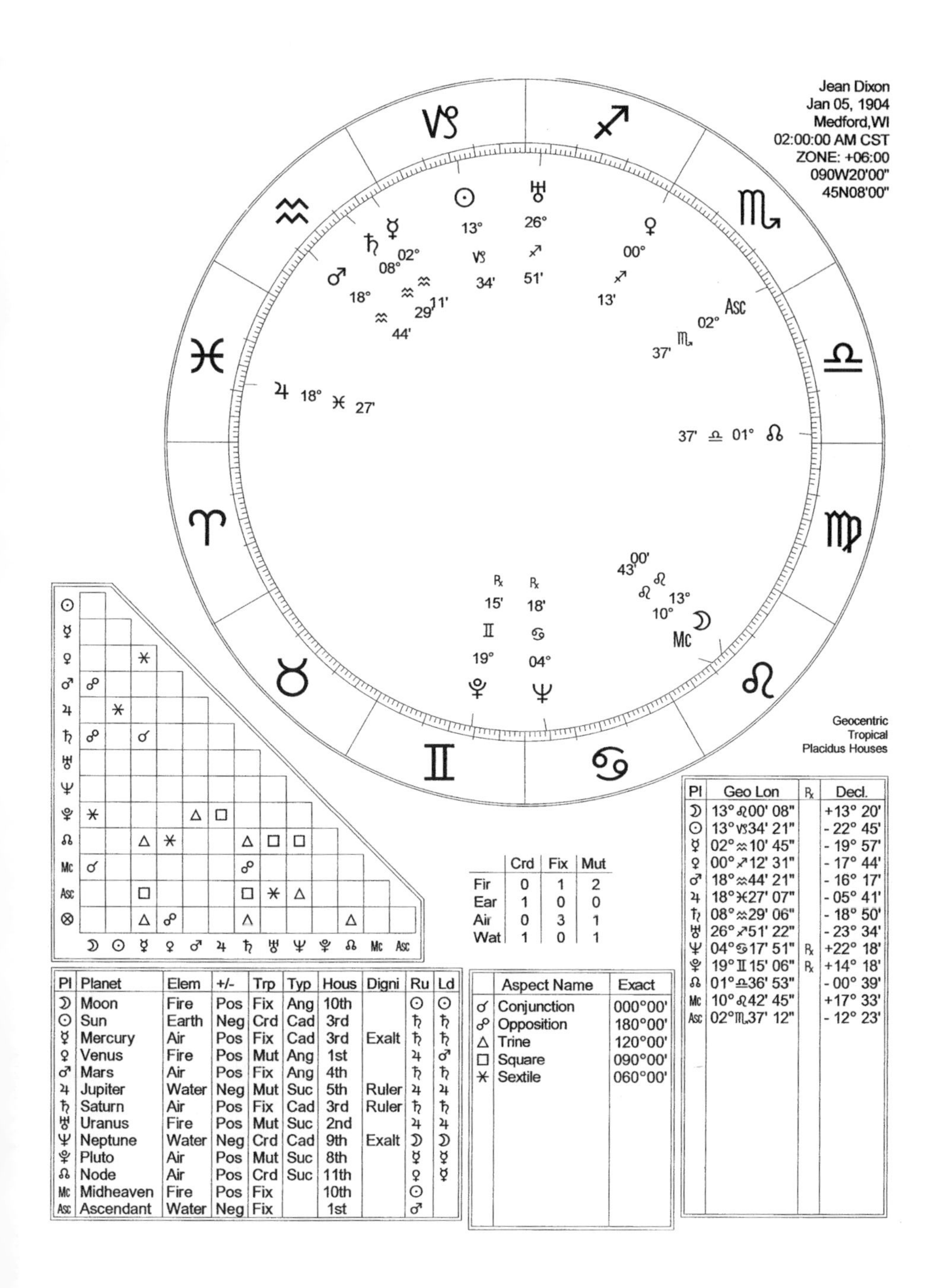

	☽	☉	☿	♀	♂	♃	♄	♅	♆	♇	☊	Mc	Asc
☉													
☿													
♀			✳										
♂	☍												
♃		✳											
♄	☍		☌										
♅													
♆													
♇	✳				△	□							
☊			△	✳			△	□	□				
Mc	☌						☍						
Asc			□				□	✳	△				
⊗			△	☍			△				△		

	Crd	Fix	Mut
Fir	0	1	2
Ear	1	0	0
Air	0	3	1
Wat	1	0	1

Pl	Geo Lon	℞	Decl.
☽	13°♌00' 08"		+13° 20'
☉	13°♑34' 21"		- 22° 45'
☿	02°♒10' 45"		- 19° 57'
♀	00°♐12' 31"		- 17° 44'
♂	18°♒44' 21"		- 16° 17'
♃	18°♓27' 07"		- 05° 41'
♄	08°♒29' 06"		- 18° 50'
♅	26°♐51' 22"		- 23° 34'
♆	04°♋17' 51"	℞	+22° 18'
♇	19°♊15' 06"	℞	+14° 18'
☊	01°♎36' 53"		- 00° 39'
Mc	10°♌42' 45"		+17° 33'
Asc	02°♏37' 12"		- 12° 23'

Pl	Planet	Elem	+/-	Trp	Typ	Hous	Digni	Ru	Ld
☽	Moon	Fire	Pos	Fix	Ang	10th		☉	☉
☉	Sun	Earth	Neg	Crd	Cad	3rd		♄	♄
☿	Mercury	Air	Pos	Fix	Cad	3rd	Exalt	♄	♄
♀	Venus	Fire	Pos	Mut	Ang	1st		♃	♂
♂	Mars	Air	Pos	Fix	Ang	4th		♄	♄
♃	Jupiter	Water	Neg	Mut	Suc	5th	Ruler	♃	♃
♄	Saturn	Air	Pos	Fix	Cad	3rd	Ruler	♄	♄
♅	Uranus	Fire	Pos	Mut	Suc	2nd		♃	♃
♆	Neptune	Water	Neg	Crd	Cad	9th	Exalt	☽	☽
♇	Pluto	Air	Pos	Mut	Suc	8th		☿	☿
☊	Node	Air	Pos	Crd	Suc	11th		♀	☿
Mc	Midheaven	Fire	Pos	Fix		10th		☉	
Asc	Ascendant	Water	Neg	Fix		1st		♂	

	Aspect Name	Exact
☌	Conjunction	000°00'
☍	Opposition	180°00'
△	Trine	120°00'
□	Square	090°00'
✳	Sextile	060°00'

Birth / Event Data

Jean Dixon
Place of birth/event (city, state, county)

1-5-1904 Medford WI 90W20 45n08
Date of birth/event

2:00Am CST Zone +6:00
Time of birth/event (exact time, i.e. birth certificate)

Client Data

First and last name

Mailing address

City, state, country, zip code

Telephone no. and fax no.

E-mail address

GENERAL PSYCHIC POTENTIAL – MARKER ASPECTS

(All aspects score 10 points each, unless otherwise indicated)

CONJUNCTIONS

- ___ Saturn - Mars
- ___ Jupiter - Saturn
- ___ Moon -Venus
- ___ Saturn - Uranus
- ___ Jupiter - Moon
- ___ Jupiter - Uranus
- ___ Sun - Mars
- ___ Uranus - Mars

TRINES

- ___ Neptune – Mars
- ___ Venus – Jupiter
- ___ Mercury - Mars
- ___ Jupiter – Uranus (25 pts)

SEXTILES

- ___ Saturn – Mercury
- ___ Pluto – Uranus (25 pts)
- ___ Sun – Uranus (25 pts)
- ___ Mercury – Mars (25 pts)
- ___ Jupiter – Mercury (25 pts)
- ___ Saturn – Pluto (25 pts)
- ___ Saturn – Sun (25 pts)
- ___ Saturn – Neptune
- ___ Sun – Mars
- ___ Uranus – Moon (25 pts)
- ___ Venus – Pluto (25 pts)
- X Mercury – Venus (25 pts)
- ___ Neptune – Moon (25 pts)
- ___ Moon – Mars
- ___ Jupiter – Moon

SQUARES

- ___ Pluto – Moon
- ___ Sun – Jupiter
- ___ Uranus – Pluto
- ___ Jupiter – Moon
- ___ Jupiter – Uranus
- ___ Venus – Jupiter
- ___ Saturn – Moon
- ___ Jupiter – Saturn
- ___ Jupiter – Neptune

OPPOSITIONS

- ___ Pluto – Mars
- X Saturn – Moon
- ___ Venus – Saturn
- ___ Saturn – Neptune

PARALLELS

- ___ Moon – Venus
- X Pluto – Moon (25 pts)
- ___ Sun – Moon
- ___ Mercury – Mars
- ___ Pluto – Mars
- ___ Jupiter – Moon
- ___ Saturn - Neptune
- ___ Venus – Neptune (25 pts)
- ___ Pluto – Uranus
- ___ Moon – Mercury
- ___ Jupiter – Mars (25 pts)
- ___ Sun – Mercury
- X Mercury – Venus (25 pts)
- ___ Jupiter – Saturn

CONTRAPARALLELS

- ___ Jupiter – Saturn (25 pts)
- ___ Moon – Mercury (25 pts)
- ___ Pluto – Moon (25 pts)
- ___ Jupiter – Mercury
- ___ Jupiter – Neptune
- ___ Jupiter – Moon
- ___ Sun – Jupiter (25 pts)
- ___ Sun – Moon (25 pts)
- X Uranus – Neptune (25 pts)
- X Pluto – Mars (25 pts)

HIDEK

- ___ Mercury
- ___ Mars

EXDEK

- ___ Venus
- ___ Mars
- X Uranus
- ___ Pluto

PROXIMITY ELEVATIONS

- ___ Pluto – Mars (parallel)
- ___ Sun – Pluto (contraparallel)

ECLIPSES

- X Saturn – Mercury
- ___ Jupiter – Uranus
- ___ Any Mars Eclipse

GRAND ELEVATIONS

- ___ + Mercury
- ___ - Sun
- ___ - Uranus
- X - Neptune
- ___ + Moon

GRAND TOTAL		SCALE
___	Below Average	0 - 30
___	Average	31 - 60
___	Above Average	61 - 100
___	Superior	101 - 140
165	Outstanding	141 - 180
___	Delphi Class	181+

JOSEPH MCMONEAGLE

Joseph McMoneagle was born in Miami Florida on January 10,1949. He is the greatest living clairvoyant in the world today. Joseph is perhaps not as well known as some of the more illustrious participants in our discussion, but he has served the United States Intelligence effort for more than 20 years. Joseph's primary affiliation is remote-viewing. Simply stated, if you give him a set of coordinates representing an unknown target or question, he is the best in the world at eliciting a correct answer to this limited amount of data. He has appeared on hundreds of television, and radio shows and has been featured in every major newspaper in the US. He has worked for the CIA, Defense Intelligence Agency, National Security Agency, Drug Enforcement Agency, Secret Service, FBI, US Customs, the National Security Council, and Project Stargate. Most of his work has been classified by these agencies and the vast majority of his successes have been related to topics vital to national security. Some of his more public exploits are listed in the book Remote Viewers by Jim Schnabel.

Early in McMoneagle's childhood when he was eleven years old he was camping with a group of friends next to an orange grove in his home state of Florida. One night he and his friends were all up late, in the grove, playing one of those primitive combat games that young boys seem to devise instinctively. One boy, designated "it", had to run and hide, while the others tried to find him. After a certain number of rounds, it was McMoneagle's turn to hide. He ran into the dark, climbed an orange tree, found a secure position, and relaxed. He had been playing the game for a few hours now, and he was very tired. He closed his eyes and fell fast asleep.

Someone tapped him. He opened his eyes. A strange, ghostlike woman was floating in space next to the tree. She gently took Joe's arm, and he floated along with her. The scenery changed. They were in a clearing somewhere, in a forest or a swamp; it felt special. The woman gently lectured Joe on the future. He would grow up to be a strong boy. He would join the Army and be sent far-off to war. Many would be killed there, but Joe would come back all right. The woman's survey of his future lasted an hour, unveiling detail after detail of Joe's life. He then woke up in the tree.

McMoneagle did go to war when he grew up. He spent much of the Vietnam War in the Vietnamese central highlands, south of the city of Da Nang. The borders of Laos and Cambodia were nearby, and the Vietcong and North Vietnamese Army criss-crossed his position regularly. Sometimes, on a perfectly sunny day or a perfectly starry evening, a strange feeling would come over him, a sense of something about to happen, and he would pack up his favorite lawn chair, put on his helmet and flak jacket, and headed for his assigned bunker. Suddenly, the mortar rounds would scream in from the surrounding forest, and he sat comfortably as his buddies scrambled for cover.

The other soldiers started noticing how often Joe seemed to anticipate these attacks. It got so that whenever he would start packing up his lawn chair, some of the rest of them would put down what they were doing and head for their bunkers. Eventually, they began to mimic his most arbitrary and inconsequential actions. When Joe tied his boots a different way one day, looping the laces around the back, suddenly half a dozen of the others started tying their boots the same way. No bullet or mortar round ever hit him, and despite a helicopter accident that left him with a chronic back condition, he made it out on his own two feet.

When Joe left Vietnam, he was recruited for an elite corp of psychic soldiers who would work on special secret projects for the government. They were called remote viewers. One of his most famous projects was Project Stargate, a top secret multimillion-dollar project at Fort Meade, MD. Using only their paranormal ability, these soldiers were asked to locate American hostages, enemy submarines, strategic buildings in foreign countries, and a host of other projects. On a typical workday, Joe would report to an old, leaky wooden barrack where he went into a one-person office. He sat at a desk with a typewriter and a mug of coffee. He was then presented with sealed envelopes, large brown ones, sometimes small white ones, all of which he was asked to supply information on whatever he sensed was inside.

Sometimes there might be a photograph of a person, and he would be asked to describe where the person was located. Over the years, Joe said that he was involved in about 450 missions. One of his favorites was in 1980, when CIA personnel captured a suspected KGB agent in South Africa. They wanted to know how the agent was communicating with the Soviet military. They put an envelope on Joe's desk, and without knowing anything of the man, he told the CIA that the man liked to use a small pocket calculator to communicate with his superiors. The calculator turned out to be a disguised short-wave radio.

Today, McMoneagle is the executive director of Intuitive Intelligence Applications, Inc. He is the author of two books, Mind Trek and the Ultimate Time Machine. He is available for private as well as corporate psychic operations. What does his birth chart have to say of his ability? McMoneagle scores in the high outstanding range of our potential scale. His chart is listed on the next page. Did the encounter with the multidimensional being during his childhood trigger his clairvoyant ability? With a score of 175 plus years of military psychic training, this man is certainly qualified to accept the mantle of world's greatest and most accurate psychic! Notably, he has the top three spiritual potential markers in all of the sky, the Moon/Mercury contraparallel, a positive Mercury grand elevation, and a positive Moon grand elevation. This alone probably elevates his chart to the heights of function that he so brilliantly displays.

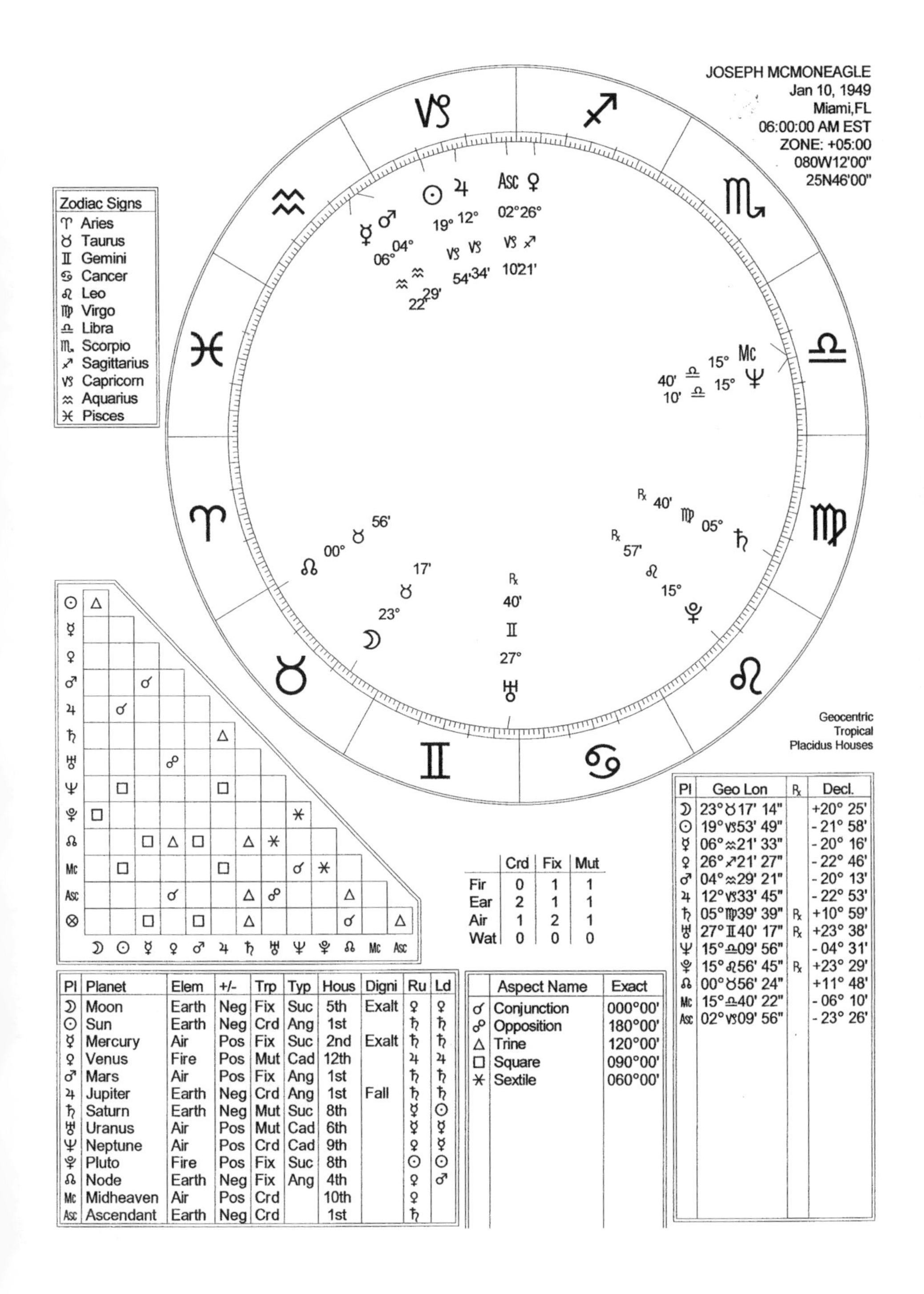

Pl	Planet	Elem	+/-	Trp	Typ	Hous	Digni	Ru	Ld
☽	Moon	Earth	Neg	Fix	Suc	5th	Exalt	♀	♀
☉	Sun	Earth	Neg	Crd	Ang	1st		♄	♄
☿	Mercury	Air	Pos	Fix	Suc	2nd	Exalt	♄	♄
♀	Venus	Fire	Pos	Mut	Cad	12th		♃	♃
♂	Mars	Air	Pos	Fix	Ang	1st		♄	♄
♃	Jupiter	Earth	Neg	Crd	Ang	1st	Fall	♄	♄
♄	Saturn	Earth	Neg	Mut	Suc	8th		☿	☉
♅	Uranus	Air	Pos	Mut	Cad	6th		☿	☿
♆	Neptune	Air	Pos	Crd	Cad	9th		♀	☿
♇	Pluto	Fire	Pos	Fix	Suc	8th		☉	☉
☊	Node	Earth	Neg	Fix	Ang	4th		♀	♂
Mc	Midheaven	Air	Pos	Crd		10th		♀	
Asc	Ascendant	Earth	Neg	Crd		1st		♄	

	Crd	Fix	Mut
Fir	0	1	1
Ear	2	1	1
Air	1	2	1
Wat	0	0	0

	Aspect Name	Exact
☌	Conjunction	000°00'
☍	Opposition	180°00'
△	Trine	120°00'
□	Square	090°00'
⚹	Sextile	060°00'

Pl	Geo Lon	Rx	Decl.
☽	23°♉17' 14"		+20° 25'
☉	19°♑53' 49"		- 21° 58'
☿	06°♒21' 33"		- 20° 16'
♀	26°♐21' 27"		- 22° 46'
♂	04°♒29' 21"		- 20° 13'
♃	12°♑33' 45"		- 22° 53'
♄	05°♍39' 39"	Rx	+10° 59'
♅	27°♊40' 17"	Rx	+23° 38'
♆	15°♎09' 56"		- 04° 31'
♇	15°♌56' 45"	Rx	+23° 29'
☊	00°♉56' 24"		+11° 48'
Mc	15°♎40' 22"		- 06° 10'
Asc	02°♑09' 56"		- 23° 26'

Birth / Event Data

Joseph McMoneagle
Place of birth/event (city, state, county)

1-10-1945 6:00AM EST
Date of birth/event

Miami, FLA 80W12 25N46
Time of birth/event (exact time, i.e. birth certificate)

Client Data

____
First and last name

____
Mailing address

____
City, state, country, zip code

____
Telephone no. and fax no.

____
E-mail address

GENERAL PSYCHIC POTENTIAL – MARKER ASPECTS

(All aspects score 10 points each, unless otherwise indicated)

CONJUNCTIONS

- ____ Saturn - Mars
- ____ Jupiter - Saturn
- ____ Moon -Venus
- ____ Saturn - Uranus
- ____ Jupiter - Moon
- ____ Jupiter - Uranus
- ____ Sun - Mars
- ____ Uranus - Mars

TRINES

- ____ Neptune – Mars
- ____ Venus – Jupiter
- ____ Mercury - Mars
- ____ Jupiter – Uranus (25 pts)

SEXTILES

- ____ Saturn – Mercury
- ____ Pluto – Uranus (25 pts)
- ____ Sun – Uranus (25 pts)
- ____ Mercury – Mars (25 pts)
- ____ Jupiter – Mercury (25 pts)
- ____ Saturn – Pluto (25 pts)
- ____ Saturn – Sun (25 pts)
- ____ Saturn – Neptune
- ____ Sun – Mars
- ____ Uranus – Moon (25 pts)
- ____ Venus – Pluto (25 pts)
- ____ Mercury – Venus (25 pts)
- ____ Neptune – Moon (25 pts)
- ____ Moon – Mars
- ____ Jupiter – Moon

SQUARES

- ____ Pluto – Moon
- ____ Sun – Jupiter
- ____ Uranus – Pluto
- ____ Jupiter – Moon
- ____ Jupiter – Uranus
- ____ Venus – Jupiter
- ____ Saturn – Moon
- ____ Jupiter – Saturn
- X Jupiter – Neptune

OPPOSITIONS

- ____ Pluto – Mars
- ____ Saturn – Moon
- ____ Venus – Saturn
- ____ Saturn – Neptune

PARALLELS

- ____ Moon – Venus
- ____ Pluto – Moon (25 pts)
- ____ Sun – Moon
- X Mercury – Mars
- ____ Pluto – Mars
- ____ Jupiter – Moon
- ____ Saturn - Neptune
- ____ Venus – Neptune (25 pts)
- X Pluto – Uranus
- ____ Moon – Mercury
- ____ Jupiter – Mars (25 pts)
- X Sun – Mercury
- X Mercury – Venus (25 pts)
- ____ Jupiter – Saturn

CONTRAPARALLELS

- ____ Jupiter – Saturn (25 pts)
- X Moon – Mercury (25 pts)
- ____ Pluto – Moon (25 pts)
- ____ Jupiter – Mercury
- ____ Jupiter – Neptune
- X Jupiter – Moon
- ____ Sun – Jupiter (25 pts)
- X Sun – Moon (25 pts)
- ____ Uranus – Neptune (25 pts)
- ____ Pluto – Mars (25 pts)

HIDEK

- ____ Mercury
- ____ Mars

EXDEK

- ____ Venus
- ____ Mars
- X Uranus
- X Pluto

PROXIMITY ELEVATIONS

- ____ Pluto – Mars (parallel)
- ____ Sun – Pluto (contraparallel)

ECLIPSES

- ____ Saturn – Mercury
- ____ Jupiter – Uranus
- X Any Mars Eclipse

GRAND ELEVATIONS

- X + Mercury
- ____ - Sun
- ____ - Uranus
- ____ - Neptune
- X + Moon

	GRAND TOTAL	SCALE
____	Below Average	0 - 30
____	Average	31 - 60
____	Above Average	61 - 100
____	Superior	101 - 140
175	Outstanding	141 - 180
____	Delphi Class	181+

PERTER HURKOS

Peter Hurkos was born in Rotterdam, Netherlands on May 21 1911. He was given the name Pieter van der Hurk but he later changed it to Peter Hurkos. There are many eerie parallels between the life of Peter Hurkos and another great psychic, Edgar Cayce. Like Edgar Cayce, he was a simple, humble man who believed that his gift should be used to help people and not for material gain. Like Cayce, he gave readings for free, to people who could not afford to pay or who for some reason felt they didn't need to. Like Cayce, he could help others become richer by exploring for gold or oil, or advising them on business ventures. However, like Cayce, he was inept in handling his own business affairs, and he gave away more than he earned with his readings.

Many of Edgar Cayce's earthshaking prophecies and remarkable medical cures came to him either while he was in a trance or while he slept. Similarly, some of Peter's most spine-chilling revelations on the Boston Strangler case came while he was talking in his sleep. Some of his most astonishingly accurate descriptions of the Strangler's victims came from sleeping with some of their clothes! Both Edgar Cayce and Peter Hurkos were psychic awake as well as asleep. Nevertheless, both were literal dreamers-that is, they dreamed voluminously, and their dreams frequently had psychical interpretations. Cayce was far more famous for his prophecies but many of Peter's prophecies were equally remarkable.

Peter Hurkos never specialized in healing but many of his psychic diagnoses were remarkably accurate and he scored well in a series of tests at the Glen Cove research labs in Maine. That series of tests was conducted by none other than Dr. Andrija Puharich. Peter is a very versatile and talented man.

As boys, Edgar Cayce and Peter Hurkos were both very poor students, sixth-grade dropouts, and both spent a great deal of their childhood outdoors, in the woods or in seclusion, lonely and brooding, dreamy and introverted, prone to fantasies and visions. Cayce was deeply religious all his life, even as a boy. Peter became religious only after he acquired his gift through his accident. Strangest of all are the physical parallels between Edgar Cayce and Peter Hurkos, the peculiar circumstances of their birth, and their accidents. Cayce was born with milk extruding from the breasts, and Peter was born blind, with an amniotic veil over his eyes. Peter fell on his head; Cayce was hit in the head by a thrown baseball.

After acquiring their gifts, both Edgar Cayce and Peter Hurkos could speak in alien tongues while asleep or in a trance. Both had an uncanny way with plants and flowers, talking to them as though they were people, making them grow, and keeping them alive. Curiously, both men were known as "the man with the X-ray eyes". They both became subject to blinding headaches, apparently related to the physical strain of their psychic forces at work. They also shared certain personality traits, such as a volatile temperament, hypersensitivity, and mercurial moods. One final similarity stretches coincidence to almost freakish disbelief.

On a very cold Sunday morning in New York on February 1964, Hurkos was roused from his sleep at 3:30 a.m., arrested for allegedly impersonating an FBI officer, and hauled off to jail. He spent only a few hours there. The incident turned out to be a political move to discredit the savant-or to embarrass the public officials who had permitted him to work on the case. Queen Juliana of the Netherlands dispatched her own private attorney, Baron von Haimstraff, whom Peter had never met, to represent him, although this turned out to be unnecessary. A quick-witted judge sensed the political hanky-panky, and quickly dropped the case. By some strange and eerie coincidence, the very jail cell that Peter had spent those few hours in had been occupied by Edgar Cayce thirty three years earlier on November 8, 1931. On that occasion, a kindly judge had listened intently to the simple recital of his work by a simple man, who candidly admitted that he himself was not quite sure how he did what he did how much good he did in the world. The judge quoted a line from Shakespeare, "There are more things in heaven and earth Horatio, than are dreamt of in your philosophy." He then dismissed the case.

Some people have conjectured that Peter Hurkos and Edgar Cayce are the same soul in different incarnations. Are the Dutch psychic and the American psychic the same soul? Both men have extraordinary psychic potential according to their life exploits and their birth charts. Though Cayce's potential was higher by birth, Hurkos' potential is well into the outstanding range at 150. He has four Delphi signs for psychic ability and his chart is listed on the following page.

After examining so many charts of gifted individuals, I posed the question, "Do miraculous events have an associated high number of spiritual marker aspects?" I wanted to know if nature marked certain dates and times for special occurrences that could ostensibly be tuned into by these gifted individuals.

THE TOP TEN MARKER ASPECTS FOR PSYCHIC ABILITY

1. JUPITER URANUS TRINE
2. MOON URANUS SEXTILE
3. MERCURY VENUS SEXTILE
4. PLUTO MOON PARALLEL
5. JUPITER MARS PARALLEL
6. MERCURY VENUS PARALLEL
7. JUPITER SATURN CONTRA-PARALLEL
8. PLUTO MOON CONTRAPARALLEL
9. URANUS NEPTUNE CONTRAPARALLEL
10. ANY MARS ECLIPSE

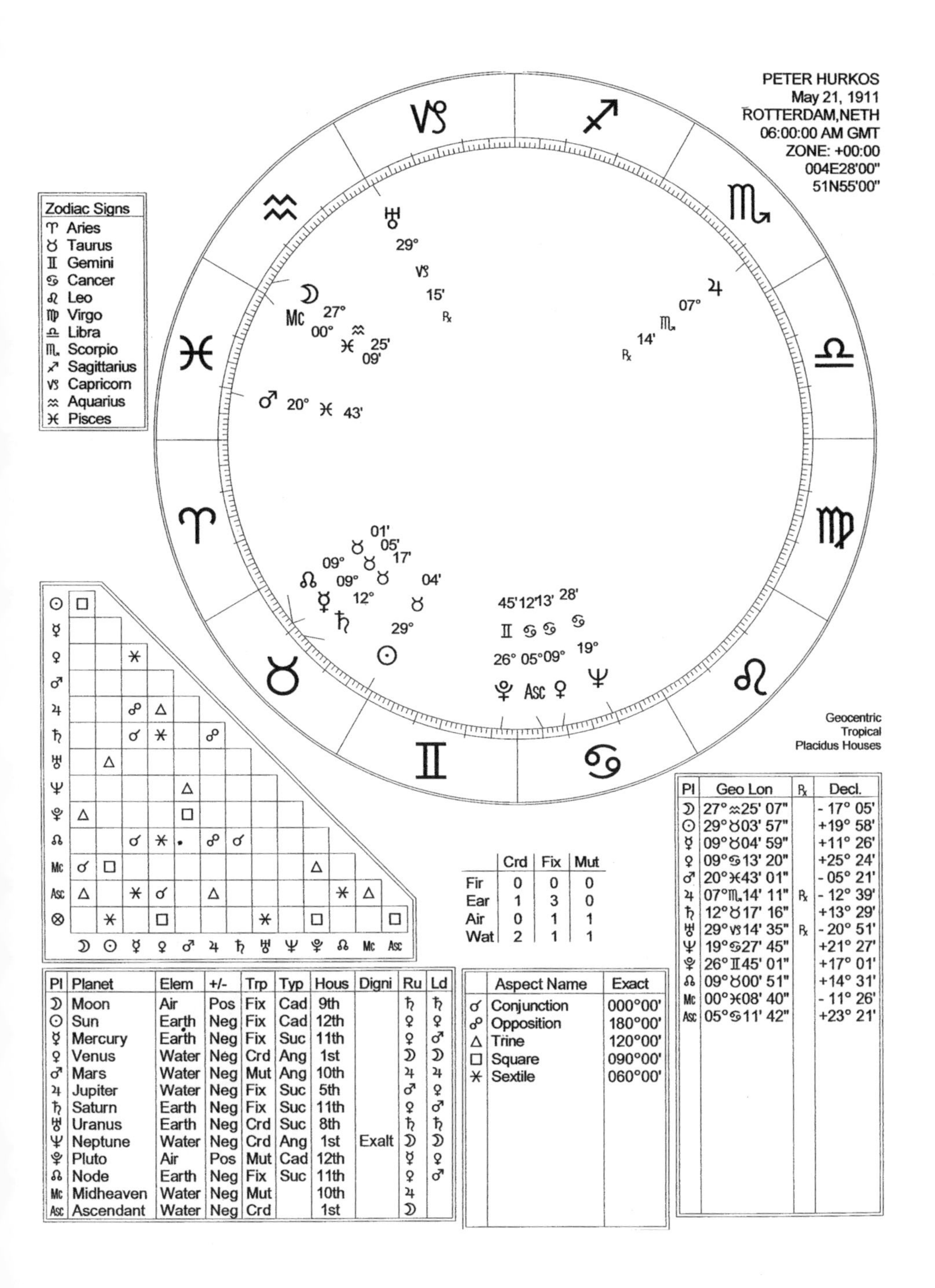

	☽	☉	☿	♀	♂	♃	♄	♅	♆	♇	☊	Mc	Asc
☉	□												
☿													
♀			✶										
♂													
♃			☍	△									
♄			☌	✶		☍							
♅		△											
♆						△							
♇	△					□							
☊			☌	✶	•	☍	☌						
Mc	☌	□								△			
Asc	△		✶	☌		△					✶	△	
⊗		✶		□				✶		□			□

	Crd	Fix	Mut
Fir	0	0	0
Ear	1	3	0
Air	0	1	1
Wat	2	1	1

Pl	Geo Lon	℞	Decl.
☽	27°♒25' 07"		- 17° 05'
☉	29°♉03' 57"		+19° 58'
☿	09°♉04' 59"		+11° 26'
♀	09°♋13' 20"		+25° 24'
♂	20°♓43' 01"		- 05° 21'
♃	07°♏14' 11"	℞	- 12° 39'
♄	12°♉17' 16"		+13° 29'
♅	29°♑14' 35"	℞	- 20° 51'
♆	19°♋27' 45"		+21° 27'
♇	26°♊45' 01"		+17° 01'
☊	09°♉00' 51"		+14° 31'
Mc	00°♓08' 40"		- 11° 26'
Asc	05°♋11' 42"		+23° 21'

Pl	Planet	Elem	+/-	Trp	Typ	Hous	Digni	Ru	Ld
☽	Moon	Air	Pos	Fix	Cad	9th		♄	♄
☉	Sun	Earth	Neg	Fix	Cad	12th		♀	♀
☿	Mercury	Earth	Neg	Fix	Suc	11th		♀	♂
♀	Venus	Water	Neg	Crd	Ang	1st		☽	☽
♂	Mars	Water	Neg	Mut	Ang	10th		♃	♃
♃	Jupiter	Water	Neg	Fix	Suc	5th		♂	♀
♄	Saturn	Earth	Neg	Fix	Suc	11th		♀	♂
♅	Uranus	Earth	Neg	Crd	Suc	8th		♄	♄
♆	Neptune	Water	Neg	Crd	Ang	1st	Exalt	☽	☽
♇	Pluto	Air	Pos	Mut	Cad	12th		☿	♀
☊	Node	Earth	Neg	Fix	Suc	11th		♀	♂
Mc	Midheaven	Water	Neg	Mut		10th		♃	
Asc	Ascendant	Water	Neg	Crd		1st		☽	

	Aspect Name	Exact
☌	Conjunction	000°00'
☍	Opposition	180°00'
△	Trine	120°00'
□	Square	090°00'
✶	Sextile	060°00'

Birth / Event Data

Peter Hurkos
Place of birth/event (city, state, county)

5-21-1911 6:02am GMT
Date of birth/event

Zone 00:00 004E28 51N55
Time of birth/event (exact time, i.e. birth certificate)

Client Data

First and last name

Mailing address

City, state, country, zip code

Telephone no. and fax no.

E-mail address

GENERAL PSYCHIC POTENTIAL – MARKER ASPECTS

(All aspects score 10 points each, unless otherwise indicated)

CONJUNCTIONS

- ___ Saturn - Mars
- ___ Jupiter - Saturn
- ___ Moon -Venus
- ___ Saturn - Uranus
- ___ Jupiter - Moon
- ___ Jupiter - Uranus
- ___ Sun - Mars
- ___ Uranus - Mars

TRINES

- X Neptune – Mars
- X Venus – Jupiter
- ___ Mercury - Mars
- ___ Jupiter – Uranus (25 pts)

SEXTILES

- ___ Saturn – Mercury
- ___ Pluto – Uranus (25 pts)
- ___ Sun – Uranus (25 pts)
- ___ Mercury – Mars (25 pts)
- ___ Jupiter – Mercury (25 pts)
- ___ Saturn – Pluto (25 pts)
- ___ Saturn – Sun (25 pts)
- ___ Saturn – Neptune
- ___ Sun – Mars
- ___ Uranus – Moon (25 pts)
- ___ Venus – Pluto (25 pts)
- X Mercury – Venus (25 pts)
- ___ Neptune – Moon (25 pts)
- ___ Moon – Mars
- ___ Jupiter – Moon

SQUARES

- ___ Pluto – Moon
- ___ Sun – Jupiter
- ___ Uranus – Pluto
- ___ Jupiter – Moon
- ___ Jupiter – Uranus
- ___ Venus – Jupiter
- ___ Saturn – Moon
- ___ Jupiter – Saturn
- ___ Jupiter – Neptune

OPPOSITIONS

- ___ Pluto – Mars
- ___ Saturn – Moon
- ___ Venus – Saturn
- ___ Saturn – Neptune

PARALLELS

- ___ Moon – Venus
- ___ Pluto – Moon (25 pts)
- ___ Sun – Moon
- ___ Mercury – Mars
- ___ Pluto – Mars
- ___ Jupiter – Moon
- ___ Saturn - Neptune
- ___ Venus – Neptune (25 pts)
- ___ Pluto – Uranus
- ___ Moon – Mercury
- ___ Jupiter – Mars (25 pts)
- ___ Sun – Mercury
- ___ Mercury – Venus (25 pts)
- ___ Jupiter – Saturn

CONTRAPARALLELS

- X Jupiter – Saturn (25 pts)
- ___ Moon – Mercury (25 pts)
- X Pluto – Moon (25 pts)
- X Jupiter – Mercury
- ___ Jupiter – Neptune
- ___ Jupiter – Moon
- ___ Sun – Jupiter (25 pts)
- ___ Sun – Moon (25 pts)
- X Uranus – Neptune (25 pts)
- ___ Pluto – Mars (25 pts)

HIDEK

- ___ Mercury
- ___ Mars

EXDEK

- X Venus
- ___ Mars
- ___ Uranus
- ___ Pluto

PROXIMITY ELEVATIONS

- ___ Pluto – Mars (parallel)
- ___ Sun – Pluto (contraparallel)

ECLIPSES

- X Saturn – Mercury
- ___ Jupiter – Uranus
- ___ Any Mars Eclipse

GRAND ELEVATIONS

- ___ + Mercury
- ___ - Sun
- ___ - Uranus
- ___ - Neptune
- ___ + Moon

	GRAND TOTAL	SCALE
___	Below Average	0 - 30
___	Average	31 - 60
___	Above Average	61 - 100
___	Superior	101 - 140
150	Outstanding	141 - 180
___	Delphi Class	181+

PSYCHIC HEALERS

Modern medical science has never truly embraced the obvious and undeniable notion that most major illnesses have never been cured. Even more undeniable is the notion that in order to cure the maladies that continue to plague mankind, allopathic medical specialists must embrace the totality of possible cures for illness. Healers have worked alongside traditional doctors for thousands of years and have been credited with an astonishing array of otherwise inexplicably successful treatments for any medical problem, which one would care to name. Yet in today's technocratic and machine dominated medical society, the healer has been relegated to the realms of charlatans and dilettantes who seek solely to bilk the unsuspecting masses out of their hard-earned dollars. Such is not the case, however, in all circumstances. In my own personal and research experience, I have witnessed a variety of remarkable treatments for disease that were performed by skilled and professional healers who have had little or no medical training. Each time I came away with one unshakable thought, how can the medical community combine this knowledge with its own in order to overcome the impasse that holds mankind in it's grip? Can the sciences of healing and allopathic medicine ever truly work together? Unfortunately, a full exploration of this subject is beyond the scope of this book. Before any meaningful examination of psychic healers can be entertained on an astrological level, we must first examine who they are and what they do.

Psychic and spiritual healers have appeared in numerous forms throughout recorded history. Healing practices differ greatly from the current accepted methods of medical science. Recently, medical science has begun to examine healing and its practitioners in order to apply the scientific method to a more thorough understanding of this art. A few scant years ago, most medical doctors would not have even discussed healing with their colleagues or clients.

Psychic healing requires that the healer draw energy from his physical body, mainly from the solar plexus in the back of the stomach and at the top of the head, where groups (ganglia) of nerves come together. This energy is then channeled through his/her hands and applies to the aura, or the magnetic field extending somewhat beyond the physical body of the patient. A good healer notices a discolored aura. Discoloration indicates illness. By placing his/her energy into the troubled areas of the aura, the healer displaces the diseased particles and momentarily creates a vacuum. Into this vacuum, healthy electrically charged particles rush to fill the gap in the aura. Instant healing is often the result, since the physical body must fall in line with its inner etheric counterpart. This type of healer rarely touches the patient's skin. The healing takes place at the periphery of the aura where it is most sensitive. Healing may take place whether the patient believes in psychic healing or not. It is a purely mechanical process, and its success depends on the healer's ability to draw enough of his life force into his hands to effect the healing.[1]

Physical healing requires that the healer touch the afflicted area of the body. This art has been practiced by many religions and it is still seen as an important symbol of the power of the Church. Although the prime force in this type of treatment is still the psychic energy of the healer, a positive attitude toward it on the part of the patient is helpful. When the healer is also a priest or minister, religious faith enters the process to some extent. [2]

Faith healing is often confused with psychic healing, but the two methods have little in common. In faith healing, everything depends on three elements. First, the afflicted person must have a religious belief in the power of healing (and in the intercession of divine forces); the deeper the belief the better. Second, the patient must have unlimited confidence in the healer from whom he expects the miracle. Third, a large audience, the larger the better, is usually a must for the faith healing to succeed.[3] The efficacy of the individual healer varies greatly. Some healers are so proficient at their work that their success rates rival those of even the best medical doctors and as such they have become world famous. One of the reasons that I have written this book is to provide the public with an astrological method of evaluating the latent ability of a given healer with whom they might choose to work. I believe that each of us is granted specific latent abilities by virtue of our natal charts and this chapter will hopefully show that it is indeed possible to demonstrate extraordinary healing ability within the birth chart.

Science has proven that the healing phenomenon exists. A series of now famous experiments designed to answer this question were performed at several prestigious universities in different parts of the world.

"The Grad experiments", performed by Bernard Grad at McGill University, involved work with a Hungarian-born healer named Colonel Oskar Estebany, who had a long history of treating both animals and people by laying his hands on the afflicted areas.In one of Grad's most famous experiments, mice received small, surgically inflicted wounds on their skins, and the rate of healing of the wounds was measured objectively on a daily basis. The mice were divided into an experimental group and a control group. Each mouse in the experimental group was put into a paper bag by an investigator, and Estabany held the bag and its contained mouse in his hands while doing the healing. Mice in the control group were put in paper bags for equivalent periods of time, but not held by Estebany. The results showed that the wounds healed more rapidly in the case of the mice which received the healing treatment. The difference in the rate of healing was statistically significant[4]

M. Justa Smith performed further testing on the healing abilities of Estebany. She discovered that the activity level of trypsin was increased by a magnetic field. Trypsin is an enzyme produced by the pancreas to assist in the digestion of proteins; it can be damaged by ultraviolet radiation. In a unique study of Estebany's abilities, Smith divided solutions of trypsin into four portions. One was treated by Estebany who put his hands around a covered glass flask containing the enzyme for a maximum of 75 minutes. Another sample was exposed to ultraviolet light at a wavelength determined to be the most damaging for enzymes, and was then treated by Estebany. The third sample was exposed to a high magnetic field for three hours. The final sample was used as a control and was untreated. The most striking finding of Smith's was that the effect of Estebany's treatment of the undamaged sample was similar to that of the enzyme's exposure to a high magnetic field. The effect of Estebany on the damaged sample was similar but not as dramatic.[5]

Graham and Anita Watkins designed an experiment in which 12 volunteers worked on animals, part of the time at a distance. The task given to these individuals, most of whom did not profess to have any "paranormal healing" abilities, was to arouse mice more quickly from anesthesia than would be expected under ordinary circumstances.

Pairs of mice were rendered unconscious with ether at the same time. These pairs were closely matched; they were of the same sex, of the same size, and had been litter mates. After both mice were unconscious, they were placed in plastic containers. One mouse was placed before one of the 12 volunteers and the volunteer was asked to "awaken" the animal. The other mouse served as a control and therefore the numbers of mice in the experimental group were the same as the number in the control group.

Tests were conducted under various circumstances. In some cases, the volunteer and the mouse were in one room while the control mouse was in another room. In some cases, the volunteer and both mice were in the same room. In some instances, both mice were in the same room with the volunteer looking through a window. And in some cases, the volunteer was blindfolded. In no instance was the volunteer allowed to do a laying on of hands with the unconscious mouse.

The overall results of this study were statistically significant; the animals assigned to the volunteers required an average of 13% less time to revive as did the control animals. There were no clear-cut differences among the various conditions. However, when the mice were viewed through a window, the unblinded volunteers did significantly better than the blindfolded volunteers.[6] Watkins and Watkins found three subjects who did exceptionally well in reviving mice, so much so that in 24 attempts, their mice revived significantly more quickly than did the control mice.

Roger Well and Judith Klein, two of Watkins and Watkins colleagues at the Foundation for Research and Nature of Man, reported significant results following an attempt to repeat the experiment themselves with an additional finding. Once a mouse revives more quickly than expected by chance, the location of the mouse is recorded. Future mice placed in the same location are more likely to revive quickly than mice placed in other locations, even though the subject does not know about the former inhabitants of that spot. This lingering effect suggests that some spots are better than others as locations for healing or that a residue of "healing power" remains there to help the next mouse revive.[7]

These experiments demonstrate several important points regarding healing. One, the healing phenomenon is real and can be demonstrated in the laboratory. Two, some individuals appear to have a natural gift for healing when compared to the normal population and in many instances the magnitude of this gift is exceptional. Third, healing appears to involve the use of a measurable form of energy which has an effect on living tissue and can be projected from the body of the healer. With these findings, modern science began to explore the myriad uses of healers in clinical settings. Today, hundreds of doctors utilize healers as an important adjunct of their clinical services. Now let us examine the astrological charts of some of the most famous healers in the world to see if we can demonstrate clearly discernible markers for this exciting gift.

In this study, I examined the charts of 28 well known healers. The natal charts of the healers were then compared to those of a group of 28 age- matched controls. The control group consisted of people who had not displayed any previous history of psychic or spiritual healing ability. I applied my modern astrology method to both sets of charts and tabulated the differences. The astrological aspects that occurred with at least a 50% increase in frequency in the healer group when compared to the control group were designated "MARKER ASPECTS" healing. Those marker aspects for healing which were at least 300% more common in the charts of healers than the controls were designated as "DELPHI MARKERS" for healing. Ordinary marker aspects for healing were assigned a point value of 10 points and delphi markers for healing were assigned a point value of 25 points. The total of points that occurred in each chart was calculated. The resulting score was called the "ASTROLOGICAL HEALING INDEX".

The control group revealed an average healing index of 41.33 points. The healing group revealed an average healing index of 151.6 points. The research showed that there is a discernible group of marker aspects for healing which occurs at a significantly increased frequency among healers when compared to the normal population. The marker aspects for healing which I discovered are as follows:

Birth / Event Data

____
Place of birth/event (city, state, county)

____
Date of birth/event

____
Time of birth/event (exact time, i.e. birth certificate)

Client Data

____
First and last name

____
Mailing address

____
City, state, country, zip code

____
Telephone no. and fax no.

____
E-mail address

HEALING POTENTIAL – MARKERS ASPECTS

(All aspects score 10 points each, unless otherwise indicated)

CONJUNCTIONS

- ____ Sun - Venus
- ____ Neptune - Pluto
- ____ Pluto – Moon (25 pts)
- ____ Saturn – Moon
- ____ Moon – Mars
- ____ Jupiter – Mars
- ____ Mars - Venus

TRINES

- ____ Venus - Saturn
- ____ Sun - Moon (25 pts)
- ____ Jupiter – Neptune
- ____ Mercury – Uranus (25 pts)
- ____ Moon – Venus
- ____ Saturn – Neptune
- ____ Jupiter – Mars
- ____ Venus - Pluto

SEXTILES

- ____ Neptune - Pluto
- ____ Sun - Saturn
- ____ Moon - Neptune (25 pts)
- ____ Saturn - Mercury
- ____ Venus – Jupiter
- ____ Pluto – Uranus
- ____ Mercury – Venus
- ____ Sun - Pluto

SQUARES

- ____ Uranus – Moon (25 pts)
- ____ Saturn – Pluto
- ____ Jupiter – Moon
- ____ Pluto – Moon (25 pts)
- ____ Sun – Saturn
- ____ Uranus – Jupiter
- ____ Venus – Uranus (25 pts)
- ____ Venus – Neptune (25 pts)
- ____ Sun – Pluto
- ____ Jupiter – Pluto
- ____ Saturn – Moon
- ____ Mercury – Uranus

OPPOSITIONS

- ____ Uranus – Neptune (25 pts)
- ____ Uranus – Pluto (25 pts)
- ____ Jupiter – Venus
- ____ Pluto – Mercury
- ____ Jupiter – Mars
- ____ Sun – Moon
- ____ Sun – Jupiter
- ____ Sun - Saturn

PARALLELS

- ____ Neptune - Moon
- ____ Neptune - Pluto (25 pts)
- ____ Pluto – Moon
- ____ Mercury – Venus
- ____ Moon – Mars
- ____ Mercury – Mars
- ____ Saturn - Sun (25 pts)
- ____ Pluto - Uranus
- ____ Sun - Mercury (25 pts)
- ____ Jupiter – Mars
- ____ Neptune - Mars

CONTRAPARALLELS

- ____ Moon – Mercury (25 pts)
- ____ Jupiter – Mars
- ____ Neptune - Mars
- ____ Venus - Pluto (25 pts)
- ____ Pluto – Mars
- ____ Sun – Jupiter
- ____ Sun – Mars
- ____ Uranus – Neptune (25 pts)
- ____ Moon – Venus
- ____ Saturn – Uranus (25 pts)
- ____ Saturn – Sun
- ____ Sun – Moon (25 pts)

QUADS

- ____ Jupiter – Mars – Uranus – Neptune (25 pts)

HIDEK

- ____ Mercury
- ____ Mars

EXDEK

- ____ Uranus

PROXIMITY ELEVATIONS

- ____ Venus – Saturn (contraparallel)
- ____ Uranus–Neptune (contraparallel)
- ____ Sun-Moon (contraparallel; 25 pts)
- ____ Venus-Neptune (contraparallel; 25 pts)

ECLIPSES

- ____ Any Uranus Eclipses

GRAND ELEVATIONS

- ____ + Moon
- ____ - Sun
- ____ - Neptune
- ____ + Mercury
- ____ - Uranus

GRAND TOTAL		SCALE
____	Below Average	0 - 30
____	Average	31 - 60
____	Above Average	61 - 100
____	Superior	101 - 140
____	Outstanding	141 - 180
____	Delphi Class	181+

The following healers were included in this study:

BIRTH DATA FOR ALL HEALERS WAS TAKEN FROM THE HUNTER DATABASE.

WALTER DEVOE
3/11/1874
6:46AM LMT
CEDAR RAPIDS, IOWA

FINBARRY NOLAN
10-1-1951
11:02 PM WET
CAVAN, IRELAND

JOMANDA
5-5-1948
1:00PM
DEVENTER, NL CET

LINDA MARTEL
8-21-1956
3:30AM WEDT
GYERNSEY,
CHANNEL ISLANDS GREAT BRITAIN

RASPUTIN
1-22-1870
11:00 PM LMT
POKROVSKOE, SIBERIA RUSSIA

FELICIANO OMILES
10-26-1937
8:OOAM ST
BAGUIO, PHILLIPPINES

GREET HOFFMANS
6-23-1894
11:30 AM LMT
AMSTERDAM NL

DIETER SCHOPFWINKEL
11-23-1876
11:25PM LMT
HAMM, NRW GERMANY

WILLIAM BRANHAM
4-6-1909
6:00AM CST
BURKESVILLE KY

YOLANDA BETEGH
12-1-1911
12:00PM EET
SATMAR, RUMANIA

SERGE LEON ALALOUF
12-24-1901
11:59PM LMT
SALONIKA, MACEDONIA GREECE

GERARD CR0ISET
3-10-1909
3:00PM LMT
AMSTERDAM NL

AINO KASSINEN
12-13-1900
5:05PM LMT
OULU, FINLAND

DAVID BRAY
3-5-1889
2:00AM LMT
HONOLULU, HI

MATTI VILOKKINEN
4-21-1945
5:50PM EET
ILOMANTSI, FINLAND

WIRKUS MIETEK
7-19-1939
3:46AM CET
RACIAZ, POLAND

KATHYRN KUHLMAN
5-9-1907
3:00PM CST
CONCORDIA , MO

GIOVANI BONI
3-15-1916
6:28 AM CET
ROME, ITALY

MASAHIRO NAKAZONO
5-22-1918
5:00AM JST
KAGOSHIMA, KAGOSHIMA JAPAN

MALCOLM BESSENT
2-8-1944
6:53AM ZONE 5.5
DEOLALI, INDIA

OLGA WORRALL
11/30/1906
CLEVELAND, OHIO CST
7:30PM

JOSEF ISSELS
11-21-1907
9:15AM CET
MONCHENGLADBACH, GERMANY

JACK SCHWARZ
4/26/1924
11:10AM
GREG SCHELKUN
1/20/1949
CHICAGO, IL 11:27PM

MAURICE MESSEGUE
12-14-1921
4:30PM
CALEGRAC SAINT CIRG-FRANCE
DORDRECHT, NETHERLANDS

DR. ERNESTO MONTGOMERY
10/02/1925
11:55PM
KINGSTON, JAMAICA EST

NIILO YLI-VAINJO
2/23/1920
ALAHARMA, FINLAND
6:30AM LMT

ANALEE SKARIN
07/07/1900
12:00PM MST
SALT LAKE CITY, UT

Let's examine the lives and birth charts of some of the great healers in our study.

DR. ERNESTO MONTGOMERY

HEALER RATING—OUTSTANDING—(165)

Dr. Ernesto Moshe Montgomery was born in Jamaica in 1925. By the age of 5, he was already manifesting his extraordinary gifts and at one point, his mother became so overwhelmed by the multitudes of people coming to their home that she sent him to Kingston to live with his aunt. His life story vividly exemplifies the skill and power which a Delphi Class healer and clairvoyant is capable of manifesting.

When he was a child, hundreds of people flocked to his home to experience his healing gift. He treated all manners of human ailments, often for free, and never turned anyone away. He believed that his gift came from God and that he would be remiss in his appointed duty to refuse anyone the chance to share in his bounty. A remarkable number of cures were credited to his administrations. Dr. Montgomery's gifts were not limited solely to the healing realm. At age 12, he began to frequent Queen Victoria Park in Kingston where he would regale audiences with vivid details of the coming great war in Europe. By the time he was 15, World War II was already in progress and when was 16 years old, the Secret British MI5 Intelligence Agency drafted him into the Jamaican D-Day offensive of Normandy. There was great concern that a tremendous storm was brewing at sea that could potentially destroy their invasion plans. Montgomery transported himself into the astral plane of the future and envisioned a date when an Allied invasion would be successful. The date that the Allies chose as D-Day was first foreseen by Montgomery! After the War, Churchill himself personally went to Jamaica to thank Montgomery for his efforts.

Dr. Montgomery explains that when he views the future, he imagines that he is looking at a movie. The images play themselves out for him in often startling and terrifying clarity. In July 1991, Dr. Montgomery wrote a letter to the Royal Family (Queen Elizabeth) to warn them that Princess Diana of Wales, would be in grave danger the latter part of August of 1997. In part the letter stated..."I am observing that Princess Diana is in very grave danger and will be involved in a fatal automobile accident, during the final weeks of August 1997 in France." The Royal family, having been aware of his work during World War II, sent a return letter assuring him that they would take his prediction seriously and would make certain that Princess Diana would not be anywhere near Paris in August 1997. Princess Diana died in an automobile accident in Paris in August 1997 just as Montgomery predicted.

Dr. Montgomery also predicted the bombing of the New York World Trade Center in 1993, the outcome of the O.J. Simpson trial, the Olympic games bombing in Atlanta, and the Oklahoma Federal building bombing in April of 1995. He now works as the Chief Rabbi of the Beta Israel Temple Black Jewish Synagogue in Los Angeles.[8] He maintains a very lucrative private practice with a large and prestigious clientele.

Montgomery's astrological chart prominently displays a large number of marker aspects that presage a phenomenal degree of latent paranormal potential. His Outstanding Class rating is in part due to the presence of no less than five delphi markers for healing ability. In addition, as is common in the case of gifted savants, his abilities extend far beyond the healing realm. The Pluto Moon square, the Sun Moon and Venus Pluto contraparallels, and the proximity elevation of the Sun Moon contraparallel are unique delphi level astrological signatures for the healing trait. His chart displays all of them. In addition, he has the rare Sun Moon Uranus triangle that is even further enhanced by proximity!

Dr. Montgomery's healing index score of 165 represents a degree of latent paranormal potential triple that of the average person. His life story is a splendid example of the power modern astrology has in predicting the paranormal potential of an individual! I have worked personally with Dr. Montgomery on several cases and I can definitely attest to his phenomenal healing prowess.

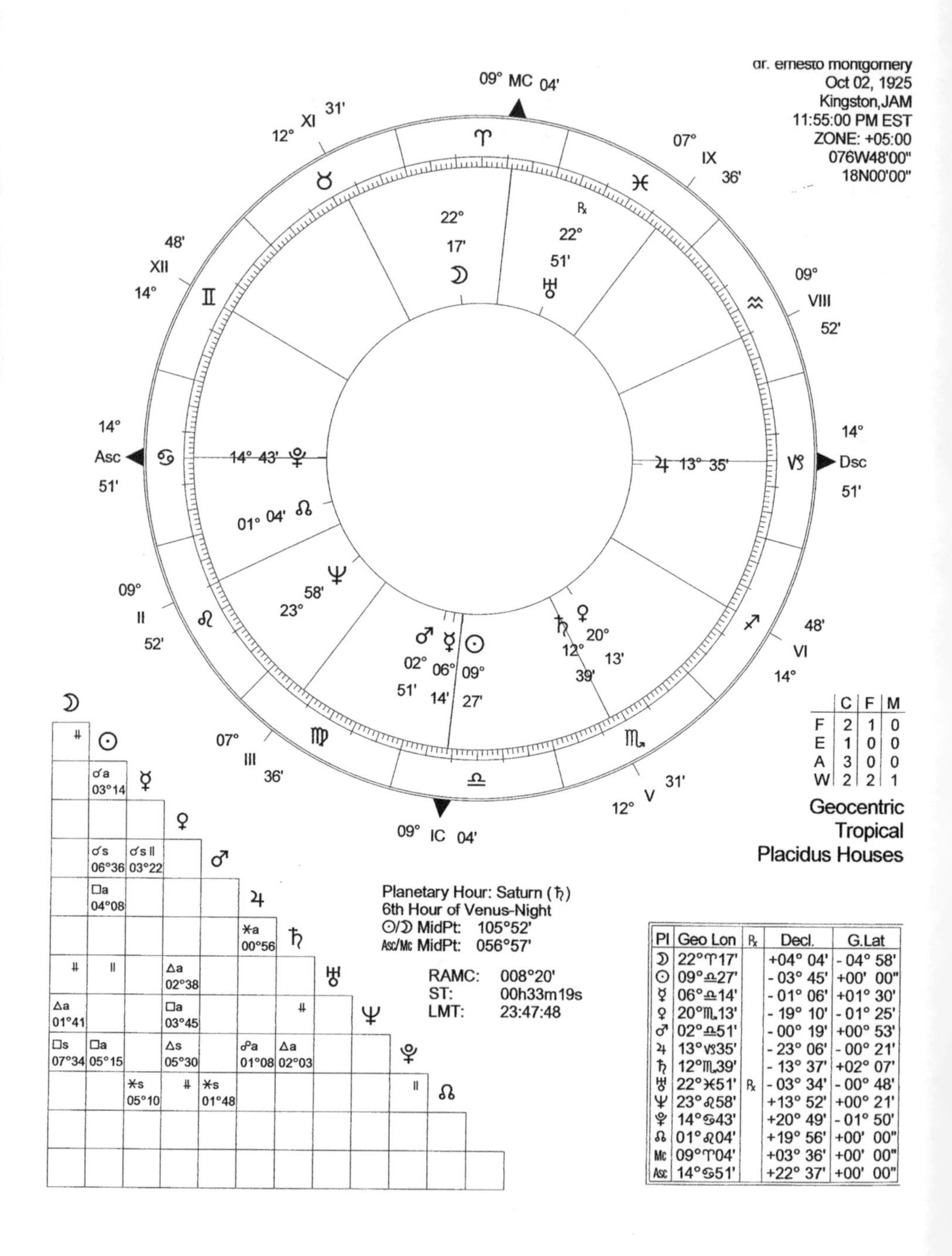

dr. ernesto montgomery
Oct 02, 1925
Kingston,JAM
11:55:00 PM EST
ZONE: +05:00
076W48'00"
18N00'00"
09° MC 04'
09° IC 04'
14° Asc 51'
14° Dsc 51'
C F M
F 2 1 0
E 1 0 0
A 3 0 0
W 2 2 1
Geocentric
Tropical
Placidus Houses
Planetary Hour: Saturn (♄)
6th Hour of Venus-Night
☉/☽ MidPt: 105°52'
Asc/Mc MidPt: 056°57'
RAMC: 008°20'
ST: 00h33m19s
LMT: 23:47:48
Pl | Geo Lon | ℞ | Decl. | G.Lat
☽ | 22°♈17' | | +04° 04' | - 04° 58'
☉ | 09°♎27' | | - 03° 45' | +00' 00"
☿ | 06°♎14' | | - 01° 06' | +01° 30'
♀ | 20°♏13' | | - 19° 10' | - 01° 25'
♂ | 02°♎51' | | - 00° 19' | +00° 53'
♃ | 13°♑35' | | - 23° 06' | - 00° 21'
♄ | 12°♏39' | | - 13° 37' | +02° 07'
♅ | 22°♓51' | ℞ | - 03° 34' | - 00° 48'
♆ | 23°♌58' | | +13° 52' | +00° 21'
♇ | 14°♋43' | | +20° 49' | - 01° 50'
☊ | 01°♌04' | | +19° 56' | +00' 00"
Mc | 09°♈04' | | +03° 36' | +00' 00"
Asc | 14°♋51' | | +22° 37' | +00' 00"

Birth / Event Data

Place of birth/event (city, state, county)

Date of birth/event

Time of birth/event (exact time, i.e. birth certificate)

Client Data

Dr. Ernesto Montgomery

First and last name

Mailing address

City, state, country, zip code

Telephone no. and fax no.

E-mail address

HEALING POTENTIAL – MARKERS ASPECTS

(All aspects score 10 points each, unless otherwise indicated)

CONJUNCTIONS

- ___ Sun - Venus
- ___ Neptune - Pluto
- ___ Pluto – Moon (25 pts)
- ___ Saturn – Moon
- ___ Moon – Mars
- ___ Jupiter – Mars
- ___ Mars - Venus

TRINES

- ___ Venus - Saturn
- ___ Sun - Moon (25 pts)
- ___ Jupiter – Neptune
- ___ Mercury – Uranus (25 pts)
- ___ Moon – Venus
- ___ Saturn – Neptune
- ___ Jupiter – Mars
- X Venus - Pluto

SEXTILES

- ___ Neptune - Pluto
- ___ Sun - Saturn
- ___ Moon - Neptune (25 pts)
- ___ Saturn - Mercury
- ___ Venus – Jupiter
- ___ Pluto – Uranus
- ___ Mercury – Venus
- ___ Sun - Pluto

SQUARES

- ___ Uranus – Moon (25 pts)
- ___ Saturn – Pluto
- ___ Jupiter – Moon
- X Pluto – Moon (25 pts)
- ___ Sun – Saturn
- ___ Uranus – Jupiter
- ___ Venus – Uranus (25 pts)
- X Venus – Neptune (25 pts)
- X Sun – Pluto
- ___ Jupiter – Pluto
- ___ Saturn – Moon
- ___ Mercury – Uranus

OPPOSITIONS

- ___ Uranus – Neptune (25 pts)
- ___ Uranus – Pluto (25 pts)
- ___ Jupiter – Venus
- ___ Pluto – Mercury
- ___ Jupiter – Mars
- ___ Sun – Moon
- ___ Sun – Jupiter
- ___ Sun - Saturn

PARALLELS

- ___ Neptune - Moon
- ___ Neptune - Pluto (25 pts)
- ___ Pluto – Moon
- ___ Mercury – Venus
- ___ Moon – Mars
- X Mercury – Mars
- ___ Saturn - Sun (25 pts)
- ___ Pluto - Uranus
- ___ Sun - Mercury (25 pts)
- ___ Jupiter – Mars
- ___ Neptune - Mars

CONTRAPARALLELS

- ___ Moon – Mercury (25 pts)
- ___ Jupiter – Mars
- ___ Neptune - Mars
- X Venus - Pluto (25 pts)
- ___ Pluto – Mars
- ___ Sun – Jupiter
- ___ Sun – Mars
- ___ Uranus – Neptune (25 pts)
- ___ Moon – Venus
- ___ Saturn – Uranus (25 pts)
- ___ Saturn – Sun
- X Sun – Moon (25 pts)

QUADS

- ___ Jupiter – Mars – Uranus – Neptune (25 pts)

HIDEK

- ___ Mercury
- ___ Mars

EXDEK

- ___ Uranus

PROXIMITY ELEVATIONS

- ___ Venus – Saturn (contraparallel)
- ___ Uranus–Neptune (contraparallel)
- X Sun-Moon (contraparallel; 25 pts)
- ___ Venus-Neptune (contraparallel; 25 pts)

ECLIPSES

- ___ Any Uranus Eclipses

GRAND ELEVATIONS

- X + Moon
- ___ - Sun
- ___ - Neptune
- ___ + Mercury
- ___ - Uranus

	GRAND TOTAL	SCALE
___	Below Average	0 - 30
___	Average	31 - 60
___	Above Average	61 - 100
165	Superior	101 - 140
	Outstanding	141 - 180
___	Delphi Class	181+

SERGE LEON ALALOUF

HEALER RATING—DELPHI CLASS—235***

Serge Leon Alalouf is said to have professed to cure only those who truly believed in his power of touch. If so, then the faithful numbered at least 276,000, for that many testimonial letters arrived at a Paris courthouse in 1957, when Alalouf was accused and acquitted of unlawfully practicing medicine. Serge Leon Alalouf was one of the greatest healers of all time.

Alalouf, born in Salonika on December 24,1901, claimed he first recognized his healing gift when, as a young man in Toulouse, he touched a man's badly wounded head and within days the injury disappeared. In over fifty years of practice, the darkly handsome healer counted among his clientele King Alfonso XIII of Spain and French playwright Jean Anouilh. Alalouf was also very clairvoyant and he accurately predicted a violent death for himself. He died in an automobile accident in 1982.[9]

Alalouf's birth chart displays an extremely high degree of latent healing potential. He has five delphi marker aspects that further add to the intensity of this gift. Let's take a look at his astrological healing aspects.

Consider for a moment the magnitude of this man's healing gift. Over a quarter of a million people signed affadavits stating that he had successfully healed them of a plethora of illnesses! The average Western physician would consider himself/herself lucky if they saw even ten percent of this number of patients in a lifetime let alone to treat them successfully. Alalouf's natal chart shows that he was predisposed to develop the healing gift to a considerable degree and he lived up to his potential admirably. Interestingly, he and Dr. Montgomery share two healing markers; the Venus Pluto trine and the Mercury Mars parallel; even though they were born almost 25 years apart and in two separate parts of the globe! They also share the hallmark of Delphi Class healers, parallel development of complimentary paranormal gifts.

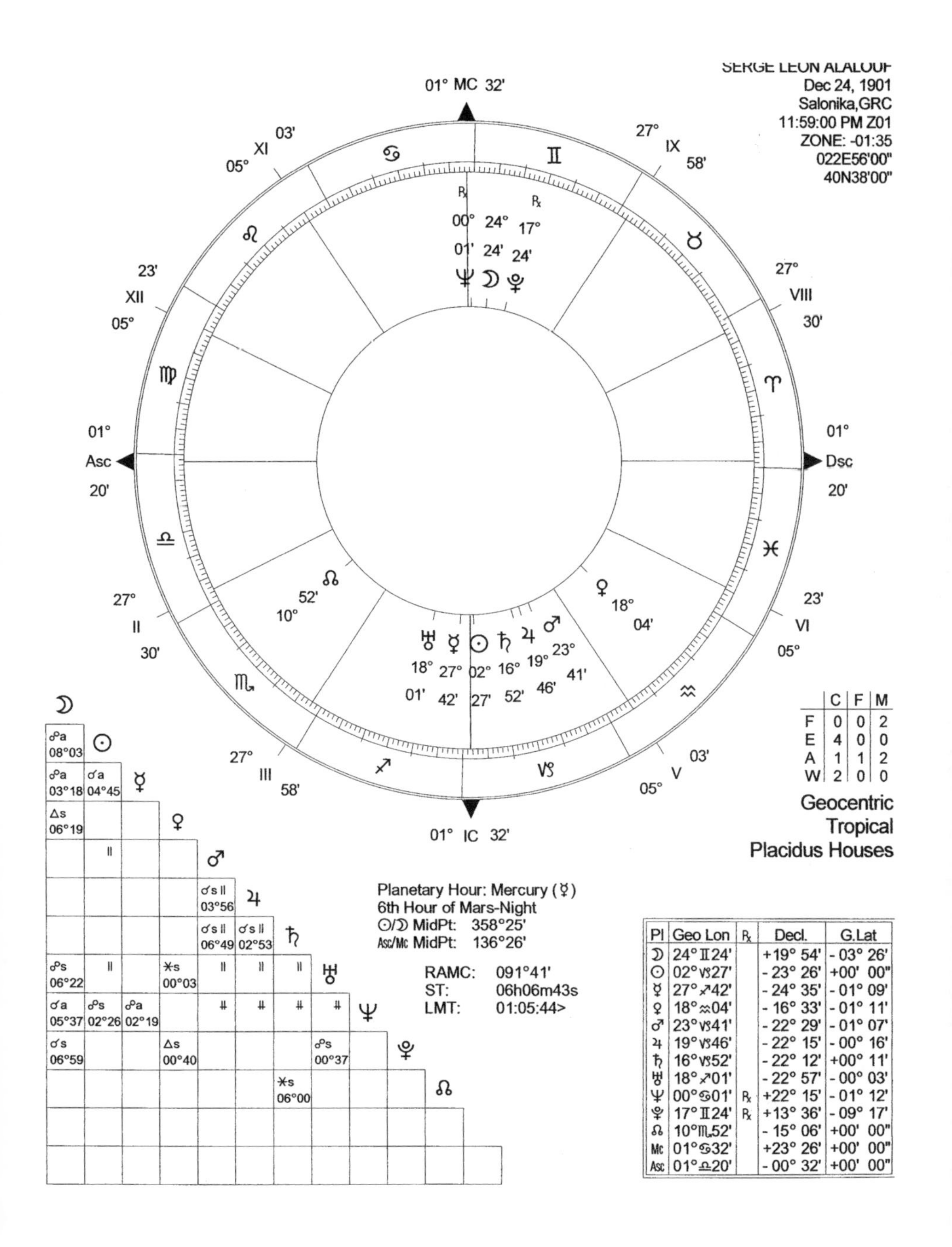

	C	F	M
F	0	0	2
E	4	0	0
A	1	1	2
W	2	0	0

Pl	Geo Lon	℞	Decl.	G.Lat
☽	24°♊24'		+19° 54'	- 03° 26'
☉	02°♑27'		- 23° 26'	+00' 00"
☿	27°♐42'		- 24° 35'	- 01° 09'
♀	18°♒04'		- 16° 33'	- 01° 11'
♂	23°♑41'		- 22° 29'	- 01° 07'
♃	19°♑46'		- 22° 15'	- 00° 16'
♄	16°♑52'		- 22° 12'	+00° 11'
♅	18°♐01'		- 22° 57'	- 00° 03'
♆	00°♋01'	℞	+22° 15'	- 01° 12'
♇	17°♊24'	℞	+13° 36'	- 09° 17'
☊	10°♏52'		- 15° 06'	+00' 00"
Mc	01°♋32'		+23° 26'	+00' 00"
Asc	01°♎20'		- 00° 32'	+00' 00"

Birth / Event Data

____
Place of birth/event (city, state, county)

____
Date of birth/event

____
Time of birth/event (exact time, i.e. birth certificate)

Client Data

Serge Leon Alalouf
First and last name

____
Mailing address

____
City, state, country, zip code

____
Telephone no. and fax no.

____
E-mail address

HEALING POTENTIAL – MARKERS ASPECTS

(All aspects score 10 points each, unless otherwise indicated)

CONJUNCTIONS

____ Sun - Venus
____ Neptune - Pluto
X Pluto – Moon (25 pts)
____ Saturn – Moon
____ Moon – Mars
X Jupiter – Mars
____ Mars - Venus

TRINES

____ Venus - Saturn
____ Sun - Moon (25 pts)
____ Jupiter – Neptune
____ Mercury – Uranus (25 pts)
X Moon – Venus
____ Saturn – Neptune
____ Jupiter – Mars
X Venus - Pluto

SEXTILES

____ Neptune - Pluto
____ Sun - Saturn
____ Moon - Neptune (25 pts)
____ Saturn - Mercury
____ Venus – Jupiter
____ Pluto – Uranus
____ Mercury – Venus
____ Sun - Pluto

SQUARES

____ Uranus – Moon (25 pts)
____ Saturn – Pluto
____ Jupiter – Moon
____ Pluto – Moon (25 pts)
____ Sun – Saturn
____ Uranus – Jupiter
____ Venus – Uranus (25 pts)
____ Venus – Neptune (25 pts)
____ Sun – Pluto
____ Jupiter – Pluto
____ Saturn – Moon
____ Mercury – Uranus

OPPOSITIONS

____ Uranus – Neptune (25 pts)
X Uranus – Pluto (25 pts)
____ Jupiter – Venus
____ Pluto – Mercury
____ Jupiter – Mars
____ Sun – Moon
____ Sun – Jupiter
____ Sun - Saturn

PARALLELS

X Neptune - Moon
____ Neptune - Pluto (25 pts)
____ Pluto – Moon
____ Mercury – Venus
____ Moon – Mars
X Mercury – Mars
X Saturn - Sun (25 pts)
____ Pluto - Uranus
X Sun - Mercury (25 pts)
X Jupiter – Mars
____ Neptune - Mars

CONTRAPARALLELS

____ Moon – Mercury (25 pts)
____ Jupiter – Mars
X Neptune - Mars
____ Venus - Pluto (25 pts)
____ Pluto – Mars
____ Sun – Jupiter
____ Sun – Mars
X Uranus – Neptune (25 pts)
____ Moon – Venus
____ Saturn – Uranus (25 pts)
____ Saturn – Sun
____ Sun – Moon (25 pts)

QUADS

____ Jupiter – Mars – Uranus – Neptune (25 pts)

HIDEK

____ Mercury
X Mars

EXDEK

____ Uranus

PROXIMITY ELEVATIONS

____ Venus – Saturn (contraparallel)
____ Uranus–Neptune (contraparallel)
____ Sun-Moon (contraparallel; 25 pts)
____ Venus-Neptune (contraparallel; 25 pts)

ECLIPSES

____ Any Uranus Eclipses

GRAND ELEVATIONS

____ + Moon
X - Sun
X - Neptune
____ + Mercury
X - Uranus

GRAND TOTAL		SCALE
____	Below Average	0 - 30
____	Average	31 - 60
____	Above Average	61 - 100
____	Superior	101 - 140
____	Outstanding	141 - 180
235	Delphi Class	181+

OLGA WORRALL

HEALER RATING—DELPHI CLASS—200

Perhaps the most famous healer of the twentieth century, Olga Worrall believed that her healing power was a direct gift from God. Mrs. Worrall first noticed her healing gift when she was only three years old, when one day her mother complained of a headache. The little girl touched the woman's forehead, and according to the story, the headache instantly disappeared. Olga said that her parents acknowledged her gift but played it down because they did not want her regarded as a freak. As we have seen in the cases of previous healers, the gift tends to present itself early in the life of the individual and in the case of these Delphi Class savants, its results are unmistakable. This observation is in direct keeping with my astrological theory that if these gifts are in some way influenced by the stars at the time of the native's birth, then they should develop in conjunction with the growing individual and present themselves as a normal part of their lives.

Worrall was taken seriously by scientific circles during her lifetime and she lectured at colleges and universities in the U.S. and abroad. She wrote about her gift extensively and three of her biographies became bestsellers. Her most famous work, ***The Gift of Healing***, is considered a classic in the genre. One letter which Worrall chronicles in the book was written by a surgeon who treated a woman with a cancerous tumor in her abdomen. According to the surgeon, the woman, who also a nurse, was given radiation and other appropriate therapies but on her own decided to seek the services of Worrall. During the laying on of hands, the nurse reported "the sensation of a big corkscrew turning in her stomach." The tumor, described as the size of a person's head, was still obviously present after the treatment. Yet as time passed, the woman became strong enough to return to work, and within six months follow up testing showed no trace of the tumor![10] Worrall is credited with thousands of healings of this sort.

The gift also worked at a distance. In 1955 she was approached by the family of a woman who suffered from a cerebral aneurysm, a dangerous swelling of a blood vessel in the brain, that needed to be repaired by surgery before it ruptured. Her surgeons had warned that her fever was too high and that the operation would have to be delayed untilit subsided. The family feared that each day they delayed would potentially lead to a spontaneous rupture of the aneurysm and in their dismay, the woman's brother called Worrall who lived in Baltimore. An arrangement was made that Olga and her husband would pray for the lady at 9:00 p.m. while she lay in her room in New York.

More than thirty years later, a healthy Eleanor Robbers said she never forgot the emanations of strength and peace that coursed through her head and body at the moment of prayer that night. By the next morning, she related that her fever was gone and the surgeons were able to operate. Subsequently, the Worralls made absent prayer a part of their normal routine. What does the natal chart of this astounding healer reveal about her healing potential?

Worrall's healer rating of 200, a Delphi Class score, is consistent with the intensity of the healing gift that she displayed in life and with the early age in which it appeared. She has six positive grand elevations in her chart and three planetary eclipses; all of which have a positive influence on her life and healing ability. She also has two of the most powerful spiritual aspects in the sky: the Moon Mercury contraparallel and the grand elevation of Mercury. The reader will see these two aspects represented in the charts of great spiritual savants over and over in this book. One could scarcely imagine the universe designing a more perfect healing vessel than this wonderful individual.

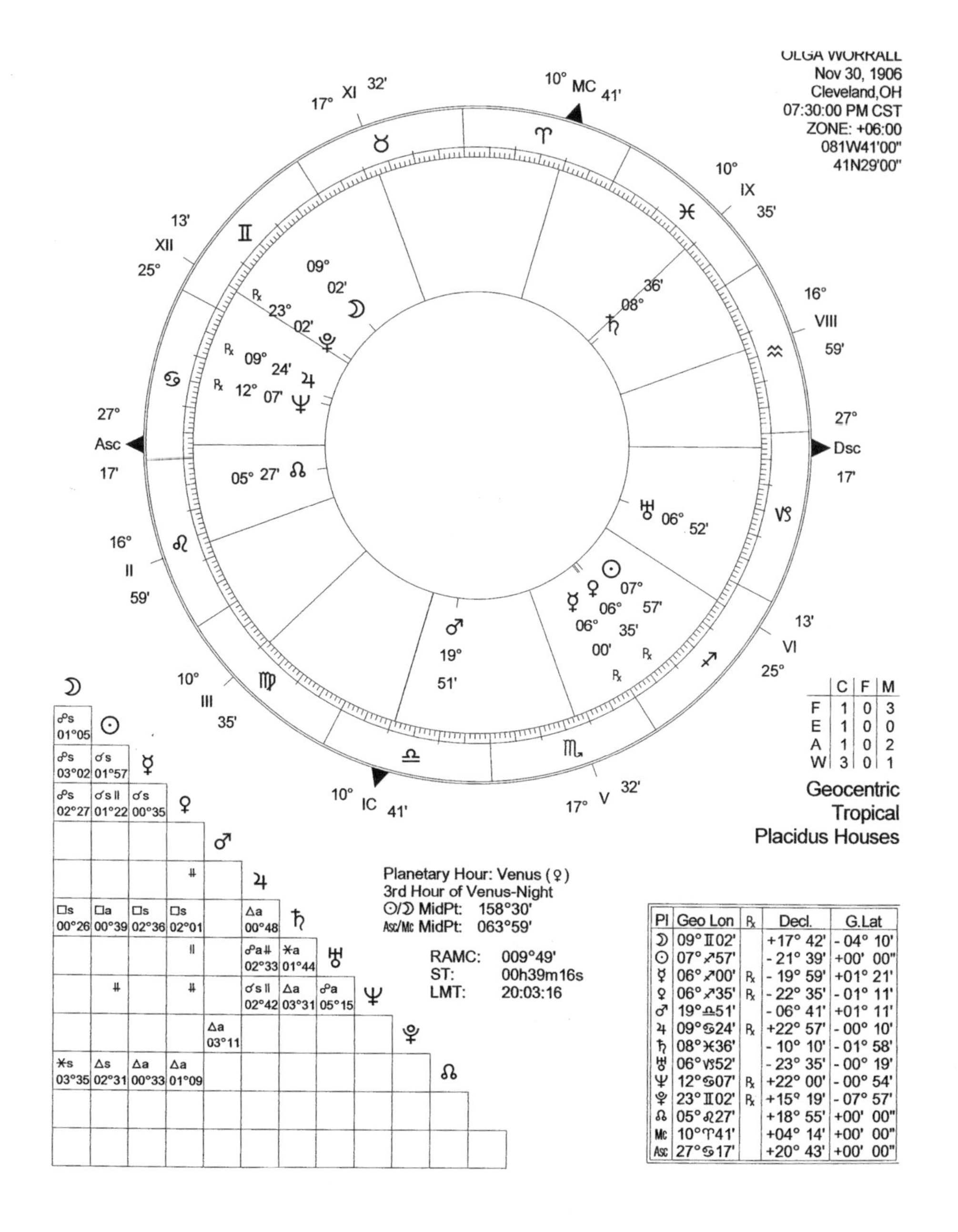
OLGA WORRALL
Nov 30, 1906
Cleveland,OH
07:30:00 PM CST
ZONE: +06:00
081W41'00"
41N29'00"
Geocentric
Tropical
Placidus Houses
Planetary Hour: Venus (♀)
3rd Hour of Venus-Night
☉/☽ MidPt: 158°30'
Asc/Mc MidPt: 063°59'
RAMC: 009°49'
ST: 00h39m16s
LMT: 20:03:16
C F M
F 1 0 3
E 1 0 0
A 1 0 2
W 3 0 1
Pl Geo Lon ℞ Decl. G.Lat
☽ 09°♊02' +17° 42' -04° 10'
☉ 07°♐57' -21° 39' +00' 00"
☿ 06°♐00' ℞ -19° 59' +01° 21'
♀ 06°♐35' ℞ -22° 35' -01° 11'
♂ 19°♎51' -06° 41' +01° 11'
♃ 09°♋24' ℞ +22° 57' -00° 10'
♄ 08°♓36' -10° 10' -01° 58'
♅ 06°♑52' -23° 35' -00° 19'
♆ 12°♋07' ℞ +22° 00' -00° 54'
♇ 23°♊02' ℞ +15° 19' -07° 57'
☊ 05°♌27' +18° 55' +00' 00"
Mc 10°♈41' +04° 14' +00' 00"
Asc 27°♋17' +20° 43' +00' 00"

Birth / Event Data

____
Place of birth/event (city, state, county)

____
Date of birth/event

____
Time of birth/event (exact time, i.e. birth certificate)

Client Data

Olga Worrall
First and last name

____
Mailing address

____
City, state, country, zip code

____
Telephone no. and fax no.

____
E-mail address

HEALING POTENTIAL – MARKERS ASPECTS

(All aspects score 10 points each, unless otherwise indicated)

CONJUNCTIONS
- X Sun - Venus
- ___ Neptune - Pluto
- ___ Pluto – Moon (25 pts)
- ___ Saturn – Moon
- ___ Moon – Mars
- ___ Jupiter – Mars
- ___ Mars - Venus

TRINES
- ___ Venus - Saturn
- ___ Sun - Moon (25 pts)
- ___ Jupiter – Neptune
- ___ Mercury – Uranus (25 pts)
- ___ Moon – Venus
- X Saturn – Neptune
- ___ Jupiter – Mars
- ___ Venus - Pluto

SEXTILES
- ___ Neptune - Pluto
- ___ Sun - Saturn
- ___ Moon - Neptune (25 pts)
- ___ Saturn - Mercury
- ___ Venus – Jupiter
- ___ Pluto – Uranus
- ___ Mercury – Venus
- ___ Sun - Pluto

SQUARES
- ___ Uranus – Moon (25 pts)
- ___ Saturn – Pluto
- ___ Jupiter – Moon
- ___ Pluto – Moon (25 pts)
- X Sun – Saturn
- ___ Uranus – Jupiter
- ___ Venus – Uranus (25 pts)
- ___ Venus – Neptune (25 pts)
- ___ Sun – Pluto
- ___ Jupiter – Pluto
- X Saturn – Moon
- ___ Mercury – Uranus

OPPOSITIONS
- X Uranus – Neptune (25 pts)
- ___ Uranus – Pluto (25 pts)
- ___ Jupiter – Venus
- ___ Pluto – Mercury
- ___ Jupiter – Mars
- X Sun – Moon
- ___ Sun – Jupiter
- ___ Sun - Saturn

PARALLELS
- ___ Neptune - Moon
- ___ Neptune - Pluto (25 pts)
- X Pluto – Moon
- ___ Mercury – Venus
- ___ Moon – Mars
- ___ Mercury – Mars
- ___ Saturn - Sun (25 pts)
- ___ Pluto - Uranus
- X Sun - Mercury (25 pts)
- ___ Jupiter – Mars
- ___ Neptune - Mars

CONTRAPARALLELS
- X Moon – Mercury (25 pts)
- ___ Jupiter – Mars
- ___ Neptune - Mars
- ___ Venus - Pluto (25 pts)
- ___ Pluto – Mars
- X Sun – Jupiter
- ___ Sun - Mars
- X Uranus – Neptune (25 pts)
- ___ Moon – Venus
- ___ Saturn – Uranus (25 pts)
- ___ Saturn – Sun
- ___ Sun – Moon (25 pts)

QUADS
- ___ Jupiter – Mars – Uranus – Neptune (25 pts)

HIDEK
- ___ Mercury
- ___ Mars

EXDEK
- X Uranus

PROXIMITY ELEVATIONS
- ___ Venus – Saturn (contraparallel)
- ___ Uranus–Neptune (contraparallel)
- ___ Sun-Moon (contraparallel; 25 pts)
- ___ Venus-Neptune (contraparallel; 25 pts)

ECLIPSES
- ___ Any Uranus Eclipses

GRAND ELEVATIONS
- ___ + Moon
- ___ - Sun
- ___ - Neptune
- X + Mercury
- ___ - Uranus

GRAND TOTAL		SCALE
___	Below Average	0 - 30
___	Average	31 - 60
___	Above Average	61 - 100
___	Superior	101 - 140
___	Outstanding	141 - 180
200	Delphi Class	181+

RASPUTIN

HEALER RATING——OUTSTANDING——160**

Grigory Rasputin is one of the most notorious personalities in modern Russian history. He is known for his almost superhuman ability to survive numerous assassination attempts but perhaps less well known is his outstanding healing gift. Through the ages, healing power has sometimes led to political power and Rasputin is a sterling example of a man whose peasant beginnings were transformed into a staggering political career by this very gift. As a young man in Siberia, Rasputin was noted both for his debauched life and for ability to heal the sick, a talent he developed as a monk in a heretical sect called the Khylsty. In 1905, he was introduced to Nicholas and Alexandra and soon demonstrated his power on their son Alexis, who was a hemophiliac. When the prince suffered a terrifying bleeding episode that confounded court physicians, Rasputin stopped the flow of blood with a few words and the touch of his hand. Needless to say, this quickly brought him into the good graces of the royal family and the grateful czarina was immediately captivated by the mysterious stranger. He soon rose to the rank of royal confidant and he was called upon to save the life of the young prince on numerous occasions. However, Rasputin never fully gave up his other passion, debauchery, and this soon proved to be his undoing. In 1916, courtiers alarmed by his influence at court made plans for his murder. Despite ingesting enough cyanide to kill a dozen men he survived, apparently none the worse for wear. The conspirators were finally reduced to shooting him three times and binding him with ropes whereupon they eventually dumped him into the icy Neva river where he died by drowning.[11]

Rasputin's natal chart reveals a strong tendency toward the development of healing and mystical powers: mystic potential rating superior 115. His Jupiter Pluto conjunction on the ascendant squared by Mars on the midheaven may be a partial explanation for his love of power in its various forms as well as his tendency toward debauchery. However, his rise to power was mainly fueled by his healing gift which is much more complex in its astrological origins. Rasputin has no less than four Delphi healing markers in his natal chart. He also has six additional marker aspects for healing which add to the overall power of his divine faculty.

Rasputin's birth chart has fascinated astrologers for decades. Within its aspectsare the secrets to one of history's most fascinating and complex human beings. Perhaps one of the mysteries has been solved regarding this enigmatic man: what was the origin of his healing ability? Using modern astrology, one can easily plot the origin of what is possibly one of the most awe-inspiring faculties a person can possess; the power of healing.

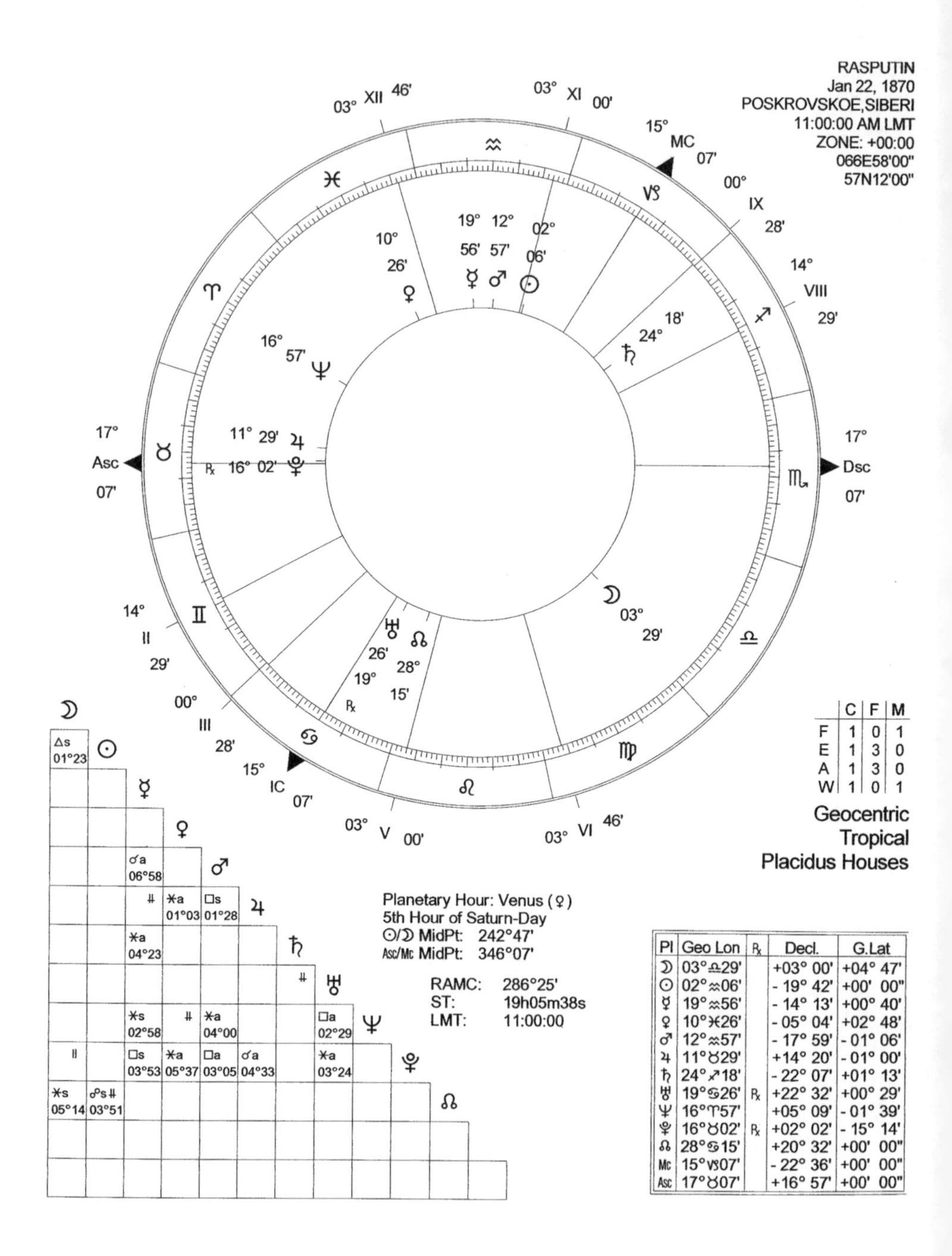

	C	F	M
F	1	0	1
E	1	3	0
A	1	3	0
W	1	0	1

Pl	Geo Lon	℞	Decl.	G.Lat
☽	03°♎29'		+03° 00'	+04° 47'
☉	02°♒06'		- 19° 42'	+00' 00"
☿	19°♒56'		- 14° 13'	+00° 40'
♀	10°♓26'		- 05° 04'	+02° 48'
♂	12°♒57'		- 17° 59'	- 01° 06'
♃	11°♉29'		+14° 20'	- 01° 00'
♄	24°♐18'		- 22° 07'	+01° 13'
♅	19°♋26'	℞	+22° 32'	+00° 29'
♆	16°♈57'		+05° 09'	- 01° 39'
♇	16°♉02'	℞	+02° 02'	- 15° 14'
☊	28°♋15'		+20° 32'	+00' 00"
Mc	15°♑07'		- 22° 36'	+00' 00"
Asc	17°♉07'		+16° 57'	+00' 00"

Birth / Event Data

Place of birth/event (city, state, county)

Date of birth/event

Time of birth/event (exact time, i.e. birth certificate)

Client Data

Rasputin

First and last name

Mailing address

City, state, country, zip code

Telephone no. and fax no.

E-mail address

HEALING POTENTIAL – MARKERS ASPECTS

(All aspects score 10 points each, unless otherwise indicated)

CONJUNCTIONS

- ___ Sun - Venus
- ___ Neptune - Pluto
- ___ Pluto – Moon (25 pts)
- ___ Saturn – Moon
- ___ Moon – Mars
- ___ Jupiter – Mars
- ___ Mars - Venus

TRINES

- X Venus - Saturn
- ___ Sun - Moon (25 pts)
- ___ Jupiter – Neptune
- ___ Mercury – Uranus (25 pts)
- ___ Moon – Venus
- ___ Saturn – Neptune
- ___ Jupiter – Mars
- ___ Venus - Pluto

SEXTILES

- ___ Neptune - Pluto
- ___ Sun - Saturn
- ___ Moon - Neptune (25 pts)
- X Saturn - Mercury
- X Venus – Jupiter
- X Pluto – Uranus
- ___ Mercury – Venus
- ___ Sun - Pluto

SQUARES

- ___ Uranus – Moon (25 pts)
- ___ Saturn – Pluto
- ___ Jupiter – Moon
- ___ Pluto – Moon (25 pts)
- ___ Sun – Saturn
- ___ Uranus – Jupiter
- ___ Venus – Uranus (25 pts)
- ___ Venus – Neptune (25 pts)
- ___ Sun – Pluto
- ___ Jupiter – Pluto
- ___ Saturn – Moon
- ___ Mercury – Uranus

OPPOSITIONS

- ___ Uranus – Neptune (25 pts)
- ___ Uranus – Pluto (25 pts)
- ___ Jupiter – Venus
- ___ Pluto – Mercury
- ___ Jupiter – Mars
- ___ Sun – Moon
- ___ Sun – Jupiter
- ___ Sun - Saturn

PARALLELS

- X Neptune - Moon
- ___ Neptune - Pluto (25 pts)
- X Pluto – Moon
- ___ Mercury – Venus
- ___ Moon – Mars
- ___ Mercury – Mars
- X Saturn - Sun (25 pts)
- ___ Pluto - Uranus
- ___ Sun - Mercury (25 pts)
- ___ Jupiter – Mars
- ___ Neptune - Mars

CONTRAPARALLELS

- ___ Moon – Mercury (25 pts)
- ___ Jupiter – Mars
- ___ Neptune - Mars
- ___ Venus - Pluto (25 pts)
- ___ Pluto – Mars
- ___ Sun – Jupiter
- ___ Sun – Mars
- ___ Uranus – Neptune (25 pts)
- X Moon – Venus
- X Saturn – Uranus (25 pts)
- ___ Saturn – Sun
- ___ Sun – Moon (25 pts)

QUADS

- ___ Jupiter – Mars – Uranus – Neptune (25 pts)

HIDEK

- ___ Mercury
- ___ Mars

EXDEK

- ___ Uranus

PROXIMITY ELEVATIONS

- ___ Venus – Saturn (contraparallel)
- ___ Uranus–Neptune (contraparallel)
- ___ Sun-Moon (contraparallel: 25 pts)
- X Venus-Neptune (contraparallel: 25 pts)

ECLIPSES

- ___ Any Uranus Eclipses

GRAND ELEVATIONS

- ___ + Moon
- ___ - Sun
- ___ - Neptune
- ___ + Mercury
- ___ - Uranus

GRAND TOTAL		SCALE
___	Below Average	0 - 30
___	Average	31 - 60
___	Above Average	61 - 100
___	Superior	101 - 140
160	Outstanding	141 - 180
___	Delphi Class	181+

ELLEN YOAKUM

HEALER RATING—DELPHI CLASS—260***

Ellen Yoakum was an American healer who was born prematurely with a "web" over her face. She had to be fed with an eyedropper for the first few weeks of her life and by the time she reached eight years of age, she weighed only 48 pounds. She noted her healing potential at a very early age and she is one of the most thoroughly tested healersof all time. She was recognized by the medical profession for her work and she has worked with allopathic healing professionals all over the world. She does not follow a particular religion, drama, or mystical pretensions. Quite simply, she displayed perhaps the highest degree of raw healing talent that has been scientifically documented in modern times. It is a fitting testament to her healing abilities that she was able to heal herself of her childhood maladies at a time when the vast majority of children died of such problems.

Astrologically, her healing potential is astounding. She has eight Delphi healing markers and six marker aspects which predispose her to the development of the healing gift. In my opinion, her life and nativity are a startling testament to the power of modern astrology to pick out individuals who could potentially develop rare latent paranormal talents to an extraordinary degree. The psychic web that she was covered with at the time of her birth has long been associated with divine gifts. It forms from remnants of amniotic tissue that adhere to the face and scalp at the time of birth. Legend holds that individuals born with this veil of tissue are marked by God for the development of great supernatural power. In the case of Ellen Yoakum, this legend crystallized magnificently into fact.

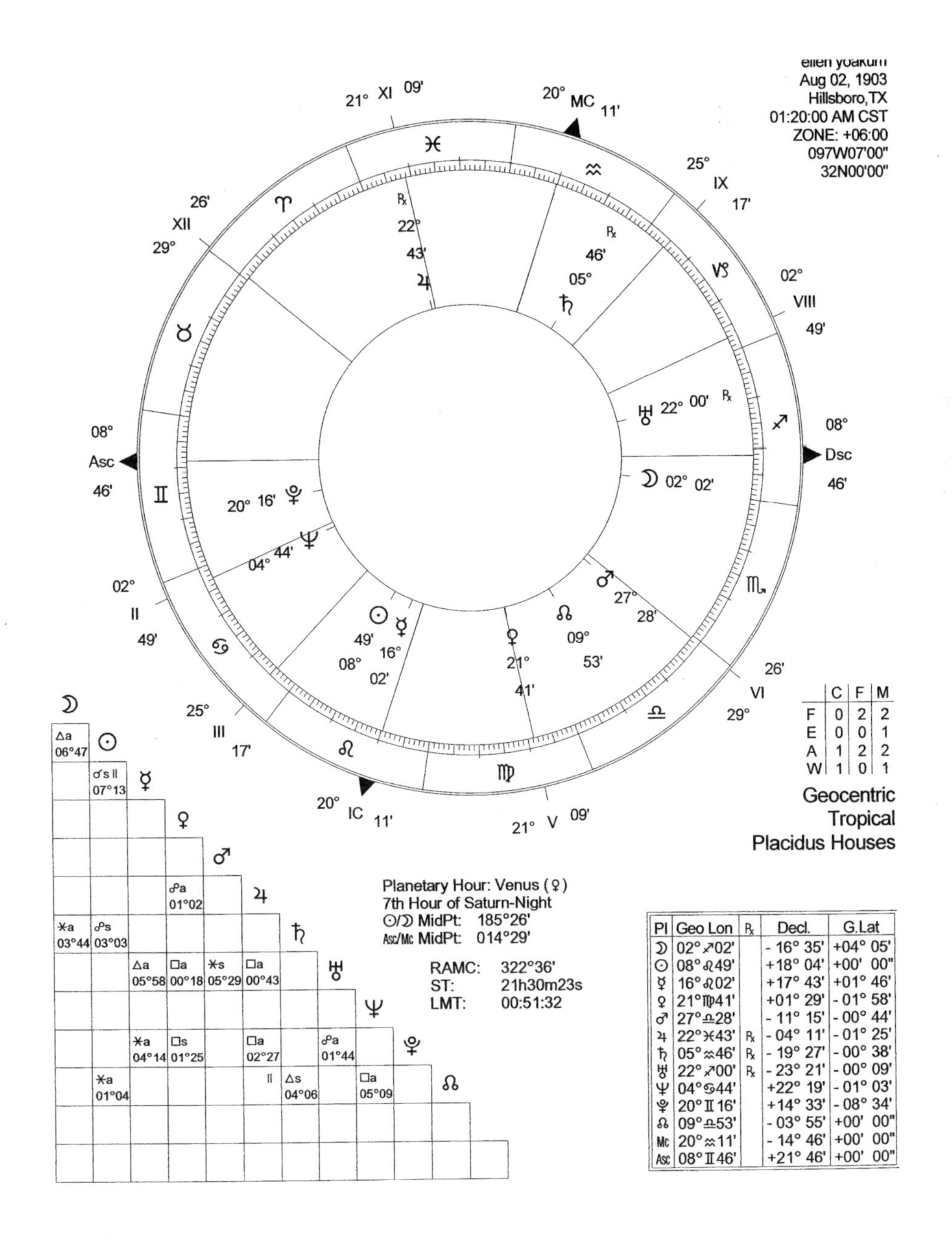

	C	F	M
F	0	2	2
E	0	0	1
A	1	2	2
W	1	0	1

Pl	Geo Lon	℞	Decl.	G.Lat
☽	02°♐02'		- 16° 35'	+04° 05'
☉	08°♌49'		+18° 04'	+00' 00"
☿	16°♌02'		+17° 43'	+01° 46'
♀	21°♍41'		+01° 29'	- 01° 58'
♂	27°♎28'		- 11° 15'	- 00° 44'
♃	22°♓43'	℞	- 04° 11'	- 01° 25'
♄	05°♒46'	℞	- 19° 27'	- 00° 38'
♅	22°♐00'	℞	- 23° 21'	- 00° 09'
♆	04°♋44'		+22° 19'	- 01° 03'
♇	20°♊16'		+14° 33'	- 08° 34'
☊	09°♎53'		- 03° 55'	+00' 00"
Mc	20°♒11'		- 14° 46'	+00' 00"
Asc	08°♊46'		+21° 46'	+00' 00"

Birth / Event Data

____
Place of birth/event (city, state, county)

____
Date of birth/event

____
Time of birth/event (exact time, i.e. birth certificate)

Client Data

Ellen Yoqkum
First and last name

____
Mailing address

____
City, state, country, zip code

____
Telephone no. and fax no.

____
E-mail address

HEALING POTENTIAL – MARKERS ASPECTS

(All aspects score 10 points each, unless otherwise indicated)

CONJUNCTIONS

- ___ Sun - Venus
- ___ Neptune - Pluto
- ___ Pluto – Moon (25 pts)
- ___ Saturn – Moon
- ___ Moon – Mars
- ___ Jupiter – Mars
- ___ Mars - Venus

TRINES

- ___ Venus - Saturn
- X Sun - Moon (25 pts)
- ___ Jupiter – Neptune
- X Mercury – Uranus (25 pts)
- ___ Moon – Venus
- ___ Saturn – Neptune
- ___ Jupiter – Mars
- ___ Venus - Pluto

SEXTILES

- ___ Neptune - Pluto
- ___ Sun - Saturn
- ___ Moon - Neptune (25 pts)
- ___ Saturn - Mercury
- ___ Venus – Jupiter
- ___ Pluto – Uranus
- ___ Mercury – Venus
- ___ Sun - Pluto

SQUARES

- ___ Uranus – Moon (25 pts)
- ___ Saturn – Pluto
- ___ Jupiter – Moon
- ___ Pluto – Moon (25 pts)
- ___ Sun – Saturn
- X Uranus – Jupiter
- X Venus – Uranus (25 pts)
- ___ Venus – Neptune (25 pts)

- ___ Sun – Pluto
- X Jupiter – Pluto
- ___ Saturn – Moon
- ___ Mercury – Uranus

OPPOSITIONS

- ___ Uranus – Neptune (25 pts)
- X Uranus – Pluto (25 pts)
- ___ Jupiter – Venus
- ___ Pluto – Mercury
- ___ Jupiter – Mars
- ___ Sun – Moon
- ___ Sun – Jupiter
- X Sun - Saturn

PARALLELS

- ___ Neptune - Moon
- ___ Neptune - Pluto (25 pts)
- ___ Pluto – Moon
- ___ Mercury – Venus
- ___ Moon – Mars
- ___ Mercury – Mars
- ___ Saturn - Sun (25 pts)
- ___ Pluto - Uranus
- X Sun - Mercury (25 pts)
- ___ Jupiter – Mars
- ___ Neptune - Mars

CONTRAPARALLELS

- X Moon – Mercury (25 pts)
- ___ Jupiter – Mars
- ___ Neptune - Mars
- ___ Venus - Pluto (25 pts)
- ___ Pluto – Mars
- ___ Sun – Jupiter
- ___ Sun – Mars
- X Uranus – Neptune (25 pts)
- ___ Moon – Venus

- ___ Saturn – Uranus (25 pts)
- X Saturn – Sun
- X Sun – Moon (25 pts)

QUADS

- ___ Jupiter – Mars – Uranus – Neptune (25 pts)

HIDEK

- ___ Mercury
- ___ Mars

EXDEK

- X Uranus

PROXIMITY ELEVATIONS

- ___ Venus – Saturn (contraparallel)
- ___ Uranus–Neptune (contraparallel)
- ___ Sun-Moon (contraparallel; 25 pts)
- ___ Venus-Neptune (contraparallel; 25 pts)

ECLIPSES

- ___ Any Uranus Eclipses

GRAND ELEVATIONS

- ___ + Moon
- X - Sun
- ___ - Neptune
- ___ + Mercury
- ___ - Uranus

	GRAND TOTAL	SCALE
___	Below Average	0 - 30
___	Average	31 - 60
___	Above Average	61 - 100
___	Superior	101 - 140
___	Outstanding	141 - 180
260	Delphi Class	181+

KATHRYN KUHLMAN

HEALER CLASS—DELPHI CLASS——230*** Kathryn Kuhlman was one of the world's most colorful and controversial healing evangelists. She was respected worldwide and she worked as a respected practitioner and soloist with Billy Graham, Rex Humbard, and Benny Hinn. After growing up in the mean streets of Baltimore as a young Christian singer and minister, she gained a reputation as a healer and missionary. Initially, many were skeptical of her "over the top" services which often involved supernatural acts and spontaneous healings. However, as her reputation grew, the legitimacy of her healing gained greater credence. Later in life, she became known as the "Miracle Lady" and her services drew audiences which numbered into the tens of thousands. Kuhlman's live telecasts that often portrayed instant healings for a variety of conditions were witnessed by millions. Astrologically, Kathryn Kuhlman's natal chart displays delphi level healing potential. Her potential rating of 230 places her in the top one-half of 1% of all individuals classified. Is this yet another example of coincidence at work?

A healing genius of this magnitude is a rare gift indeed! Kuhlman's chart displays a very rare and powerful combination of healing markers. The Jupiter-Mars-Uranus-Neptune is an extraordinarily rare celestial configuration that occurs only once every 18.6 years for a period of 14.1 days. It is so rare that no one in the control group that I studied displayed this aspect in their charts. However, it was revealed to be a delphi marker for healers and a number of prominent healers possessed this aspect in their nativity. Once again, we see that a truly gifted healer's gift is revealed in the natal chart.

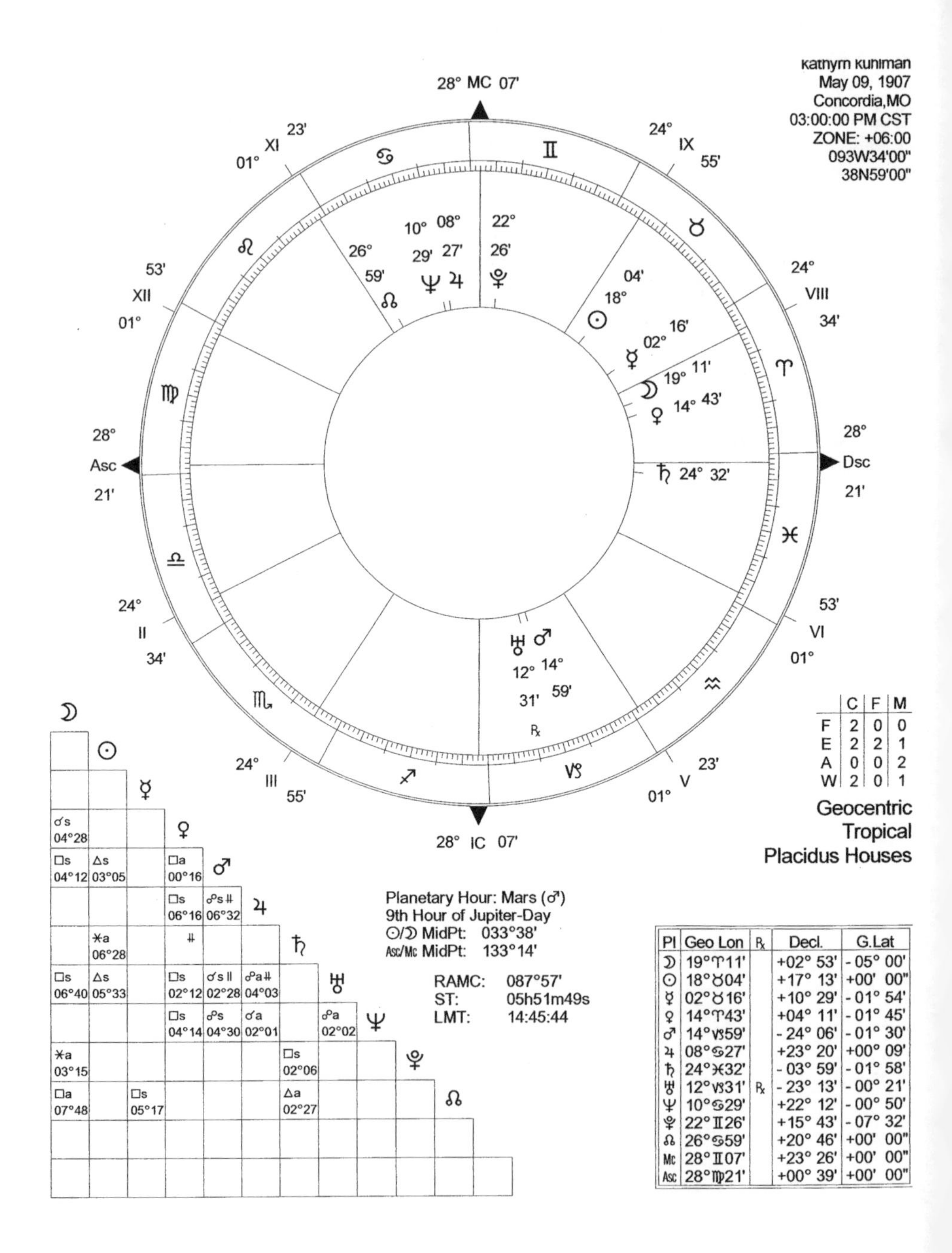
Kathyrn Kuhlman
May 09, 1907
Concordia,MO
03:00:00 PM CST
ZONE: +06:00
093W34'00"
38N59'00"
28° MC 07'
28° Asc 21'
28° Dsc 21'
28° IC 07'
Geocentric
Tropical
Placidus Houses
Planetary Hour: Mars (♂)
9th Hour of Jupiter-Day
☉/☽ MidPt: 033°38'
Asc/Mc MidPt: 133°14'
RAMC: 087°57'
ST: 05h51m49s
LMT: 14:45:44
	C	F	M
F	2	0	0
E	2	2	1
A	0	0	2
W	2	0	1
Pl	Geo Lon	Rx	Decl.	G.Lat
---	---	---	---	---
☽	19°♈11'		+02° 53'	- 05° 00'
☉	18°♉04'		+17° 13'	+00' 00"
☿	02°♉16'		+10° 29'	- 01° 54'
♀	14°♈43'		+04° 11'	- 01° 45'
♂	14°♑59'		- 24° 06'	- 01° 30'
♃	08°♋27'		+23° 20'	+00° 09'
♄	24°♓32'		- 03° 59'	- 01° 58'
♅	12°♑31'	Rx	- 23° 13'	- 00° 21'
♆	10°♋29'		+22° 12'	- 00° 50'
♇	22°♊26'		+15° 43'	- 07° 32'
☊	26°♋59'		+20° 46'	+00' 00"
Mc	28°♊07'		+23° 26'	+00' 00"
Asc	28°♍21'		+00° 39'	+00' 00"

Birth / Event Data

Place of birth/event (city, state, county)

Date of birth/event

Time of birth/event (exact time, i.e. birth certificate)

Client Data

Kathryn Kuhlman

First and last name

Mailing address

City, state, country, zip code

Telephone no. and fax no.

E-mail address

HEALING POTENTIAL – MARKERS ASPECTS

(All aspects score 10 points each, unless otherwise indicated)

CONJUNCTIONS

- ____ Sun - Venus
- ____ Neptune - Pluto
- ____ Pluto – Moon (25 pts)
- ____ Saturn – Moon
- ____ Moon – Mars
- ____ Jupiter – Mars
- ____ Mars - Venus

TRINES

- ____ Venus - Saturn
- ____ Sun - Moon (25 pts)
- ____ Jupiter – Neptune
- ____ Mercury – Uranus (25 pts)
- ____ Moon – Venus
- ____ Saturn – Neptune
- ____ Jupiter – Mars
- ____ Venus - Pluto

SEXTILES

- __X__ Neptune - Pluto
- ____ Sun - Saturn
- ____ Moon - Neptune (25 pts)
- ____ Saturn - Mercury
- ____ Venus – Jupiter
- ____ Pluto – Uranus
- ____ Mercury – Venus
- ____ Sun - Pluto

SQUARES

- __X__ Uranus – Moon (25 pts)
- __X__ Saturn – Pluto
- __X__ Jupiter – Moon
- ____ Pluto – Moon (25 pts)
- ____ Sun – Saturn
- __X__ Uranus – Jupiter
- __X__ Venus – Uranus (25 pts)
- ____ Venus – Neptune (25 pts)
- ____ Sun – Pluto
- ____ Jupiter – Pluto
- ____ Saturn – Moon
- ____ Mercury – Uranus

OPPOSITIONS

- __X__ Uranus – Neptune (25 pts)
- ____ Uranus – Pluto (25 pts)
- ____ Jupiter – Venus
- __X__ Pluto – Mercury
- ____ Jupiter – Mars
- ____ Sun – Moon
- ____ Sun – Jupiter
- ____ Sun - Saturn

PARALLELS

- ____ Neptune - Moon
- ____ Neptune - Pluto (25 pts)
- ____ Pluto – Moon
- ____ Mercury – Venus
- ____ Moon – Mars
- ____ Mercury – Mars
- ____ Saturn - Sun (25 pts)
- ____ Pluto - Uranus
- ____ Sun - Mercury (25 pts)
- ____ Jupiter – Mars
- ____ Neptune - Mars

CONTRAPARALLELS

- __X__ Moon – Mercury (25 pts)
- __X__ Jupiter – Mars
- ____ Neptune - Mars
- ____ Venus - Pluto (25 pts)
- ____ Pluto – Mars
- ____ Sun – Jupiter
- __X__ Sun – Mars
- ____ Uranus – Neptune (25 pts)
- ____ Moon – Venus
- ____ Saturn – Uranus (25 pts)
- ____ Saturn – Sun
- ____ Sun – Moon (25 pts)

QUADS

- __X__ Jupiter – Mars – Uranus – Neptune (25 pts)

HIDEK

- ____ Mercury
- ____ Mars

EXDEK

- ____ Uranus

PROXIMITY ELEVATIONS

- __X__ Venus – Saturn (contraparallel)
- ____ Uranus–Neptune (contraparallel)
- ____ Sun-Moon (contraparallel; 25 pts)
- ____ Venus-Neptune (contraparallel; 25 pts)

ECLIPSES

- __X__ Any Uranus Eclipses

GRAND ELEVATIONS

- ____ + Moon
- ____ - Sun
- ____ - Neptune
- ____ + Mercury
- ____ - Uranus

GRAND TOTAL		SCALE
____	Below Average	0 - 30
____	Average	31 - 60
____	Above Average	61 - 100
____	Superior	101 - 140
____	Outstanding	141 - 180
230	Delphi Class	181+

The birth data of these remarkable healers reveals that using these new techniques which I have applied from modern astrology, yet another paranormal ability may be detected within the birth chart. Not only is it possible to detect the gift, but also by using the techniques, it is also possible to presage the intensity of the faculty and the degree to which it may be developed in the individual. Admittedly this is not a perfect tool but after testing more than 80 healers, I have found that this system detects their ability more than 92% of the time! I have also noticed that great healings tend to take place on days when the aggregate number of healing markers in the sky approaches a critical level. I will give a few startling examples of this remarkable and uncanny phenomenon.

On May 18, 1534 Simon Vela, the only son of a wealthy and prominent family in France, dreamt a vision of a spot where the image of the Virgin Mary was buried. Initially his family and friends considered him to be quite mad and attributed his vision to the product of a vivid hallucination. He was on his way to visit the professors at the university in Salamanca when he encountered two vendors who were arguing about the quality of the coal which they were selling. One claimed his products were superior because they had been taken from the slopes of Pena de Francia, the very place that had been referred to in his dreams that he had almost believed to be entirely fictitious! He had been instructed in the dream to proceed to the mountains which bordered that area and to take witnesses. He then ventured into the village and employed the assistance of four prominent men including the Notary Public.

On the morning of May 19, 1534, the five men removed a large stone from the spot which Simon had seen in his vision. Underneath the stone, lay a miraculous sight; a perfectly preserved beautiful image of the Virgin of Pena de Francia. Each man was instantly restored from bodily infirmities or weaknesses to his health. One man regained his hearing, another recovered from defects of birth, and still another was totally healed from a chronic joint condition. This event was documented in the archives of San Martin de Castanar, a village at the foot of Pena de Francia.

Astrologically speaking, May 19, 1534 Salamanca Spain presented exactly what one would expect from a day when a series of famous documented healings took place. The healing potential of that date is also rated at 175; near delphi level! At first glance one would almost accept that just about any day would yield a near delphi level rating given the numbers of such days that we have presented in this chapter. However, this type of astrological rating for the healing potential of any given day is rare and occurs in one percent of all the days that were tested. As such, they merit more than a cursory discussion in this chapter. I do not believe that it is mere coincidence that this degree of latent healing potential on that particular day is also associated with a series of notable healings.

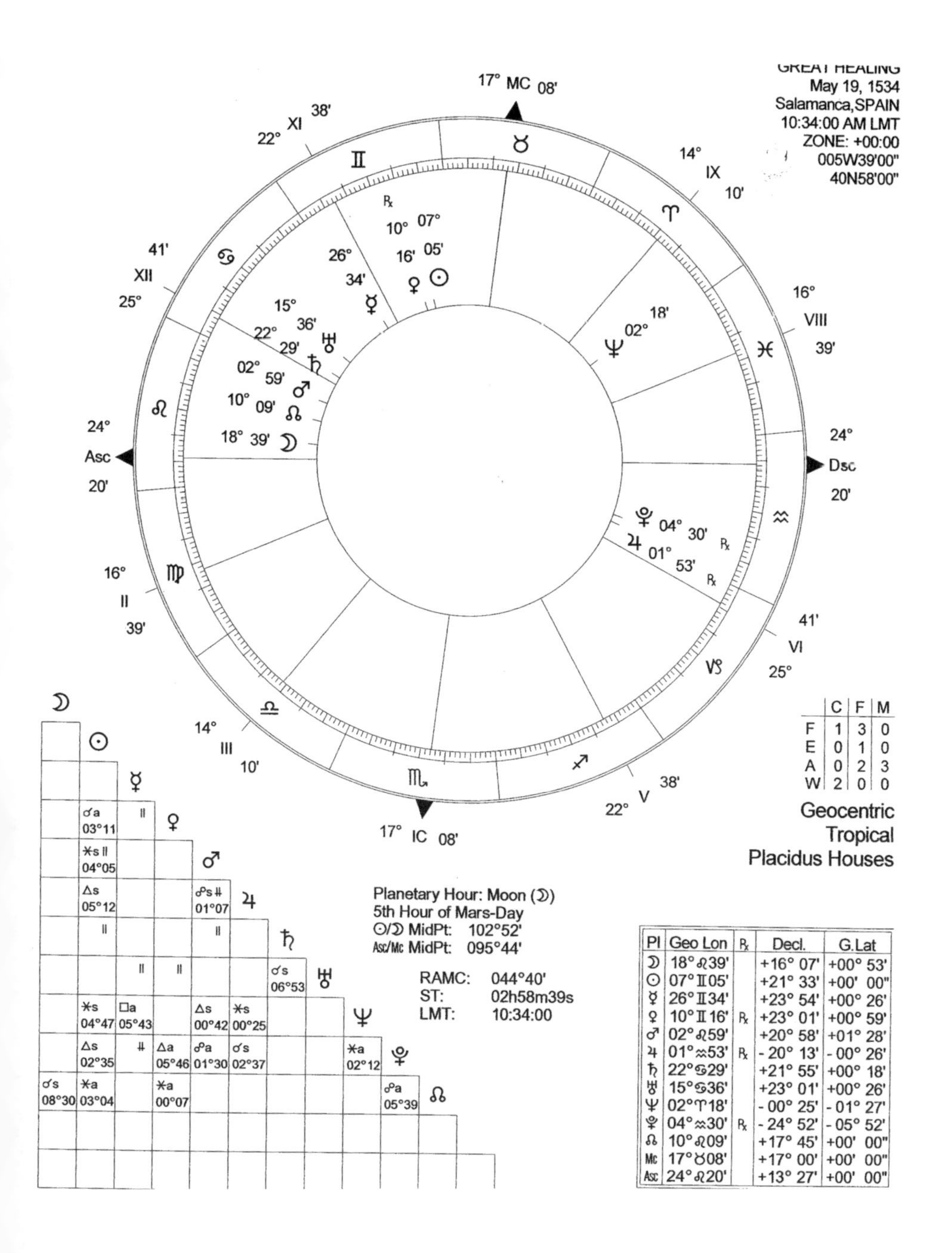
GREAT HEALING
May 19, 1534
Salamanca,SPAIN
10:34:00 AM LMT
ZONE: +00:00
005W39'00"
40N58'00"
17° MC 08'
Asc
Dsc
17° IC 08'
Geocentric
Tropical
Placidus Houses
Planetary Hour: Moon (☽)
5th Hour of Mars-Day
☉/☽ MidPt: 102°52'
Asc/Mc MidPt: 095°44'
RAMC: 044°40'
ST: 02h58m39s
LMT: 10:34:00
Pl | Geo Lon | Rx | Decl. | G.Lat
☽ 18°♌39' +16° 07' +00° 53'
☉ 07°♊05' +21° 33' +00' 00"
☿ 26°♊34' +23° 54' +00° 26'
♀ 10°♊16' Rx +23° 01' +00° 59'
♂ 02°♌59' +20° 58' +01° 28'
♃ 01°♒53' Rx - 20° 13' - 00° 26'
♄ 22°♋29' +21° 55' +00° 18'
♅ 15°♋36' +23° 01' +00° 26'
♆ 02°♈18' - 00° 25' - 01° 27'
♇ 04°♒30' Rx - 24° 52' - 05° 52'
☊ 10°♌09' +17° 45' +00' 00"
Mc 17°♉08' +17° 00' +00' 00"
Asc 24°♌20' +13° 27' +00' 00"
C F M
F 1 3 0
E 0 1 0
A 0 2 3
W 2 0 0

Birth / Event Data

____
Place of birth/event (city, state, county)

____
Date of birth/event

____
Time of birth/event (exact time, i.e. birth certificate)

Client Data

Salamanca Spain
First and last name

____
Mailing address

____
City, state, country, zip code

____
Telephone no. and fax no.

____
E-mail address

HEALING POTENTIAL – MARKERS ASPECTS

(All aspects score 10 points each, unless otherwise indicated)

CONJUNCTIONS

X Sun - Venus
—— Neptune - Pluto
—— Pluto – Moon (25 pts)
—— Saturn – Moon
—— Moon – Mars
—— Jupiter – Mars
—— Mars - Venus

TRINES

—— Venus - Saturn
—— Sun - Moon (25 pts)
—— Jupiter – Neptune
—— Mercury – Uranus (25 pts)
—— Moon – Venus
—— Saturn – Neptune
—— Jupiter – Mars
X Venus - Pluto

SEXTILES

X Neptune - Pluto
—— Sun - Saturn
—— Moon - Neptune (25 pts)
—— Saturn - Mercury
—— Venus – Jupiter
—— Pluto – Uranus
—— Mercury – Venus
—— Sun - Pluto

SQUARES

—— Uranus – Moon (25 pts)
—— Saturn – Pluto
—— Jupiter – Moon
—— Pluto – Moon (25 pts)
—— Sun – Saturn
—— Uranus – Jupiter
—— Venus – Uranus (25 pts)
—— Venus – Neptune (25 pts)
—— Sun – Pluto
—— Jupiter – Pluto
—— Saturn – Moon
—— Mercury – Uranus

OPPOSITIONS

—— Uranus – Neptune (25 pts)
—— Uranus – Pluto (25 pts)
—— Jupiter – Venus
—— Pluto – Mercury
X Jupiter – Mars
—— Sun – Moon
—— Sun – Jupiter
—— Sun - Saturn

PARALLELS

—— Neptune - Moon
—— Neptune - Pluto (25 pts)
—— Pluto – Moon
X Mercury – Venus
—— Moon – Mars
—— Mercury – Mars
X Saturn - Sun (25 pts)
—— Pluto - Uranus
X Sun - Mercury (25 pts)
—— Jupiter – Mars
—— Neptune - Mars

CONTRAPARALLELS

—— Moon – Mercury (25 pts)
X Jupiter – Mars
—— Neptune - Mars
X Venus - Pluto (25 pts)
—— Pluto – Mars
X Sun – Jupiter
—— Sun – Mars
—— Uranus – Neptune (25 pts)
—— Moon – Venus
—— Saturn – Uranus (25 pts)
—— Saturn – Sun
—— Sun – Moon (25 pts)

QUADS

—— Jupiter – Mars – Uranus – Neptune (25 pts)

HIDEK

—— Mercury
X Mars

EXDEK

—— Uranus

PROXIMITY ELEVATIONS

—— Venus – Saturn (contraparallel)
—— Uranus–Neptune (contraparallel)
—— Sun-Moon (contraparallel; 25 pts)
—— Venus-Neptune (contraparallel; 25 pts)

ECLIPSES

—— Any Uranus Eclipses

GRAND ELEVATIONS

—— + Moon
X - Sun
—— - Neptune
—— + Mercury
X - Uranus

GRAND TOTAL		SCALE
——	Below Average	0 - 30
——	Average	31 - 60
——	Above Average	61 - 100
——	Superior	101 - 140
175	Outstanding	141 - 180
——	Delphi Class	181+

Another now famous healing miracle began on November 22, 1982 in Damascus, Syria. Mirna Nazour was kneeling next to her sister-in-law Layia's sick bed, praying for her recovery, when oil suddenly began to flow from her hands. She quickly and spontaneously placed her hands on Layia, who recovered instantly. This event occurred a second time that day when she was praying next to the bed of her sick mother. Again, the oil began to flow and once again the cure was instantaneous. Two days later, Mirna's icon of the Virgin Mary and Child began to exude oil. This miracle continues to the present day and numerous healings are ascribed to the oils. This oil continues to exude from Mirna's face and hands and it has been the subject of exhaustive investigation. No trickery has been discovered and a chemical analysis of the oil reveals an unusually pure, one hundred percent, olive oil of unknown origin. The mechanics of how the oil exudes from Mirna's body and the icons remain a mystery. The healings and miraculous events surrounding the mysterious oils has received approval by the local bishops of Damascus. The factual details of these ecstasies, healings and miracles have been documented on video recordings and may be obtained for private collections from the Pittsburgh Center for Peace.

The astrological chart of November 22, 1982 Damascus reveals no less than 14 healing aspects! The total potential of that day is clearly in the superior range (135) and there are two powerful healing and mystical configurations in aspect: the positive grand elevation of Mercury and the Sun Venus conjunction. As a matter of fact, nine of these ten markers are also marker aspects for mystical events! It is amazing that a healing event such as this with such obvious associations to the mystical also shares a high number of similar paranormal markers. This chart also displays a very rare celestial event: a plenary eclipse of the planet Uranus. Any eclipse of the planet Uranus is listed as a marker aspect for healing. On this day, Uranus was eclipsed by three different planet; Sun, Venus, and Mercury. We add to this extraordinarily rare event the miraculous nature of the healing just described and we come to an inescapable conclusion; great healings can be observed during celestial events that presage a predisposition for the expression of healing energy.

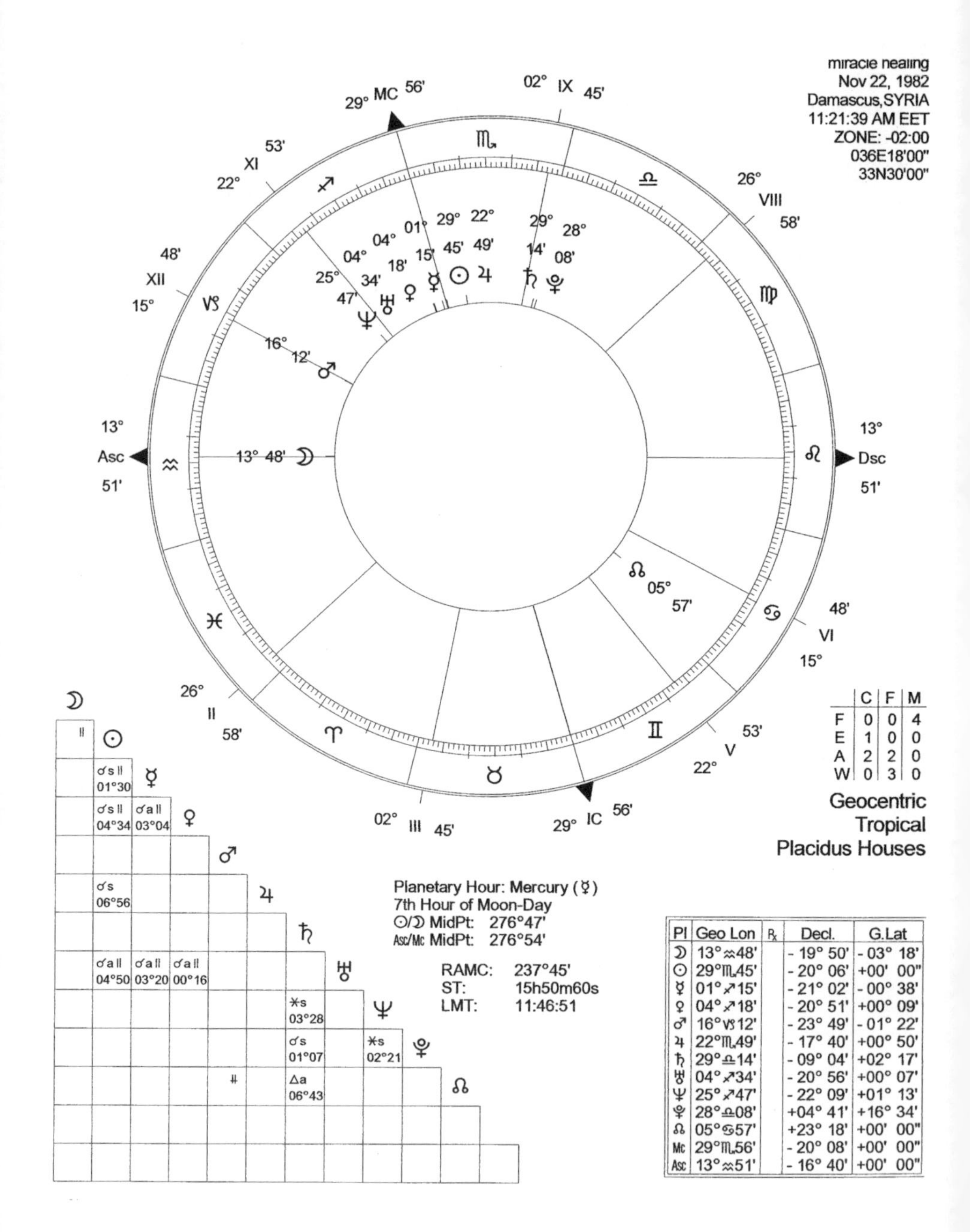

	C	F	M
F	0	0	4
E	1	0	0
A	2	2	0
W	0	3	0

Pl	Geo Lon	℞	Decl.	G.Lat
☽	13°♒48'		- 19° 50'	- 03° 18'
☉	29°♏45'		- 20° 06'	+00' 00"
☿	01°♐15'		- 21° 02'	- 00° 38'
♀	04°♐18'		- 20° 51'	+00° 09'
♂	16°♑12'		- 23° 49'	- 01° 22'
♃	22°♏49'		- 17° 40'	+00° 50'
♄	29°♎14'		- 09° 04'	+02° 17'
♅	04°♐34'		- 20° 56'	+00° 07'
♆	25°♐47'		- 22° 09'	+01° 13'
♇	28°♎08'		+04° 41'	+16° 34'
☊	05°♋57'		+23° 18'	+00' 00"
Mc	29°♏56'		- 20° 08'	+00' 00"
Asc	13°♒51'		- 16° 40'	+00' 00"

Birth / Event Data

____
Place of birth/event (city, state, county)

____
Date of birth/event

____
Time of birth/event (exact time, i.e. birth certificate)

Client Data

Miracle Healing
First and last name

____
Mailing address

____
City, state, country, zip code

____
Telephone no. and fax no.

____
E-mail address

HEALING POTENTIAL – MARKERS ASPECTS

(All aspects score 10 points each, unless otherwise indicated)

CONJUNCTIONS

X Sun - Venus
___ Neptune - Pluto
___ Pluto - Moon (25 pts)
___ Saturn – Moon
___ Moon – Mars
___ Jupiter – Mars
___ Mars - Venus

TRINES

___ Venus - Saturn
___ Sun - Moon (25 pts)
___ Jupiter – Neptune
___ Mercury – Uranus (25 pts)
___ Moon – Venus
___ Saturn – Neptune
___ Jupiter – Mars
___ Venus - Pluto

SEXTILES

X Neptune - Pluto
___ Sun - Saturn
___ Moon - Neptune (25 pts)
___ Saturn - Mercury
___ Venus – Jupiter
___ Pluto – Uranus
___ Mercury – Venus
___ Sun - Pluto

SQUARES

___ Uranus – Moon (25 pts)
___ Saturn – Pluto
___ Jupiter – Moon
___ Pluto – Moon (25 pts)
___ Sun – Saturn
___ Uranus – Jupiter
___ Venus – Uranus (25 pts)
___ Venus – Neptune (25 pts)

___ Sun – Pluto
___ Jupiter – Pluto
___ Saturn – Moon
___ Mercury – Uranus

OPPOSITIONS

___ Uranus – Neptune (25 pts)
___ Uranus – Pluto (25 pts)
___ Jupiter – Venus
___ Pluto – Mercury
___ Jupiter – Mars
___ Sun – Moon
___ Sun – Jupiter
___ Sun - Saturn

PARALLELS

X Neptune - Moon
___ Neptune - Pluto (25 pts)
___ Pluto – Moon
X Mercury – Venus
___ Moon – Mars
___ Mercury – Mars
___ Saturn - Sun (25 pts)
___ Pluto - Uranus
X Sun - Mercury (25 pts)
___ Jupiter – Mars
X Neptune - Mars

CONTRAPARALLELS

___ Moon – Mercury (25 pts)
___ Jupiter – Mars
___ Neptune - Mars
___ Venus - Pluto (25 pts)
___ Pluto – Mars
___ Sun – Jupiter
___ Sun – Mars
___ Uranus – Neptune (25 pts)
___ Moon – Venus

___ Saturn – Uranus (25 pts)
___ Saturn – Sun
___ Sun – Moon (25 pts)

QUADS

___ Jupiter – Mars – Uranus – Neptune (25 pts)

HIDEK

X Mercury
___ Mars

EXDEK

___ Uranus

PROXIMITY ELEVATIONS

___ Venus – Saturn (contraparallel)
___ Uranus–Neptune (contraparallel)
___ Sun-Moon (contraparallel; 25 pts)
___ Venus-Neptune (contraparallel; 25 pts)

ECLIPSES

(XXX) Any Uranus Eclipses

GRAND ELEVATIONS

X + Moon
___ - Sun
___ - Neptune
X + Mercury
___ - Uranus

GRAND TOTAL		SCALE
___	Below Average	0 - 30
___	Average	31 - 60
___	Above Average	61 - 100
135	Superior	101 - 140
___	Outstanding	141 - 180
___	Delphi Class	181+

Perhaps the universe has given us a guide which we can use to heal ourselves if wetake advantage of the astrological information present on these special days. Prayer,surgeries, healing rituals, and other restorative techniques may well work better when we follow these rhythms. Now with the advent of this new astrological information, we may be privy to the secrets of nature's healing rhythms. How would the treatment rates for most of the illnesses which plaque mankind be affected if we held mass= prayers and healing rituals on days which were rated in the delphi range for healing? Is it possible to induce miraculous healings in this manner? I sincerely hope that this data and the potential which it holds for our world will become a regular part of our medical treatment lexicons.

How does a special alignment of planets and stars influence the healing phenomenon? I have formulated a general theory as to how these movements may mediate the presence of paranormal abilities and events on this planet. In a later chapter entitled "Toward a General Theory of Astrology and the Paranormal," I will expand upon this idea further.

THE TEN MOST POWERFUL HEALING TRANSITS

1. PLUTO MOON CONJUNCTION
2. MOON MERCURY CONTRAPARALLEL
3. NEPTUNE PLUTO PARALLEL
4. SATURN SUN PARALLEL
5. PLUTO MOON SQUARE
6. VENUS URANUS SQUARE
7. VENUS NEPTUNE SQUARE
8. SATURN URANUS CONTRAPARALLEL
9. JUPITER MARS URANUS NEPTUNE QUAD
10. SUN MOON TRINE

The above transits displayed the strongest association to healing events according to my research results. These transits are not ranked in order of power or degree of influence. When these particular transits occur, healing phenomena may more easily be precipitated, even when compared to the other healing transits listed in the earlier part of the chapter...

---

[1] The Directory of Psychics, Hanz Holzer; p.123-124. Genuine Psychic Healing and Healers, Contemporary Books; 1995 Chicago.
[2] Ibid; p.124.
[3] Ibid;p.125
[4] Realms of Healing, p. 26. Stanley Krippner, Alfredo Villodo; Paranormal Healing in the Laboratory, Celestial Arts, Millbrae, California; 1976.
[5] Ibid. p.27-28
[6] Ibid. p.33-34
[7] Ibid. p.34
[8] Seeing Beyond the Veil: The Man Who Looks to the Future; Deardra Shuler, Black History World Today....Internet Website, 1997.
[9] Powers of Healing: Europe's Healer of Thousands; p.91, Time-Life Books, Alexandria Va..1989
[10] Ibid; p.93.
[11] Ibid; p.86.

ASTROLOGICAL MARKERS OF MYSTICAL ABILITY

Mysticism may be defined as the attempt of man to attain the ultimate reality of things and enjoy communion with the Creator. Mysticism maintains the possibility of intercourse with God, not by means of revelation, or the ordinary religious channels, but by dint of introspection, culminating in the feeling that the individual partakes of the divine nature. The name mysticism cannot be applied to any particular system of religious or spiritual study. Religion teaches submission of the will and the ethical harmonies of life while mysticism strives after the realization of a direct union with God himself. The mystic desires to be as close to God as possible, if not indeed part of the Divine Essence Itself. This fact is a sharp contrast to the obeisanceses of the ordinary religious devotee who seeks only to walk in God's way and to obey His will.

The mystic differs greatly from the psychic in that the primary impetus for their experiences derive from a union with the Creator. Psychics identify the source of their power in a personal, often mental persona while mystics readily attribute their energies to the Divine. The art of Mysticism may be said to have originated from the East, where it probably derived from kindred philosophic concepts. The Sufis of Persia may be said to be a link between the more austere Indian mystics and those of Europe. Sufism first arose in the ninth century among the Persian Mahommedans, probably as a protest against the severe monotheism of their religion. In Sufism, the concept of God begins to take on a more tangible, approachable construct.

Some writers believed that religious truth is external to the mind but this view is fundamentally opposed by the mystic. The mystic places every confidence in human reason, and it is essential that it should have the unity of the human mind with the divine as its main tenet. The higher faculties of human reason and perception are central to the mystics ability to progress along the Path to Divinity. Some mystics are quite practical in their approach to the knowledge of God while some prefer the scholastic approach. Monasteries and spiritual temples have become the main centers for mystical development and experience. Contemplation and withdrawal from the material world are seen as necessary refinements for the mind on its Path to the Divine. Through this withdrawal, the faculty of mystical or divine intuition may be developed and enhanced. Mystics believe that all people possess this faculty in one degree or another and proper development of this intuition is a prerequisite for further attainment. Once the mystic perceives that there is no distinction between the spirit and the Divine, they believe that the mind then escapes the limitations of the personality and finite reason. The human ego then evolves into the divine ego, the next incarnation of mental awareness or understanding. The divine ego remains intimately tied to the human ego throughout the remainder of the aspirants life, but it defines and directs the human experience and its ties to the Divine for the duration of that incarnation. Some believe that once developed, the divine ego is a permanent fixture within the spirit. All future incarnations of that spirit are then marked by the presence of a heightened awareness and sensitivity to the presence of God and to techniques by which the mind may seek direct communion with Him. It is the presence of this divine ego that marks the mystic as a separate and distinct entity from all other spiritual aspirants. Through the divine ego, the mystic cements his relationship with the Creator and physical manifestations of this union are the hallmark of mystical attainment.

The divine ego allows the mystic to experience the physical and mental presence of God without the dissolution of personality that the otherwise human ego would encounter. Through the aegis of the divine ego, the mystic may enter samadhi, a meditative state that allows him to speak with and commune directly with the Creator on a variety of levels. The seven successive levels of samadhi lead to higher levels of communion with the Creator. The highest level of samadhi is said to lead to dissolution of even the divine ego and ultimate reemergence of the spirit into the infinite Light of the Creator. Most mystics avoid frequent visits to the uppermost levels of samadhi for this very reason. However, at the end of human life, all true and highly evolved mystics seek this level of attainment as a respite from human existence.

In this study, I examined the charts of 29 noted mystics and saints. These individuals are world renowned for their spiritual attainment and wisdom. The mystical potential score that I developed from this work was determined by comparing the average number of mystical markers in these charts with a database of 30 control charts. Overall, these charts revealed the highest overall average score for any of the groups tested; 213. The average score for the control group was 39. This indicates a tremendous difference between the number of mystical marker aspects for persons who have led lives without particular spiritual distinction and the gifted savants within the database. The question that this type of data generates is important. Do the stars influence the occurrence of spiritual events and powers? A more than five-fold increase above normal in mystical marker activity in this group would definitely seem to indicate the presence of an active principle within the movements of celestial bodies.

The following natal charts were used as part of this aspect of our study:

1. THERESE OF LISIEUX- 1/2/1873- 11:30 PM LMT ALENCON,ORNE FRANCE, 0E05:00 48N26:00

2. OLNEY RICHMOND- 2/22/1844- 3:11PM LMT GRAND RAPIDS, MI 85W40:05 42N57:48

3. SWAMI VIVEKANANDA- 1/12/1863 6:33AM LMT CALCUTTA INDIA 88E20:00 22N34:00

4. ABDUL BAHA 5-23 1844, 11:59 PM LMT TEHERAN PERSIA 51E26:00 35N40:00

5. GEORGES GURDJIEFF 1/13/1866 12:00AM LMT ALEXANDROPOL RUSSIA 43E50:00 40N 48:00

6. SRI MEHER BABA 2/25/1894 5:00AM LMT POONA INDIA 73E52 18N32

7. LOUIS CLAUDE ST. MARTIN 1/18/1743 1:30AM LMT AMBOISE FRANCE OE59:00 47N25:00

8. SRI JADGURU 5/20/1894 1:16PM LMT VILLUPURAM INDIA 79E29 11N56

9. ANTOINETTE BOURIGNON 1/13/1616 11:00AM LMT LILLE, FRANCE 3E4:00 50N38:00

10. WILLIAM BLAKE 11/28/1757 07:45PM LMT LONDON ENGLAND 0W10:00 51N30:00

11. DAVID SPANGLER 1/7/1945 3:34AM CWT COLUMBUS OHIO 82W49:56 39N57:40

12. SRI AUROBINDO 8/15/1872 5:17AM LMT CALCUTTA INDIA 88E20 22N 34

13. PARAMANHANSA YOGANANDA 1/5/1893 8:38PM LMT GORAKHPUR INDIA 8E22 26N46

14. PIR KHAN 6/19/1916 LONDON,ENGLAND OW10 51N30

15. ELIZABETH BURROWS 1/30/1930 9:40PM PST PORTLAND OR 122W40:30 45N31:25

16. GOPO KRISHNA 5/30/1903 12:14AM GAIROO KASHMIR,INDIA 12:14PM LMT 74E50 33N33

17. COUNT KARL FRIED VON DURCKHEIM 10-24-1896 12:00PM CET (-1) MUNICH GERMANY 11E34 48NO8

18. GURU NANAK 11/17/1470 12:01 AM LMT LAHORE INDIA 74E47 31N39

19. MA AMRITANANDAMAYI 9/27/1953 9:10AM (ZONE –5.5) VALLICKAVU, INDIA 76E31 9N10

20. ALICE BAILEY 6/16/1880 MANCHESTER ENGLAND 002W15 53N30 ZONE 00:00

21. HENRY JAMES 5/9/1893 ISLINGTON ENGLAND 6:00AM GMT ZONE 00:00 00W06 51N33

22. PAUL CASE 3/10/1884 FAIRPORT NY 6:00AM ZONE 05:00 77W27 43N06

23. SRI CHAITANYA 2/27/1486 NAVADWEEP, INDIA 8:56AM LMT ZONE 00:00 88E25 23N23

24. HARLEY SWIFT DEER 9/6/1941 LUBBOCK TEXAS 6:41AM CST ZONE 06:00 101W51'17" 33N34'40"

25. PAUL BRUNTON 10/21/1898 AMSTERDAM, NETHERLANDS 11:30AM LMT ZONE 00:00 OO4E54 52N22

26. SATHYA SAI BABA 11/23/1926 6:26AM PUTTAPARTHI INDIA 77E45 14N15 ZONE (-5.30)

27. SYBIL LEEK 2/22/1922 STAFFORDSHIRE ENGLAND 11:52AM GMT ZONE 00:00 002W07 52N48

28. JIDDU KRISHNAMURTHI 5/12/1895 12:30PM MADRAS INDIA 80E17 13N05 ZONE (-5.30)

29. SRI RAMAKRISHNA 2/18/1836 KAMARPUKUR, INDIA 06:22AM LMT ZONE 00:00 87E52 22N42

The following list of markers are associated with increased mystical potential. Most of the markers are worth 10 points but the Delphi aspects are valued at 25 points.

Birth / Event Data

____
Place of birth/event (city, state, county)

____
Date of birth/event

____
Time of birth/event (exact time, i.e. birth certificate)

Client Data

____
First and last name

____
Mailing address

____
City, state, country, zip code

____
Telephone no. and fax no.

____
E-mail address

MYSTICAL POTENTIAL – MARKER ASPECTS

(All aspects score 10 points each, unless otherwise indicated)

CONJUNCTIONS

—— Sun – Venus (25 pts)
—— Pluto – Moon (25 pts)
—— Neptune – Pluto (25 pts)
—— Saturn – Venus (25 pts)
—— Jupiter – Venus (25 pts)

TRINES

—— Venus – Jupiter
—— Venus –Saturn (25 pts)
—— Mercury – Jupiter (25 pts)
—— Sun – Pluto (25 pts)
—— Neptune – Moon
—— Jupiter – Saturn (25 pts)
—— Uranus – Mars
—— Saturn – Mercury
—— Venus – Pluto
—— Saturn - Neptune

SEXTILES

—— Moon – Mars
—— Neptune – Moon (25 pts)
—— Venus – Saturn (25 pts)
—— Neptune – Mars
—— Sun – Jupiter (25 pts)
—— Jupiter – Mars (25 pts)
—— Venus – Neptune (25 pts)
—— Sun – Moon
—— Mercury – Venus
—— Sun – Uranus (25 pts)
—— Venus - Jupiter

SQUARES

—— Saturn – Neptune (25 pts)
—— Jupiter – Venus (25 pts)
—— Jupiter – Neptune
—— Jupiter – Moon (25 pts)
—— Neptune – Mars (25 pts)
—— Jupiter - Mercury

OPPOSITIONS

—— Pluto – Moon (25 pts)
—— Saturn – Mars (25 pts)
—— Jupiter - Saturn

PARALLELS

—— Neptune – Mars
—— Pluto – Moon (25 pts)
—— Sun – Saturn (25 pts)
—— Jupiter – Mars (25 pts)
—— Mercury – Venus (25 pts)
—— Saturn – Neptune (25 pts)
—— Sun – Mercury (25 pts)
—— Neptune – Mercury (25 pts)
—— Uranus – Moon
—— Neptune - Pluto

CONTRAPARALLELS

—— Moon – Mercury (25 pts)
—— Uranus – Mars (25 pts)
—— Saturn – Uranus (25 pts)
—— Pluto – Mars (25 pts)
—— Saturn – Mars
—— Sun – Pluto
—— Neptune – Mars (25 pts)
—— Mercury – Uranus (25 pts)
—— Venus – Neptune

TRIANGLES

—— Sun–Venus–Saturn (25 pts)

QUADS

—— Mercury – Mars - Saturn - Neptune (25 pts)

PROXIMITY ELEVATIONS

—— Sun – Venus (parallel; 25 pts)
—— Pluto–Mars (contraparallel; 25 pts)
—— Neptune – Moon (parallel)
—— Sun – Mercury (parallel)

HIDEK

—— Mercury (25 pts)
—— Venus
—— Mars

EXDEK

—— Moon
—— Mars
—— Uranus

ECLIPSES

—— Uranus – Moon
—— Mercury – Venus
—— Mercury – Neptune
—— Sun – Venus (25 pts)
—— Any Mars eclipse
—— Any Sun eclipse
—— Any Venus eclipse

GRAND ELEVATIONS

—— + Moon
—— + Uranus
—— + Mercury (25 pts)

GRAND TOTAL		SCALE
-------	Below Average	0 - 30
-------	Average	31 - 60
-------	Above Average	61 - 100
-------	Superior	101 - 140
-------	Outstanding	141 - 180
-------	Delphi Class	181+

Let's examine some of the more famous mystics in our database as some very interesting additions who were not part of our original study.

MA AMRITANANDAMAYI (AMMACHI) MYSTICAL POTENTIAL SCORE 215

Sudhamani, the birth name of Holy Mother Ammachi, was born to an extremely poor but pious family in the lush state of Kerala on the west coast of India. She underwent many severe hardships and encountered a number of obstacles in her young life, including near starvation, cold, disease, and malnutrition, but she persevered in her search for union with the Divine. She was required to work long hours in the service of her family, and she could not continue her schooling beyond the fourth year. In addition to looking after all the household chores, she served the elderly, the poor and the sick in her seaside village. One day, she gave away her mother's only gold bangle to a poor starving man. She received a severe beating when her father found out, yet she was happy that she could relieve someone's suffering.

Sudhamani worshipped God in the form of the cowherd Krishna, considered in India to be a Divine incarnation born thousands of years ago. She used to carry a little picture of Him and she talked to the picture of her problems and worries. When she went to graze the family's cows, she felt that she herself was Krishna and that her playmates were the cowherds, the childhood friends of the Lord. She was often seen singing in a mood of ecstatic devotion or blissfully immersed in meditation. Her family did not understand her meditations and eventually they locked her out of the house and she was not given any food to eat. When sympathetic local women tried to bring her food and care for her, they were sent away by the family. Some of the local villagers who could not understand her state of divine bliss ridiculed her by throwing stones at her. They placed thorns where she walked and even went to the extreme of trying to poison her. Once, a villager actually threatened to kill her by stabbing her with a knife.

Despite all of these threats and abuses, Sudhamani remained steadfast in her prayers and meditations. She slept outdoors as the family no longer permitted her into the home. A dog brought her packets of food in his mouth and a cow is said to have given her milk from its udder. During the time period that she was rejected by her family, Sudhamani attained mystical union with the Lord.

Her first miracle happened in the village of her birth. One day the villagers asked, "Show us a miracle, for how can we believe that you are really one with Him?" She replied, "Children, do not ask to see miracles. The greatest miracle of all is for man to realize his True Self." She then asked one of the villagers to bring her a pitcher of milk. When she dipped her finger into it, it immediately changed into sweet jam that was distributed to the hundreds of people there. This miracle created a vast change in the minds of the people and from that day forward, large crowds gathered around the Holy Mother. On another occasion she caused an oil lamp to burn the entire night without any fuel whatsoever as a show of her love for a group of followers.

One day, while she was sitting alone in a meditative state, a beautiful orb of brilliant light appeared before her. As she looked on in wonder, the orb then materialized into a vision of the Divine Mother herself. The vision lingered for a few minutes and then faded. Following this experience, Sudhamani withdrew herself from everything and everyone, and remained immersed in the intense inner bliss of God –Consciousness. But suddenly one day she heard a voice from within her say, "I am in all as the One Essence and do not have any particular abode. It is to give solace to suffering humanity that you have come into the world and not merely for enjoying Divine Bliss. Therefore, worship Me by showing mankind the way back to Me." This was a major turning point in the Mother's life and from this time forward she was called "Ammachi". Since 1981 Ammachi has been disseminating spiritual knowledge to a dedicated group of spiritual aspirants who have come to study with her, training them with practical spiritual discipline. She feels that the greatest of all blessings is to rouse an aspirant to the glory of the divinity within. The awakened man solves all his problems for himself and becomes a blessing to society. Today her work has blossomed into a worldwide organization, the Mata Amritanadamayi Mission Trust, which is engaged in many spiritual and charitable activities.

One of Ammachi's most famous attributes is her spiritual touch. She is said to imbue the aspirant with a special energy from the Creator himself simply by hugging them or touching them upon the forehead. Her seminars and weekend intensives attract thousands of people from all around the world who seek this Gift. Ammachi's natal chart is a splendid example of a Delphi level mystic. Her Mystical potential score of 210 places her in the top 1% of all people in the world.

The Holy Mother's chart reveals no less than six delphi aspects for mystical ability. The Mercury/Mars/Saturn/Neptune quad elevation in her chart is one of the rarest aspect for mystical ability and it did not occur at all in any of the control charts. Overall, her chart is a sterling example of the predictive power of this system. The gifts of one of the world's most precious spiritual leaders were in evidence even from the moment of her birth. Discoveries like these are the reason that I love this work.

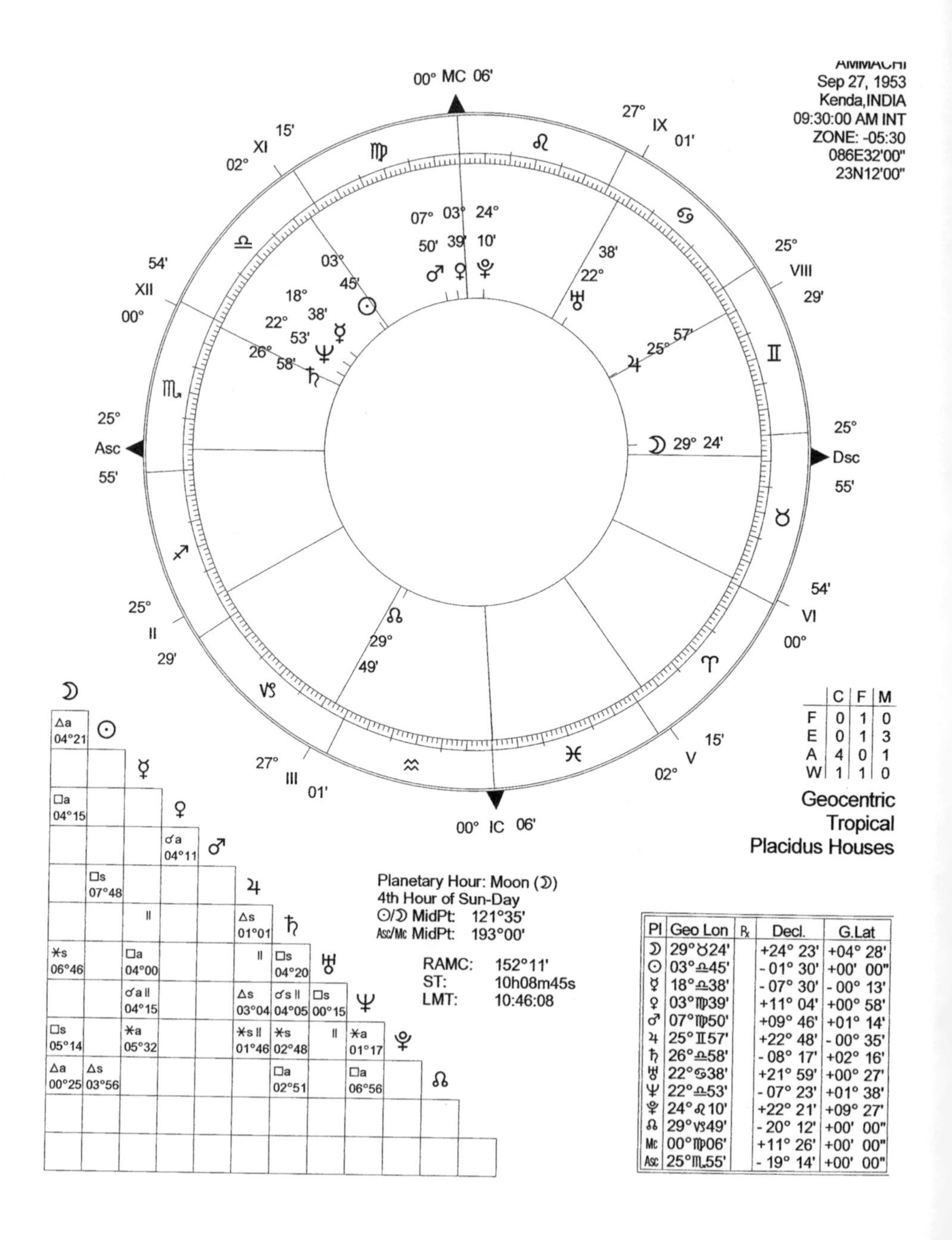

	C	F	M
F	0	1	0
E	0	1	3
A	4	0	1
W	1	1	0

Pl	Geo Lon	℞	Decl.	G.Lat
☽	29°♉24'		+24° 23'	+04° 28'
☉	03°♎45'		- 01° 30'	+00' 00"
☿	18°♎38'		- 07° 30'	- 00° 13'
♀	03°♍39'		+11° 04'	+00° 58'
♂	07°♍50'		+09° 46'	+01° 14'
♃	25°♊57'		+22° 48'	- 00° 35'
♄	26°♎58'		- 08° 17'	+02° 16'
♅	22°♋38'		+21° 59'	+00° 27'
♆	22°♎53'		- 07° 23'	+01° 38'
♇	24°♌10'		+22° 21'	+09° 27'
☊	29°♑49'		- 20° 12'	+00' 00"
Mc	00°♍06'		+11° 26'	+00' 00"
Asc	25°♏55'		- 19° 14'	+00' 00"

Birth / Event Data

____
Place of birth/event (city, state, county)

____
Date of birth/event

____
Time of birth/event (exact time, i.e. birth certificate)

Client Data

AMMACHI
First and last name

____
Mailing address

____
City, state, country, zip code

____
Telephone no. and fax no.

____
E-mail address

MYSTICAL POTENTIAL – MARKER ASPECTS

(All aspects score 10 points each, unless otherwise indicated)

CONJUNCTIONS

- ___ Sun – Venus (25 pts)
- ___ Pluto – Moon (25 pts)
- ___ Neptune – Pluto (25 pts)
- ___ Saturn – Venus (25 pts)
- ___ Jupiter – Venus (25 pts)

TRINES

- ___ Venus – Jupiter
- ___ Venus –Saturn (25 pts)
- ___ Mercury – Jupiter (25 pts)
- ___ Sun – Pluto (25 pts)
- _X_ Neptune – Moon
- _X_ Jupiter – Saturn (25 pts)
- ___ Uranus – Mars
- ___ Saturn – Mercury
- ___ Venus – Pluto
- ___ Saturn - Neptune

SEXTILES

- ___ Moon – Mars
- ___ Neptune – Moon (25 pts)
- ___ Venus – Saturn (25 pts)
- ___ Neptune – Mars
- ___ Sun – Jupiter (25 pts)
- ___ Jupiter – Mars (25 pts)
- ___ Venus – Neptune (25 pts)
- ___ Sun – Moon
- ___ Mercury – Venus
- ___ Sun – Uranus (25 pts)
- ___ Venus - Jupiter

SQUARES

- ___ Saturn – Neptune (25 pts)
- ___ Jupiter – Venus (25 pts)
- ___ Jupiter – Neptune
- ___ Jupiter – Moon (25 pts)
- ___ Neptune – Mars (25 pts)
- ___ Jupiter - Mercury

OPPOSITIONS

- ___ Pluto – Moon (25 pts)
- ___ Saturn – Mars (25 pts)
- ___ Jupiter - Saturn

PARALLELS

- _X_ Neptune – Mars
- _X_ Pluto – Moon (25 pts)
- ___ Sun – Saturn (25 pts)
- ___ Jupiter – Mars (25 pts)
- _X_ Mercury – Venus (25 pts)
- _X_ Saturn – Neptune (25 pts)
- _X_ Sun – Mercury (25 pts)
- _X_ Neptune – Mercury (25 pts)
- ___ Uranus – Moon
- ___ Neptune - Pluto

CONTRAPARALLELS

- ___ Moon – Mercury (25 pts)
- ___ Uranus – Mars (25 pts)
- ___ Saturn – Uranus (25 pts)
- _X_ Pluto – Mars (25 pts)
- _X_ Saturn – Mars
- _X_ Sun – Pluto
- _X_ Neptune – Mars (25 pts)
- ___ Mercury – Uranus (25 pts)
- ___ Venus – Neptune

TRIANGLES

- ___ Sun–Venus–Saturn (25 pts)

QUADS

- _X_ Mercury – Mars - Saturn - Neptune (25 pts)

PROXIMITY ELEVATIONS

- ___ Sun – Venus (parallel; 25 pts)
- ___ Pluto–Mars (contraparallel; 25 pts)
- ___ Neptune – Moon (parallel)
- ___ Sun – Mercury (parallel)

HIDEK

- ___ Mercury (25 pts)
- ___ Venus
- ___ Mars

EXDEK

- _X_ Moon
- ___ Mars
- ___ Uranus

ECLIPSES

- ___ Uranus – Moon
- _X_ Mercury – Venus
- _X_ Mercury – Neptune
- _X_ Sun – Venus (25 pts)
- _X_ Any Mars eclipse
- ___ Any Sun eclipse
- ___ Any Venus eclipse

GRAND ELEVATIONS

- _X_ + Moon
- _X_ + Uranus
- ___ + Mercury (25 pts)

GRAND TOTAL		SCALE
___	Below Average	0 - 30
___	Average	31 - 60
___	Above Average	61 - 100
___	Superior	101 - 140
___	Outstanding	141 - 180
210	Delphi Class	181+

SYBIL LEEK (WORLD FAMOUS WICCAN MYSTIC) DELPHI SCORE 315

Sybil Leek was one of the most famous wiccan mystics of the 20th century. She was born into a life of wealth and comfort in the city of Staffordshire England. She was taken to see her first eclipse by the author H.G. Wells and she was often consulted by Aleister Crowley. Sybil Leek foresaw the charismatic success of an obscure French captain name Charles DeGaulle, and predicted the literary achievements and death of Ian Fleming years before he set James Bond to paper.

The dawn of Goddess-centered astrology was first heralded by Sybil Leek, who was notably kicked out of England for being a Wiccan. This move reflected the country's repressive societal attitude toward basically everything. She was one of the Pagan community's most esteemed elders. She was known for her psychic readings for the elite of the political and entertainment worlds. Perhaps her most salient legacy is the ratification of the religion of Wicca as a true and viable alternative to the repressive monotheistic faiths that dominate much of the world today. Her mystical potential score of 315 is extraordinary. She scores very high in all of the psychic and spiritual categories that are listed in this book. Sadly, Sybil Leek left this world on October 26 1982.

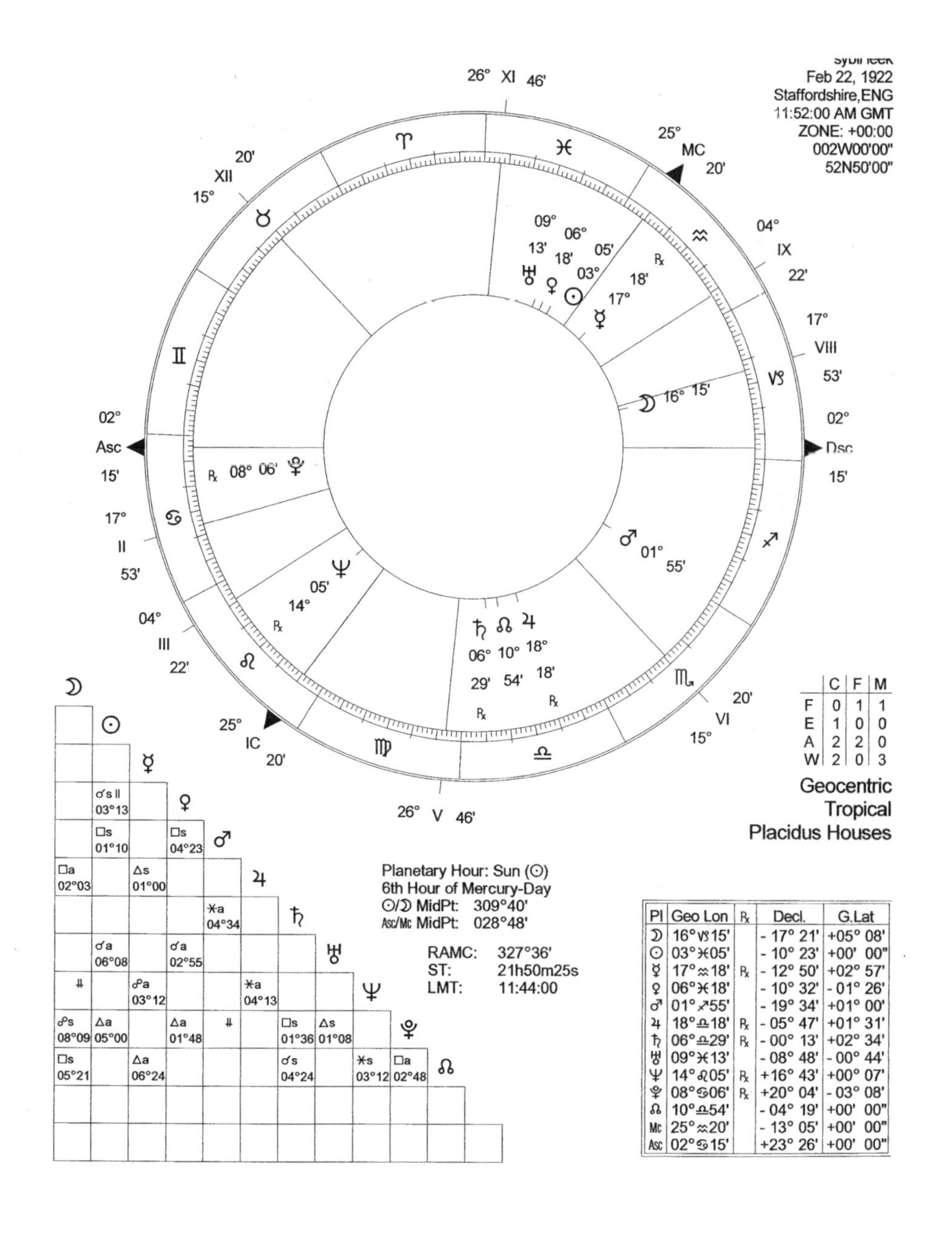

	C	F	M
F	0	1	1
E	1	0	0
A	2	2	0
W	2	0	3

Pl	Geo Lon	℞	Decl.	G.Lat
☽	16°♑15'		- 17° 21'	+05° 08'
☉	03°♓05'		- 10° 23'	+00' 00"
☿	17°♒18'	℞	- 12° 50'	+02° 57'
♀	06°♓18'		- 10° 32'	- 01° 26'
♂	01°♐55'		- 19° 34'	+01° 00'
♃	18°♎18'	℞	- 05° 47'	+01° 31'
♄	06°♎29'	℞	- 00° 13'	+02° 34'
♅	09°♓13'	℞	- 08° 48'	- 00° 44'
♆	14°♌05'	℞	+16° 43'	+00° 07'
♇	08°♋06'	℞	+20° 04'	- 03° 08'
☊	10°♎54'		- 04° 19'	+00' 00"
Mc	25°♒20'		- 13° 05'	+00' 00"
Asc	02°♋15'		+23° 26'	+00' 00"

Birth / Event Data

Place of birth/event (city, state, county)

Date of birth/event

Time of birth/event (exact time, i.e. birth certificate)

Client Data

SYBIL LEEK

First and last name

Mailing address

City, state, country, zip code

Telephone no. and fax no.

E-mail address

MYSTICAL POTENTIAL – MARKER ASPECTS

(All aspects score 10 points each, unless otherwise indicated)

CONJUNCTIONS

X Sun – Venus (25 pts)
___ Pluto – Moon (25 pts)
___ Neptune – Pluto (25 pts)
___ Saturn – Venus (25 pts)
___ Jupiter – Venus (25 pts)

TRINES

___ Venus – Jupiter
___ Venus –Saturn (25 pts)
X Mercury – Jupiter (25 pts)
X Sun – Pluto (25 pts)
___ Neptune – Moon
___ Jupiter – Saturn (25 pts)
___ Uranus – Mars
___ Saturn – Mercury
X Venus – Pluto
___ Saturn - Neptune

SEXTILES

___ Moon – Mars
___ Neptune – Moon (25 pts)
___ Venus – Saturn (25 pts)
___ Neptune – Mars
___ Sun – Jupiter (25 pts)
___ Jupiter – Mars (25 pts)
___ Venus – Neptune (25 pts)
___ Sun – Moon
___ Mercury – Venus
___ Sun – Uranus (25 pts)
___ Venus - Jupiter

SQUARES

___ Saturn – Neptune (25 pts)
___ Jupiter – Venus (25 pts)
___ Jupiter – Neptune
X Jupiter – Moon (25 pts)

___ Neptune – Mars (25 pts)
___ Jupiter - Mercury

OPPOSITIONS

X Pluto – Moon (25 pts)
___ Saturn – Mars (25 pts)
___ Jupiter - Saturn

PARALLELS

___ Neptune – Mars
___ Pluto – Moon (25 pts)
___ Sun – Saturn (25 pts)
___ Jupiter – Mars (25 pts)
X Mercury – Venus (25 pts)
___ Saturn – Neptune (25 pts)
X Sun – Mercury (25 pts)
___ Neptune – Mercury (25 pts)
___ Uranus – Moon
___ Neptune - Pluto

CONTRAPARALLELS

___ Moon – Mercury (25 pts)
___ Uranus – Mars (25 pts)
___ Saturn – Uranus (25 pts)
X Pluto – Mars (25 pts)
___ Saturn – Mars
___ Sun – Pluto
___ Neptune – Mars (25 pts)
___ Mercury – Uranus (25 pts)
___ Venus – Neptune

TRIANGLES

___ Sun–Venus–Saturn (25 pts)

QUADS

___ Mercury – Mars - Saturn - Neptune (25 pts)

PROXIMITY ELEVATIONS

X Sun – Venus (parallel; 25 pts)

X Pluto–Mars (contraparallel; 25 pts)
___ Neptune – Moon (parallel)
___ Sun – Mercury (parallel)

HIDEK

___ Mercury (25 pts)
___ Venus
___ Mars

EXDEK

___ Moon
___ Mars
___ Uranus

ECLIPSES

___ Uranus – Moon
___ Mercury – Venus
___ Mercury – Neptune
X Sun – Venus (25 pts)
X Any Mars eclipse
X Any Sun eclipse
___ Any Venus eclipse

GRAND ELEVATIONS

___ + Moon
X + Uranus
___ + Mercury (25 pts)

GRAND TOTAL		SCALE
___	Below Average	0 - 30
___	Average	31 - 60
___	Above Average	61 - 100
___	Superior	101 - 140
___	Outstanding	141 - 180
315	Delphi Class	181+

JOAN OF ARC- FRENCH SAINT MYSTICAL POTENTIAL SCORE 240

Joan of Arc, also called the Maid of Orleans, is a national heroine and patron saint. She successfully led the resistance to the English invasion of France in the Hundreds Years War. She was born the third of five children to a farmer, Jacques d'Arc and his wife Isabelle de Vouthon in the town of Domremy on the border of the provinces of Champagne and Lorranine. Her childhood was spent attending her father's herds in the fields and learning religion and housekeeping skills from her mother. Her parents were intensely pious.

When Joan was about 12 years old, she began to hear the voices of St. Michael, St. Catherine, and St. Margaret, believing them to have been sent by God. These voices told her that it was her divine mission to free her country from the English and help the dauphin gain the French throne. They told her to cut her hair, dress in a man's uniform, and to pick up arms. By 1429, the English, with the help of their Burgundian allies occupied Paris and all of France north of the Loire. The resistance was minimal due to lack of leadership and a sense of hopelessness. Henry VI of England was claiming the French throne.

Joan convinced the captain of the dauphin's forces, and then the dauphin himself of her calling. After passing an examination by a board of theologians, she was given troops to command and the rank of captain. In those days it was not unusual for women to fight side by side with the men. There were thirty women wounded in the battle of Amiens. A number of women soldiers fought among the followers of Johannes Huss in Bohemia. There was hardly a medieval siege in which some woman was not conspicuous for heroism. It was therefore quite natural for Charles to accept military services of Joan of Arc.

At the battle of Orleans in May 1429, Joan led the troops to a miraculous victory over the English. She continued fighting the enemy in other locations along the Loire. Fear of her troops was so formidable that when she approached Lord Talbot's army at Patay, most of the English troops and Commander Sir John Fastolfe fled the battlefield! Fastolfe was later stripped of his Order of the Garter for this act of cowardice. Although Lord Talbot stood his ground, he lost the battle and was captured along with a hundred English noblemen and lost 1800 of his soldiers. Charles VII was crowned king of France on July 17, 1429 in Reims Cathedral. At the coronation, Joan was given a place of honor next to the king. Later, she was ennobled for her services to her country.

In 1430, she was captured by the Burgundians while defending Compiegne near Paris and was sold to the English. The English, in turn, handed her over to the ecclesiastical court at Rouen to be tried for witchcraft, heresy, and for wearing male clothing, which was considered an offense against the church. Joan was convicted after a fourteen-month interrogation and on May 30, 1431 she was burned at the stake in the Rouen marketplace. She was nineteen years old. Charles VII had made no attempt to come to her rescue.

Joan's Delphi level mystical potential is a testament to her staggering spiritual power. Even by today's liberated standards, it would be a daunting task for a woman to approach the ruler of a major world power and request command of a battalion of strategic troops! If said person were to then invoke the guidance of divine powers as the impetus for their inspiration, such a request would almost certainly lead to incarceration and psychiatric examination. However, her determination and prowess clearly shone through the overwhelming repression and derision that peasant women faced during that time. Joan of Arc is one of the greatest mystics of all time.

The grand elevation of Mercury is the most potent of all of the mystical markers. This aspect is twelve times more common in the charts of mystics than in the control group. As you will soon see, several major mystical leaders have this aspect and even the transiting power of this aspect is something to be reckoned with. In Joan's chart, once again we see that her spiritual greatness was presaged by more than seven delphi aspects that transited over her birthplace.

TOP TEN ASTRO MARKERS FOR MISTICAL POTENTIAL

1. POSITIVE GRAND ELEVATION OF MERCURY
2. SUN VENUS ECLIPSE
3. MOON MERCURY CONTRAPARALLEL
4. SUN VENUS CONJUNCTION
5. JUPITER SATURN TRINE
6. SUN URANUS SEXTILE
7. NEPTUNE MERCURY PARALLEL
8. PLUTO MARS CONTRAPARALLEL
9. MERCURY MARS SATURN NEPTUNE QUAD
10. HIDEK MERCURY

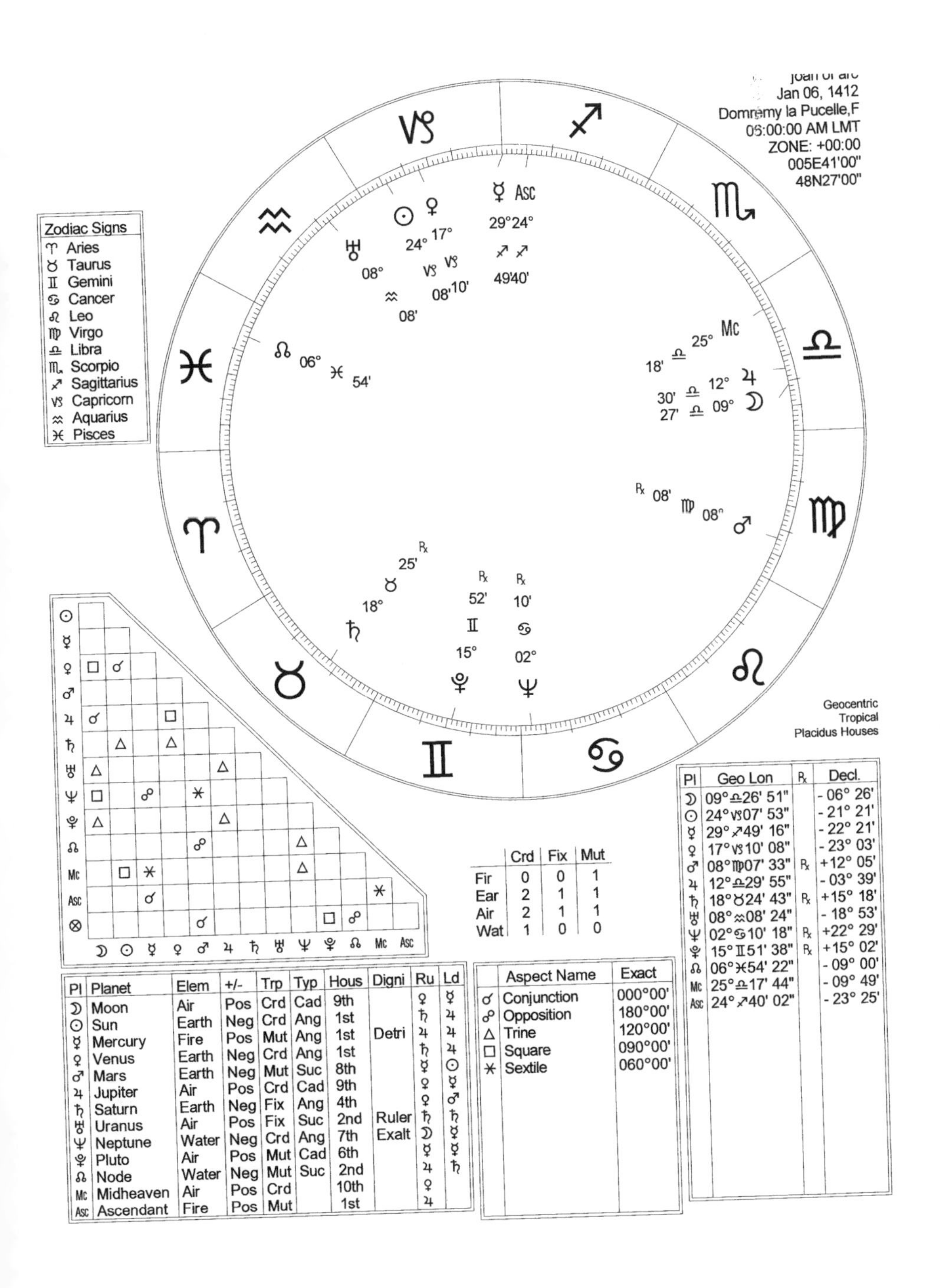

Zodiac Signs
♈ Aries
♉ Taurus
♊ Gemini
♋ Cancer
♌ Leo
♍ Virgo
♎ Libra
♏ Scorpio
♐ Sagittarius
♑ Capricorn
♒ Aquarius
♓ Pisces

	☽	☉	☿	♀	♂	♃	♄	♅	♆	♇	☊	Mc	Asc
☉													
☿													
♀	□	☌											
♂													
♃	☌			□									
♄		△		△									
♅	△					△							
♆	□		☍		✶								
♇	△					△							
☊					☍				△				
Mc		□	✶						△				
Asc			☌									✶	
⊗					☌					□	☍		

	Crd	Fix	Mut
Fir	0	0	1
Ear	2	1	1
Air	2	1	1
Wat	1	0	0

Pl	Geo Lon	℞	Decl.
☽	09°♎26' 51"		- 06° 26'
☉	24°♑07' 53"		- 21° 21'
☿	29°♐49' 16"		- 22° 21'
♀	17°♑10' 08"		- 23° 03'
♂	08°♍07' 33"	℞	+12° 05'
♃	12°♎29' 55"		- 03° 39'
♄	18°♉24' 43"	℞	+15° 18'
♅	08°♒08' 24"		- 18° 53'
♆	02°♋10' 18"	℞	+22° 29'
♇	15°♊51' 38"	℞	+15° 02'
☊	06°♓54' 22"		- 09° 00'
Mc	25°♎17' 44"		- 09° 49'
Asc	24°♐40' 02"		- 23° 25'

Pl	Planet	Elem	+/-	Trp	Typ	Hous	Digni	Ru	Ld
☽	Moon	Air	Pos	Crd	Cad	9th		♀	☿
☉	Sun	Earth	Neg	Crd	Ang	1st		♄	♃
☿	Mercury	Fire	Pos	Mut	Ang	1st	Detri	♃	♃
♀	Venus	Earth	Neg	Crd	Ang	1st		♄	♃
♂	Mars	Earth	Neg	Mut	Suc	8th		☿	☉
♃	Jupiter	Air	Pos	Crd	Cad	9th		♀	☿
♄	Saturn	Earth	Neg	Fix	Ang	4th		♀	♂
♅	Uranus	Air	Pos	Fix	Suc	2nd	Ruler	♄	♄
♆	Neptune	Water	Neg	Crd	Ang	7th	Exalt	☽	☿
♇	Pluto	Air	Pos	Mut	Cad	6th		☿	☿
☊	Node	Water	Neg	Mut	Suc	2nd		♃	♄
Mc	Midheaven	Air	Pos	Crd		10th		♀	
Asc	Ascendant	Fire	Pos	Mut		1st		♃	

	Aspect Name	Exact
☌	Conjunction	000°00'
☍	Opposition	180°00'
△	Trine	120°00'
□	Square	090°00'
✶	Sextile	060°00'

Birth / Event Data

____
Place of birth/event (city, state, county)

____
Date of birth/event

____
Time of birth/event (exact time, i.e. birth certificate)

Client Data

Joan of Arc
First and last name

____
Mailing address

____
City, state, country, zip code

____
Telephone no. and fax no.

____
E-mail address

MYSTICAL POTENTIAL – MARKER ASPECTS

(All aspects score 10 points each, unless otherwise indicated)

CONJUNCTIONS

- X Sun – Venus (25 pts)
- ___ Pluto – Moon (25 pts)
- ___ Neptune – Pluto (25 pts)
- ___ Saturn – Venus (25 pts)
- ___ Jupiter – Venus (25 pts)

TRINES

- ___ Venus – Jupiter
- X Venus –Saturn (25 pts)
- ___ Mercury – Jupiter (25 pts)
- ___ Sun – Pluto (25 pts)
- ___ Neptune – Moon
- ___ Jupiter – Saturn (25 pts)
- ___ Uranus – Mars
- ___ Saturn – Mercury
- ___ Venus – Pluto
- ___ Saturn - Neptune

SEXTILES

- ___ Moon – Mars
- ___ Neptune – Moon (25 pts)
- ___ Venus – Saturn (25 pts)
- ___ Neptune – Mars
- ___ Sun – Jupiter (25 pts)
- ___ Jupiter – Mars (25 pts)
- ___ Venus – Neptune (25 pts)
- ___ Sun – Moon
- ___ Mercury – Venus
- ___ Sun – Uranus (25 pts)
- ___ Venus - Jupiter

SQUARES

- ___ Saturn – Neptune (25 pts)
- X Jupiter – Venus (25 pts)
- ___ Jupiter – Neptune
- ___ Jupiter – Moon (25 pts)

- ___ Neptune – Mars (25 pts)
- ___ Jupiter - Mercury

OPPOSITIONS

- ___ Pluto – Moon (25 pts)
- ___ Saturn – Mars (25 pts)
- ___ Jupiter - Saturn

PARALLELS

- ___ Neptune – Mars
- ___ Pluto – Moon (25 pts)
- ___ Sun – Saturn (25 pts)
- ___ Jupiter – Mars (25 pts)
- X Mercury – Venus (25 pts)
- ___ Saturn – Neptune (25 pts)
- X Sun – Mercury (25 pts)
- ___ Neptune – Mercury (25 pts)
- ___ Uranus – Moon
- ___ Neptune - Pluto

CONTRAPARALLELS

- ___ Moon – Mercury (25 pts)
- ___ Uranus – Mars (25 pts)
- ___ Saturn – Uranus (25 pts)
- ___ Pluto – Mars (25 pts)
- ___ Saturn – Mars
- ___ Sun – Pluto
- ___ Neptune – Mars (25 pts)
- ___ Mercury – Uranus (25 pts)
- X Venus – Neptune

TRIANGLES

- ___ Sun–Venus–Saturn (25 pts)

QUADS

- ___ Mercury – Mars - Saturn - Neptune (25 pts)

PROXIMITY ELEVATIONS

- ___ Sun – Venus (parallel; 25 pts)

- ___ Pluto–Mars (contraparallel; 25 pts)
- ___ Neptune – Moon (parallel)
- ___ Sun – Mercury (parallel)

HIDEK

- X Mercury (25 pts)
- X Venus
- ___ Mars

EXDEK

- ___ Moon
- ___ Mars
- ___ Uranus

ECLIPSES

- ___ Uranus – Moon
- ___ Mercury – Venus
- ___ Mercury – Neptune
- X Sun – Venus (25 pts)
- ___ Any Mars eclipse
- X Any Sun eclipse
- X Any Venus eclipse

GRAND ELEVATIONS

- ___ + Moon
- ___ + Uranus
- X + Mercury (25 pts)

GRAND TOTAL		**SCALE**
___	Below Average	0 - 30
___	Average	31 - 60
___	Above Average	61 - 100
___	Superior	101 - 140
___	Outstanding	141 - 180
240	Delphi Class	181+

MEDIUMSHIP

The term *"medium" came into widespread use in the 19th century, to designate individuals who claimed to "mediate" communications between the living and the spirits of the deceased. The wave of spiritualism which overtook America and Europe in the latter 19th century brought forth a multitude of mediums who were able to contact the spirits of the departed or to invoke physical manifestations (e.g., levitations or materializations). Most often mediums began the séance by putting themselves into a trance state. A spirit or several of them, taking turns, would come forth and speak through the medium for a certain time. Then the person would come out of the trance, usually recalling nothing of what had been said. Spirit communication was also mediated by other means, such as automatic writing, raps or tapping noises, Ouija boards, and a pointer held by the medium, but usually guided by the spirit.*

Extremely talented mediums manifest an extreme dedication to scientific research and have collaborated with researchers over several decades, while accepting some very extreme constraints on their personal freedom. Often, their mail, their movements and personal relationships were constantly surveyed by detectives, to eliminate any chance of deception. The famous American medium Leonora Piper was one such medium. William James and Richard Hodgson concluded that Ms. Piper had repeatedly demonstrated very strong psychic talents over a number of years. Similarly, in the 1950's, Eileen Garrett a medium and a brilliant psychic showed an active interest in scientific investigations of her psi capacities. She was not only proven to be a genuine medium, but she later founded the Parapsychology Foundation, which has helped to advance scientific psi research after her passing.

Trance mediumship is in some ways related to multiple personality disorder. However, trance mediums do not display the psychopathology often seen in these patients. Scientists are intensely studying the phenomenon of multiple personality disorder in order to better understand mediumship. Channeling is similar to mediumship but its focus tends to shift toward higher entities such as angels and cosmic beings. Mediumship is a discrete spiritual ability and as such is a rare gift indeed. The essential qualification of a medium is an abnormal sensitiveness, which enables him to be readily "controlled" by disembodies spirits. For this reason mediums are also known as sensitives. There is a belief that all men are mediums, though in varying degrees, and consequently that all of us are in communication with the spirits from whom proceeds what is called inspiration. Those who are ordinarily designated as mediums are gifted with this common faculty in a higher degree than their fellows.

Mediumship, like all central doctrines of spiritualism, dates back to very early times. In its usual application, the term medium is used only of those sensitives who belong to the modern spiritualistic movement, which had its origin in America in 1848. In this sense, then, Mrs. Fox and her daughters, the heroines of the Rochester Rappings, were the earliest mediums. The phenomena of their séances consisted mainly of knockings, by means of which messages were conveyed from the spirits to the sitters. Other mediums rapidly sprang up, first in America, and later in Britain and the Continent. Their mediumship was of two kinds, "physical" and "automatic". These phases were to be found either separately or combined in one person, as in the case of Rev. Stanton Moses. The early rappings speedily developed into more elaborate manifestations. For a few years, an epidemic of table-turning caused wide-spread excitement, and the motions of the table became a favorite means of communicating with the spirits. The playing of musical instruments without visible agency was a form of manifestation which received the attention of mediums from an early date, as was the bringing into the séance room of "apports" of fruit, flowers, perfume, and all manner of portable property. Darkness was found to facilitate the spirit manifestations, and as there are certain physical manifestations, such as photography, to which darkness is essential, no logical objection could be offered to the dimness of the séance room. As time went on, and the demand for physical manifestations increased, seances became more daring and more varied. The moving of objects without contact, the levitation of heavy furniture, and of the persons mediums or sitters, the elongation of the human body, the fire ordeal, were all practiced by mediums at one point or another. The tying of knots in endless cords, the passage of solids, through solids, were commonplace occurrences in mediumistic circles. The crowning achievement of the medium however was the materialization of the spirit form. Early in the history of spiritualism, hands were materialized, the faces, and finally the complete form of the control. Thereafter the materialized spirits allowed themselves to be touched, and even condescended, on occasion, to hold conversations with the sitters. Further proof of the actuality of the spirit control was offered by spirit photography.

Misuse of the divine gift of mediumship carries with it its own punishment, for the medium becomes the sport of base human spirits and elementals, his will sapped, and his whole being degraded. Likewise, he must be wary of giving up his personality to the first spirit who comes his way, for the low and earth-bound spirits have least difficulty in communicating with the living. They still have more affinity with the things of the earth than with those of spirit.

Of the various theories advanced to explain the mediumistic manifestations the most important is the spiritualistic explanation, which claims that the phenomena are produced by the spirits of the dead acting on the sensitive organism of the medium. The evidence for such a theory, though some investigators of highest distinction have found it satisfactory, it is not accepted by all. Conscious fraud, though it is no longer considered to cover the whole ground, plays a definite part in the phenomena of both the physical and trance medium. The spiritualist's explanation of the lapses into fraud is that they are instigated by the spirits themselves. And it does not seem impossible that a genuine medium might have to resort to fraud during a temporary failure of his psychic powers.

The diagnosis and cure of disease has been extensively practiced by mediums. The healing medium is able not only to diagnose and describe the process of an illness, but they have often been able to prescribe a mode of treatment. The medium will consult with a suitable spirit with whom he has a rapport and then be guided as to the proper course of treatment for a number of illnesses. Some mediums do not accept any remuneration for their services but many healers depend upon their practices for their entire livelihood. Mediumistic healers have cured heart disease, cancer, pneumonia, paralysis, and many other illnesses. Some have been credited with the power to heal instantaneously, as did the Cure d' Ars and other miraculous healers. The marvelous potency of the waters of Lourdes is considered by spiritualists to be the gift of discarnate beings, having been first empowered by the Virgin Mary and a young white angel who appeared to the now sainted Bernadette Soubourious.

This is the first astrological study of the phenomenon of mediumship. As I examined the various birth charts and potential markers for the mediumship, I was awestruck by the repeated correlations between the higher rates of potential gift marker activity in very gifted individuals. The control individuals who had not displayed any unusual tendency toward mediumistic ability consistently revealed much lower scores than the test group.

In this study, I examined the charts of 27 noted mediums. These individuals are world renowned for their spiritual attainment and wisdom. The mediumship potential score that I developed from this work was determined by comparing the average number of mediumship markers in these charts with a database of 27 control charts. Overall, the charts of the gifted mediums revealed an average score of 156.67. The average score for the control group was 54.33. This indicates a tremendous difference between the number of mediumship marker aspects for persons who have led lives without particular distinction and the gifted savants within the database. The question that this study as well as the others brings up is very important. Do the stars influence the occurrence of spiritual events and powers? An almost three-fold increase above normal in astrological mediumship marker activity in this group would definitively seem to indicate the presence of an active principle within the movements of celestial bodies.

The following natal charts were used as part of this aspect of our study:

1. Eleanor Zugan 5/24/1913, Iozna, Rumania 1:50 pm EET
   ZONE –02:00 EET 026E36 47N50
2. Madam Davia 10/25/1861 Savoie France, 10:00 am
   ZONE –01:00 CET 006E25 45N30
3. David Home 3/20/1883 Edinburgh Scotland 6:00 am GMT
   ZONE 00:00 003W13 55N57
4. Maxine Bell 6/25/1916 Ames, IA 6:26 am
   ZONE +6:00 093W37'11 42N02'05"
5. Emmanuel Swedenborg 2/08/1688 Stockholm Sweden 5:30 am
   LMT 018E03 59N20
6. Katie Crookes 1/22/1859 Kensington England 6:00 am GMT
   000W12 51N30

7. Edgar Cayce 3/18/1877 London England 1:30 am GMT 1:30 AM ZONE 00:00 000W10 51N30
8. Eliane Guerri 5/29/1942 Algiers, AlG 8:10 am ZONE –1:00 003E03 36N47
9. Reverend Owen 6/26/1869 Birmingham, ENG 6:00 am ZONE 00:00 001W50 52N30
10. Aulikki Plaami 8/14/1941 Kajaani, FIN 5:30 AM EET ZONE -02:00 27E41 64N14
11. Eileen Garrett 3/17/1893 Luimneach, IRE 6:00 am ZONE 00:25 008W38 52N40
12. Brenda Crenshaw 3/01/1909 London, ENG 2:00 am GMT ZONE 00:00 000W10 51N30
13. Henry Nusselein 4/20/1879 Nurnberg, Germany 12:00 pm LMT ZONE 00:00 011E04 49N27
14. Mrs. Meurig Morris 11/17/1899 London, ENG 2:30 pm GMT ZONE 00:00 000W10 51N30
15. Beline 6/12/1924 Paris, France 1:40 am GMD ZONE –01:00 002E20 48N52
16. Nancy Rubin 8/24/1953 Fort Bragg, CA 8:54 am PDT ZONE +07:00 123W48 39N27
17. Madame Freya 5/20/1871 Velleneuve de Marsan 10:00 pm LMT Zone 00:00 000w18 43n54
18. Maria Silbert 12/25/1866 St. Stephens Austria 00:43 am LMT ZONE 00:00 13E31 46N37
19. Elise Wheeler 9/30/1887 Norris City, IL 9:45 AM EST ZONE +05:00 85W29 43N42
20. Maria de Sabato 5/12/1933 Bordeaux France, 5:00 am GMD ZONE –01:00 000W34 44N50
21. Dortha Fretz 6/30/1909 Bourbon, Indiana 3:17 am EST ZONE +05:00 86W07 41N18
22. Helen Duncan 3/20/1883 Edinburgh, Scotland 6:00 am ZONE 00:00 003W13 55N57
23. Nancy Mikuriya 6/25/1943 Chicago, IL 5:20 am CWT ZONE +05:00 087W39 41N51
24. Edward Gurney 3/23/1847 Sutton, ENG 6:00 am LMT 000W26 51N12
25. Arthur Ford 1/08/1896 Atlanta, GA 2:34 am LMT 84W23 33N45
26. P.B. Randolph 10/08/1825 New York, NY 6:00 am LMT 074W00 40N43
27. Rudi Schneider 7/27/1908 Braunau am Inn, AUS 6:00 am ZONE –01:00 013E02 48N15 CET

Birth / Event Data

Place of birth/event (city, state, county)

Date of birth/event

Time of birth/event (exact time, i.e. birth certificate)

Client Data

First and last name

Mailing address

City, state, country, zip code

Telephone no. and fax no.

E-mail address

MEDIUMSHIP POTENTIAL – MARKERS ASPECTS

(All aspects score 10 points each, unless otherwise indicated)

CONJUNCTIONS

- ____ Neptune – Pluto (25 pts)
- ____ Saturn – Uranus
- ____ Venus –Pluto (25 pts)
- ____ Jupiter - Saturn

TRINES

- ____ Neptune – Moon
- ____ Jupiter – Neptune (25 pts)
- ____ Uranus – Moon
- ____ Mercury – Uranus
- ____ Saturn – Neptune
- ____ Mercury – Mary (25 pts)

SEXTILES

- ____ Jupiter – Pluto
- ____ Uranus – Pluto (25 pts)

SQUARES

- ____ Pluto – Moon (25 pts)
- ____ Venus – Neptune (25 pts)
- ____ Saturn – Neptune
- ____ Saturn – Moon
- ____ Saturn – Mars
- ____ Venus – Jupiter

OPPOSITIONS

- ____ Uranus – Neptune
- ____ Sun - Jupiter

LONGITUDINAL PROXIMITY

- ____ Jupiter – Mars (25 pts)

PARALLELS

- ____ Sun – Mercury
- ____ Neptune – Pluto (25 pts)
- ____ Moon – Mercury
- ____ Uranus – Moon
- ____ Saturn – Sun (25 pts)
- ____ Jupiter – Uranus
- ____ Saturn – Neptune (25 pts)
- ____ Mercury – Venus (25 pts)
- ____ Neptune – Mars (25 pts)
- ____ Jupiter – Mars (25 pts)
- ____ Mercury – Neptune (25 pts)
- ____ Saturn – Mercury (25 pts)
- ____ Sun – Jupiter (25 pts)

CONTRAPARALLELS

- ____ Moon – Mercury (25 pts)
- ____ Uranus – Moon
- ____ Uranus – Neptune (25 pts)
- ____ Neptune – Mars (25 pts)
- ____ Sun – Saturn
- ____ Saturn – Uranus (25 pts)
- ____ Mercury – Uranus (25 pts)
- ____ Sun – Jupiter
- ____ Pluto – Moon (25 pts)
- ____ Uranus - Pluto

HIDEK

- ____ Mercury
- ____ Venus
- ____ Mars

PROXIMITY ELEVATIONS

- ____ Neptune – Mars (parallel)
- ____ Venus – Uranus (parallel)
- ____ Venus – Mars (parallel)
- ____ Pluto – Mercury (parallel)
- ____ Sun – Uranus (parallel)
- ____ Jupiter – Uranus (parallel)
- ____ Saturn – Mars (parallel)
- ____ Mercury – Mars (parallel)

ECLIPSES

- ____ Neptune - Mars
- ____ Any Pluto eclipse
- ____ Any Venus eclipse (25 pts)

GRAND ELEVATIONS

- ____ + Moon
- ____ + Mars
- ____ – Sun
- ____ – Uranus
- ____ + Mercury (25 pts)
- ____ + Uranus
- ____ – Mercury
- ____ – Neptune (25 pts)

GRAND TOTAL		SCALE
____	Below Average	0 - 30
____	Average	31 - 60
____	Above Average	61 - 100
____	Superior	101 - 140
____	Outstanding	141 - 180
____	Delphi Class	181+

The following list of markers are associated with increased mediumship potential. Most of the markers are worth 10 points but the Delphi aspects are valued at 25 points.

Let's examine the birth charts of some of the more famous mediums in history.

PASCHAL BEVERLY RANDOLPH

P. B. Randolph was born and raised in the slums of New York city. A freed slave, he was self-taught, always poor, and was something of a nomad. He was the son of a black woman (Flora Clark), and a white land owner William Beverly Randolph. His father abandoned him when he was a young boy and his mother died of small pox when he was a child. The loss of his mother at such an early age is thought to have greatly saddened the young Paschal. In his later writings, he credits this trauma with triggering his latent mediumistic abilities. After his mother's death he worked as a bootblack on the streets of New York, and by his early teens, he had moved himself to New England to live with his mother's relatives. He then went to sea as a cabin boy, another common occupation for blacks at the time, on the brig of the Phoebe out of New Bedford. His travels took him to Cuba, England, and Europe. He was miserable as a cabin boy, bullied and brutalized by the older sailors. He even thought of suicide to escape, but finally left the sea after an accident chopping wood.

Randolph's formal education was minimal and largely obtained the hard way. He taught himself to read and write from posters on the streets and with bits of chalk he found in the gutters. Despite these handicaps, Randolph became and was recognized as a remarkably literate and even learned man. His writings about mediumship and mysticism were lively, clear, and even humorous at times. His writings above all revealed him to be a seer, a man who was trying to relate what he knew first-hand rather than from merely recapitulating the works of his predecessors. He was also a linguist, acquiring a good knowledge of French and probably more than a smattering of Arabic and Turkish in his travels. His Rosicrucian novels (Ravalette and the Rosicrucian's Story) were well received by the critics and are still quite readable today. He is quite well known as a trance medium and spiritualist and he regaled the courts of Europe with his séances and mediumistic displays. His investigations into Rosicrucianism led him into the then highly controversial field of sex-magic, and along the way he wrote the definitive treatise on the use of hashish as an aid to trance possession and an equally important work on clairvoyant scrying with magic mirrors. As a self-trained medical doctor, he practiced a form of psychiatry and medicine in defiance of the racial stereotyping and coercion that was so pervasive in the United States at the time.

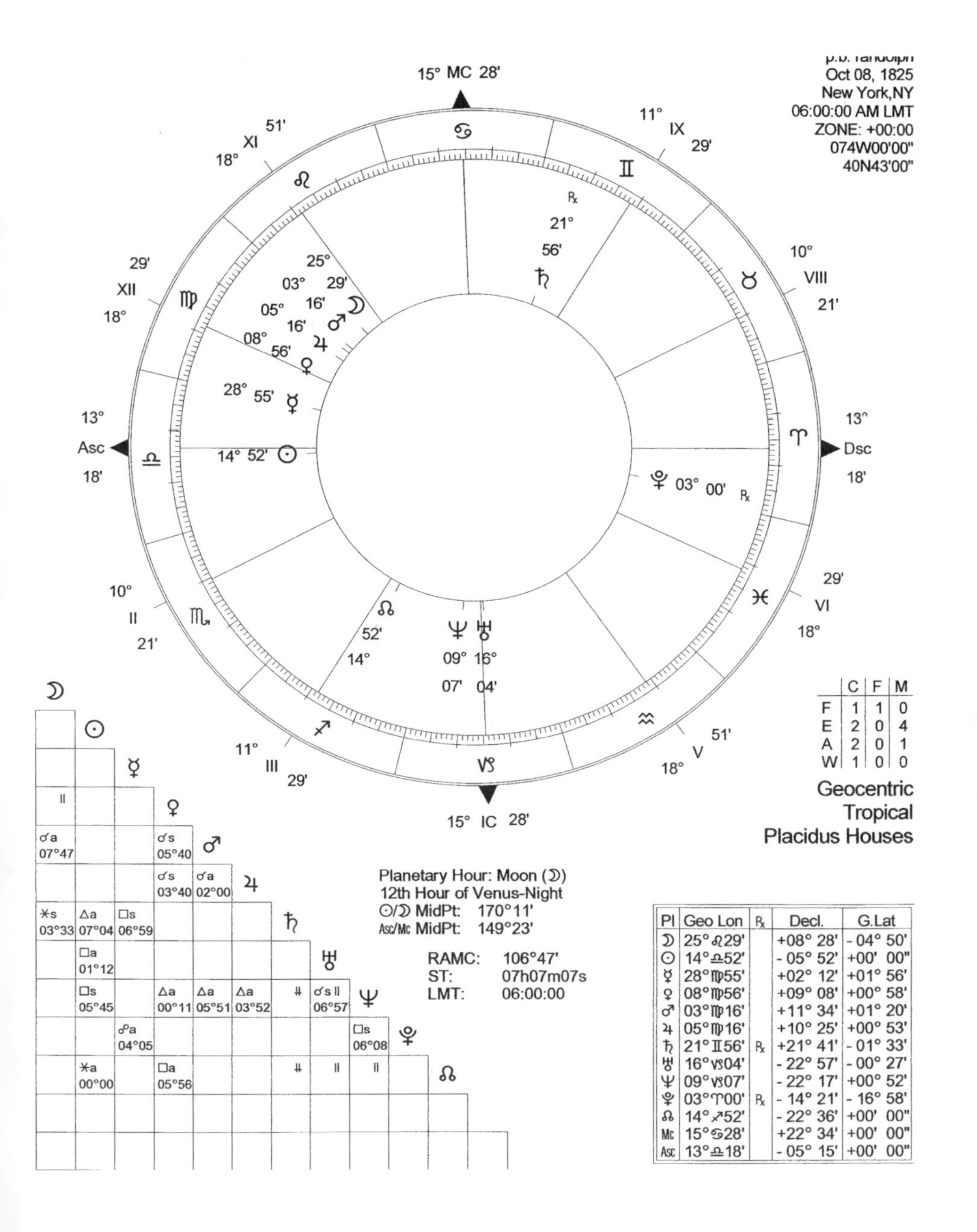

	C	F	M
F	1	1	0
E	2	0	4
A	2	0	1
W	1	0	0

Pl	Geo Lon	℞	Decl.	G.Lat
☽	25°♌29'		+08° 28'	- 04° 50'
☉	14°♎52'		- 05° 52'	+00' 00"
☿	28°♍55'		+02° 12'	+01° 56'
♀	08°♍56'		+09° 08'	+00° 58'
♂	03°♍16'		+11° 34'	+01° 20'
♃	05°♍16'		+10° 25'	+00° 53'
♄	21°♊56'	℞	+21° 41'	- 01° 33'
♅	16°♑04'		- 22° 57'	- 00° 27'
♆	09°♑07'		- 22° 17'	+00° 52'
♇	03°♈00'	℞	- 14° 21'	- 16° 58'
☊	14°♐52'		- 22° 36'	+00' 00"
Mc	15°♋28'		+22° 34'	+00' 00"
Asc	13°♎18'		- 05° 15'	+00' 00"

Birth / Event Data

Place of birth/event (city, state, county)

Date of birth/event

Time of birth/event (exact time, i.e. birth certificate)

Client Data

Paschal Beverly Randolph

First and last name

Mailing address

City, state, country, zip code

Telephone no. and fax no.

E-mail address

MEDIUMSHIP POTENTIAL – MARKERS ASPECTS

(All aspects score 10 points each, unless otherwise indicated)

CONJUNCTIONS

- ------ Neptune – Pluto (25 pts)
- ------ Saturn – Uranus
- ------ Venus –Pluto (25 pts)
- ------ Jupiter - Saturn

TRINES

- ------ Neptune – Moon
- X Jupiter – Neptune(25 pts)
- ------ Uranus – Moon
- ------ Mercury – Uranus
- ------ Saturn – Neptune
- ------ Mercury – Mars (25 pts)

SEXTILES

- ------ Jupiter – Pluto
- ------ Uranus – Pluto (25 pts)

SQUARES

- ------ Pluto – Moon (25 pts)
- ------ Venus – Neptune (25 pts)
- ------ Saturn – Neptune
- ------ Saturn – Moon
- ------ Saturn – Mars
- ------ Venus – Jupiter

OPPOSITIONS

- ------ Uranus – Neptune
- ------ Sun - Jupiter

LONGITUDINAL PROXIMITY

- ------ Jupiter – Mars (25 pts)

PARALLELS

- ------ Sun – Mercury
- ------ Neptune – Pluto (25 pts)
- ------ Moon – Mercury
- ------ Uranus – Moon
- ------ Saturn – Sun (25 pts)
- ------ Jupiter – Uranus
- ------ Saturn – Neptune (25 pts)
- ------ Mercury – Venus (25 pts)
- ------ Neptune – Mars (25 pts)
- X Jupiter – Mars (25 pts)
- ------ Mercury – Neptune (25 pts)
- ------ Saturn – Mercury (25 pts)
- ------ Sun – Jupiter (25 pts)

CONTRAPARALLELS

- ------ Moon – Mercury (25 pts)
- ------ Uranus – Moon
- ------ Uranus – Neptune(25 pts)
- ------ Neptune – Mars (25 pts)
- ------ Sun – Saturn
- X Saturn – Uranus (25 pts)
- ------ Mercury – Uranus (25 pts)
- ------ Sun – Jupiter
- ------ Pluto – Moon (25 pts)
- ------ Uranus - Pluto

HIDEK

- ------ Mercury
- ------ Venus
- ------ Mars

PROXIMITY ELEVATIONS

- ------ Neptune – Mars(parallel)
- ------ Venus – Uranus (parallel)
- ------ Venus – Mars (parallel)
- ------ Pluto – Mercury (parallel)
- ------ Sun – Uranus (parallel)
- ------ Jupiter – Uranus(parallel)
- ------ Saturn – Mars (parallel)
- ------ Mercury – Mars (parallel)

ECLIPSES

- ------ Neptune - Mars
- ------ Any Pluto eclipse
- X Any Venus eclipse(25 pts)

GRAND ELEVATIONS

- ------ + Moon
- ------ + Mars
- ------ – Sun
- ------ – Uranus
- ------ + Mercury (25 pts)
- ------ + Uranus
- ------ – Mercury
- X – Neptune (25 pts)

	GRAND TOTAL	SCALE
------	Below Average	0 - 30
------	Average	31 – 60
------	Above Average	61 - 100
125	Superior	101 - 140
------	Outstanding	141 - 180
------	Delphi Class	181+

Randolph is credited with starting the Rosicrucian movement in the United States. His writings on sex magic and magical alchemy are still considered to be classics in their genre. When you examine Randolph's chart, you find that all of his marker aspects for mediumship are Delphi aspects! His potential score places him squarely in the Superior range for mediumship. His Jupiter Mars parallel and the binary eclipse of Jupiter, Mars, and Venus are perhaps his strongest markers for the gift. The fact that all of his markers are Delphi in nature probably adds to the strength of his gift. Randolph died at the age of 50.

GLADYS OSBORNE LEONARD

Gladys Osborne was born on May 28, 1882, at Lythom, on the coast of Lancaster England. She was the eldest of four children born of Isabel and William Osborne. Her father was a wealthy yachting entrepeneur, and for the first part of Gladys' life, money was no problem. Ms. Leonard exhibited early signs of her sensitive nature. In her book, "My Life in Two Worlds", she explains:

"Every morning....I saw visions of the most beautiful places. In whatever direction I happened to be looking would gradually come valleys, gentle slopes, lovely trees and banks covered with flowers of every shape and hue.....The most entrancing part to me was the restful velvety green of the grass that covered the ground of the valley and the hills. Walking about.......were people who looked radiantly happy. They were dressed in graceful flowing draperies, for the greater part, but every movement, gesture and expression suggested in an indefinable and yet positive way a condition of deep happiness, and a state of quiet ecstasy."

She did not look upon these visions as anything abnormal. However, an inner sense guided her to keep silent about them, until one morning, at breakfast, she said to her father, "Isn't that an especially beautiful place we are seeing this morning?" Her father did not understand about these visions, and from that time forward, she was forbidden to speak about these visions. As Mrs. Leonard approached adolescence, she experienced great changes in her life. Her family underwent great financial loss, and from then on, she had to manage for herself. She trained her already lovely voice and then did some work in opera and theatrical companies, singing and dancing in various leads and comedy parts. During this part of her life, while she was singing at a local Spiritualist church, a medium told her that her guides were preparing her for a "great spiritual work." She accepted the message but was not quite sure what to do with it.

On December 18, 1906, her mother died. That evening, she had been staying with a friend. Although her mother had not been well, no one suspected that she was seriously ill. At 2:00 am., Gladys awakened with a strange feeling. She relates the story:

"I looked up and saw in front of me, but about five feet above the level of my body, a large, circular patch of light. In this light I saw my mother quite distinctly. Her face looked several years younger than I had seen it a few hours before....She gazed down on me for a moment, seeming to convey to me an intense feeling of relief and a sense of safety and well-being. Then the vision faded. I was wide awake all the time, quite conscious of my surroundings."

The next morning she learned that her mother had died at 2:00 am. Shortly thereafter, she met and married an actor named Frederick Leonard, who became her devoted husband and lifelong friend. From this point forward, her life as a medium took some definite directions.

Mrs. Leonard became one of the most thoroughly investigated mediums of the twentieth century. For more than fifty years she gave remarkable evidence of personal survival to countless sitters. Perhaps the most significant sittings of her life were the ones that she gave to Sir Oliver Lodge, the renowned physicist. In 1915, he and Lady Lodge visited Mrs. Leonard anonymously at first. With the information given her guide Feda, they were convinced that they were communicating with their son Raymond, who had recently been killed in the war. Sir Oliver was not one to accept mediumistic utterances blindly, and he put Mrs. Leonard through a severe series of tests. But the evidence kept coming forth, and it became impossible to deny the obvious: Raymond lived on. Sir Oliver Lodge's book, "Raymond", or "Life After Death", is a remarkable examination of his search for evidence of survival after death.

Investigations into Mrs. Leonard's mediumship were conducted by the world's most noted psychic researcher of the time: Rev. C. Drayton Thomas, Rev. Vale Owen, James Hewat McKenzie, and Whately Carington, to name but a few. A complete list of investigations on Mrs. Leonard's mediumship may be found in the Society for Psychical Research-Combined Indes, Part III, pages 50-52, and Part IV, page 104.

Mrs. Leonard functioned as a trance medium, with Feda controlling her. In that state, Feda, herself acted as a message medium and related what she saw and heard from others in Spirit. Essentially, this served as an example of two mediums working together, one in body and one in Spirit. A good deal of research done with Mrs. Leonard revolved around Feda's relating how she worked with the medium and how she was able to link with the various Spirit people and relate their messages through Mrs. Leonard. Even though Feda was in Spirit, she had to mentally reach out to the various Spirit communicators and invite them to draw closer to the circle of energy consciousness which was established around Mrs. Leonard at the time of the sitting. In other words, until they stepped into the Light, Feda was neither able to see or hear the Spirit people with any real degree of clarity.

Her work, recorded in the annals of psychic research, represents a great source of understanding and dedication to the work of Spirit. In her work, she set an example of honesty, integrity, and professionalism which to this day may be used as a basis of all types of mediumship. On March 19, 1968, during her sleep, Mrs. Gladys Osborne Leonard quietly passed out of the body, in order to continue her work in Spirit. Let's examine the marker aspects for mediumship in this great Lady's chart.

Mrs. Leonard's chart contains six Delphi aspects for mediumship and two non-Delphi aspects. Her overall rating of 170 is squarely in the outstanding range and actually places her very close to the Delphi range of talent. All of her marker aspects for mediumship exist in the declinational measurements. The strength of her gift is greatly accentuated by the presence of her Pluto Moon contraparallel and her Jupiter Mars parallel. The Jupiter Mars parallel is especially important in clarifying and amplifying the gift of spiritual sight.

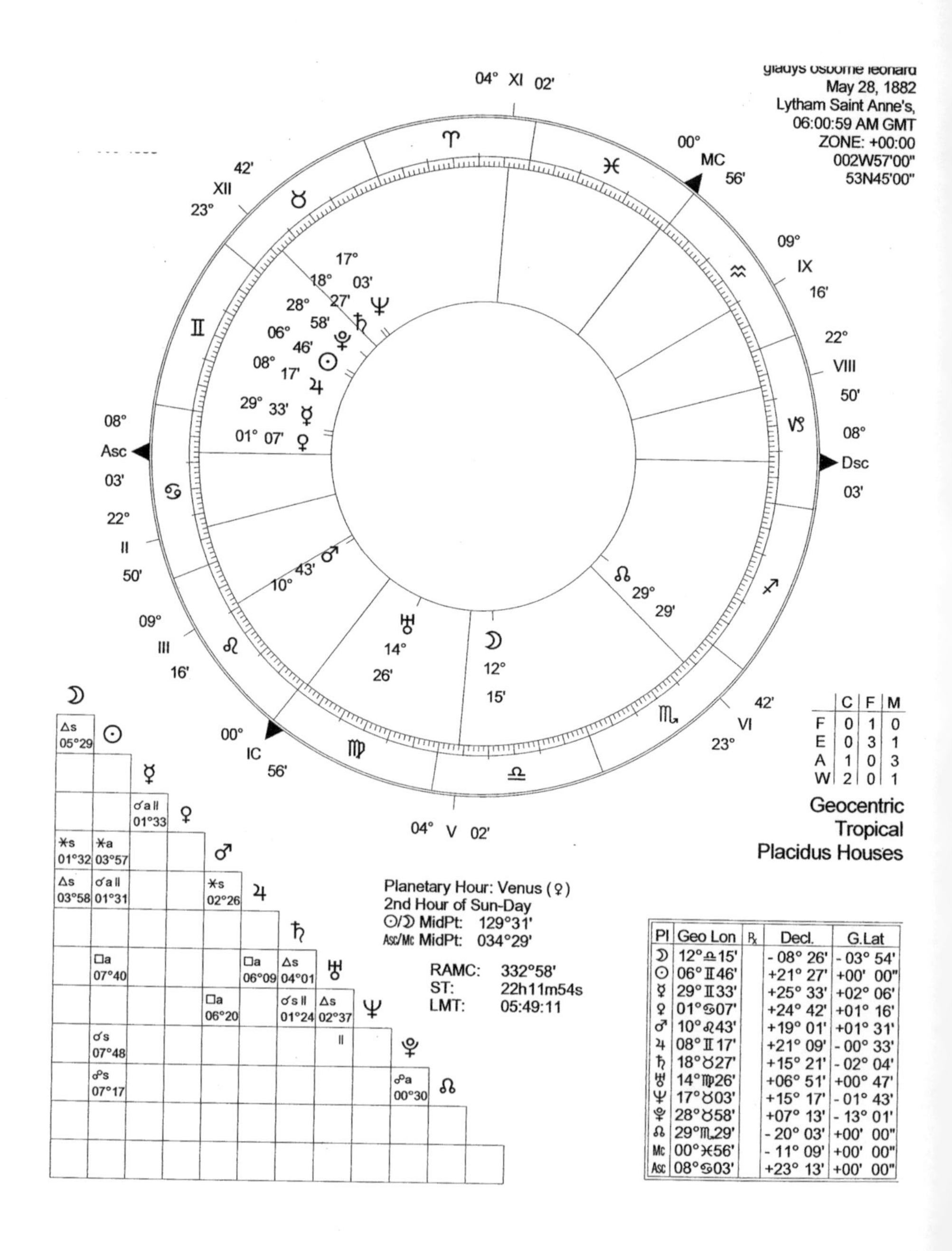

	C	F	M
F	0	1	0
E	0	3	1
A	1	0	3
W	2	0	1

Pl	Geo Lon	℞	Decl.	G.Lat
☽	12°♎15'		- 08° 26'	- 03° 54'
☉	06°♊46'		+21° 27'	+00' 00"
☿	29°♊33'		+25° 33'	+02° 06'
♀	01°♋07'		+24° 42'	+01° 16'
♂	10°♌43'		+19° 01'	+01° 31'
♃	08°♊17'		+21° 09'	- 00° 33'
♄	18°♉27'		+15° 21'	- 02° 04'
♅	14°♍26'		+06° 51'	+00° 47'
♆	17°♉03'		+15° 17'	- 01° 43'
♇	28°♉58'		+07° 13'	- 13° 01'
☊	29°♏29'		- 20° 03'	+00' 00"
Mc	00°♓56'		- 11° 09'	+00' 00"
Asc	08°♋03'		+23° 13'	+00' 00"

Birth / Event Data

Place of birth/event (city, state, county)

Date of birth/event

Time of birth/event (exact time, i.e. birth certificate)

Client Data

Gladys Leonard
First and last name

Mailing address

City, state, country, zip code

Telephone no. and fax no.

E-mail address

MEDIUMSHIP POTENTIAL – MARKERS ASPECTS

(All aspects score 10 points each, unless otherwise indicated)

CONJUNCTIONS

- ------ Neptune – Pluto (25 pts)
- ------ Saturn – Uranus
- ------ Venus –Pluto (25 pts)
- ------ Jupiter - Saturn

TRINES

- ------ Neptune – Moon
- ------ Jupiter – Neptune(25 pts)
- ------ Uranus – Moon
- ------ Mercury – Uranus
- ------ Saturn – Neptune
- ------ Mercury – Mars (25 pts)

SEXTILES

- ------ Jupiter – Pluto
- ------ Uranus – Pluto (25 pts)

SQUARES

- ------ Pluto – Moon (25 pts)
- ------ Venus – Neptune (25 pts)
- ------ Saturn – Neptune
- ------ Saturn – Moon
- ------ Saturn – Mars
- ------ Venus – Jupiter

OPPOSITIONS

- ------ Uranus – Neptune
- ------ Sun - Jupiter

LONGITUDINAL PROXIMITY

- ------ Jupiter – Mars (25 pts)

PARALLELS

- ------ Sun – Mercury
- ------ Neptune – Pluto (25 pts)
- ------ Moon – Mercury
- ------ Uranus – Moon
- ------ Saturn – Sun (25 pts)
- ------ Jupiter – Uranus
- X Saturn – Neptune (25 pts)
- X Mercury – Venus (25 pts)
- ------ Neptune – Mars (25 pts)
- X Jupiter – Mars (25 pts)
- ------ Mercury – Neptune (25 pts)
- ------ Saturn – Mercury (25 pts)
- X Sun – Jupiter (25 pts)

CONTRAPARALLELS

- ------ Moon – Mercury (25 pts)
- X Uranus – Moon
- ------ Uranus – Neptune(25 pts)
- ------ Neptune – Mars (25 pts)
- ------ Sun – Saturn
- ------ Saturn – Uranus (25 pts)
- ------ Mercury – Uranus (25 pts)
- ------ Sun – Jupiter
- X Pluto – Moon (25 pts)
- X Uranus - Pluto

HIDEK

- ------ Mercury
- ------ Venus
- ------ Mars

PROXIMITY ELEVATIONS

- ------ Neptune – Mars(parallel)
- ------ Venus – Uranus (parallel)
- ------ Venus – Mars (parallel)
- ------ Pluto – Mercury (parallel)
- ------ Sun – Uranus (parallel)
- ------ Jupiter – Uranus(parallel)
- ------ Saturn – Mars (parallel)
- ------ Mercury – Mars (parallel)

ECLIPSES

- ------ Neptune - Mars
- ------ Any Pluto eclipse
- X Any Venus eclipse(25 pts)

GRAND ELEVATIONS

- ------ + Moon
- ------ + Mars
- ------ – Sun
- ------ – Uranus
- ------ + Mercury (25 pts)
- ------ + Uranus
- ------ – Mercury
- ------ – Neptune (25 pts)

	GRAND TOTAL	**SCALE**
------	Below Average	0 - 30
------	Average	31 – 60
------	Above Average	61 - 100
------	Superior	101 - 140
170	Outstanding	141 - 180
------	Delphi Class	181+

EDGAR CAYCE

Edgar Cayce was born on a farm near Hopkinsville, Kentucky. At an early age he gave evidence of his budding talent: he was able to master his school lessons by sleeping on his books. At the age of twenty-one he developed a gradual throat paralysis which threatened the loss of his voice. When doctors were unable to find a cause for his condition, Cayce entered the same hypnotic sleep that had enabled him to learn his school lessons years before. In that state, he was able to recommend a cure which successfully repaired his throat muscles and restored his voice. He soon discovered that he could do the same for others.

Cayce began his readings in the early 1920's and continued until his death in January 1945. During the latter years, his predictions took a new turn and while in a trance he began foretelling major world events. He predicted the exact date for the end of World War II, and the assassination of President John F. Kennedy. His prophecies went further into the future, predicting major earthquakes and natural disasters occurring all over the world during our present time and he foresaw the destruction of both California and New York City.

Cayce also went into the past. A firm believer in reincarnation he based much of his information on data that he gleaned from the Akashic Records. These Records gave a full accounting of information relating to the entirety of space and time, including the past life details of everyone who ever lived. Many of his readings centered on the continent of Atlantis, which he believed to have existed 12,000 years ago. He said that the Atlanteans were a technologically advanced civilization having aircraft, electricity and weapons of destruction. Cayce referred to their "death ray" or super cosmic ray as the primary means of their own destruction. He predicted that the western edge of Atlantis would begin to reappear near the island of Bimini in the Bahamas. He said the discovery would appear between 1968 or 1969. In fact, in 1968 divers found the apparent ruins of prehistoric roads and walls off the coast of Bimini- perhaps the remnants of the lost continent of Atlantis!

Cayce's gift is probably the result of trance mediumship. His association with spirits of an exceptionally high level of integrity, accuracy, and intellect is affirmed by the legacy he has left with the world. Cayce gave over 14,000 readings on more than 10,000 different topics to people all over the world. These readings continue to be researched and written about over 50 years after his death. What are the astrological markers in his chart that relate to his phenomenal gift?

Cayce's birth chart gives ample evidence of the magnitude of his outstanding gift for mediumship. His mediumship potential score of 180 is in part a testament to this fact. He has the exceptionally powerful Jupiter Mars parallel and this aspect is doubly amplified in power by a longitudinal proximity enhancement between these two planets. In addition to this, he has no fewer than six Delphi markers for the gift of mediumship. Interestingly, the grand elevation of Mercury is a marker for mediumship whether it is positive or negative. Cayce has a negative grand elevation of Mercury which may to some extent explain the need for unconsciousness when he engages in his trance work. Cayce could not recall any of his readings upon awakening. Once again, we see that the chart of a great medium is associated with a high level of potential markers.

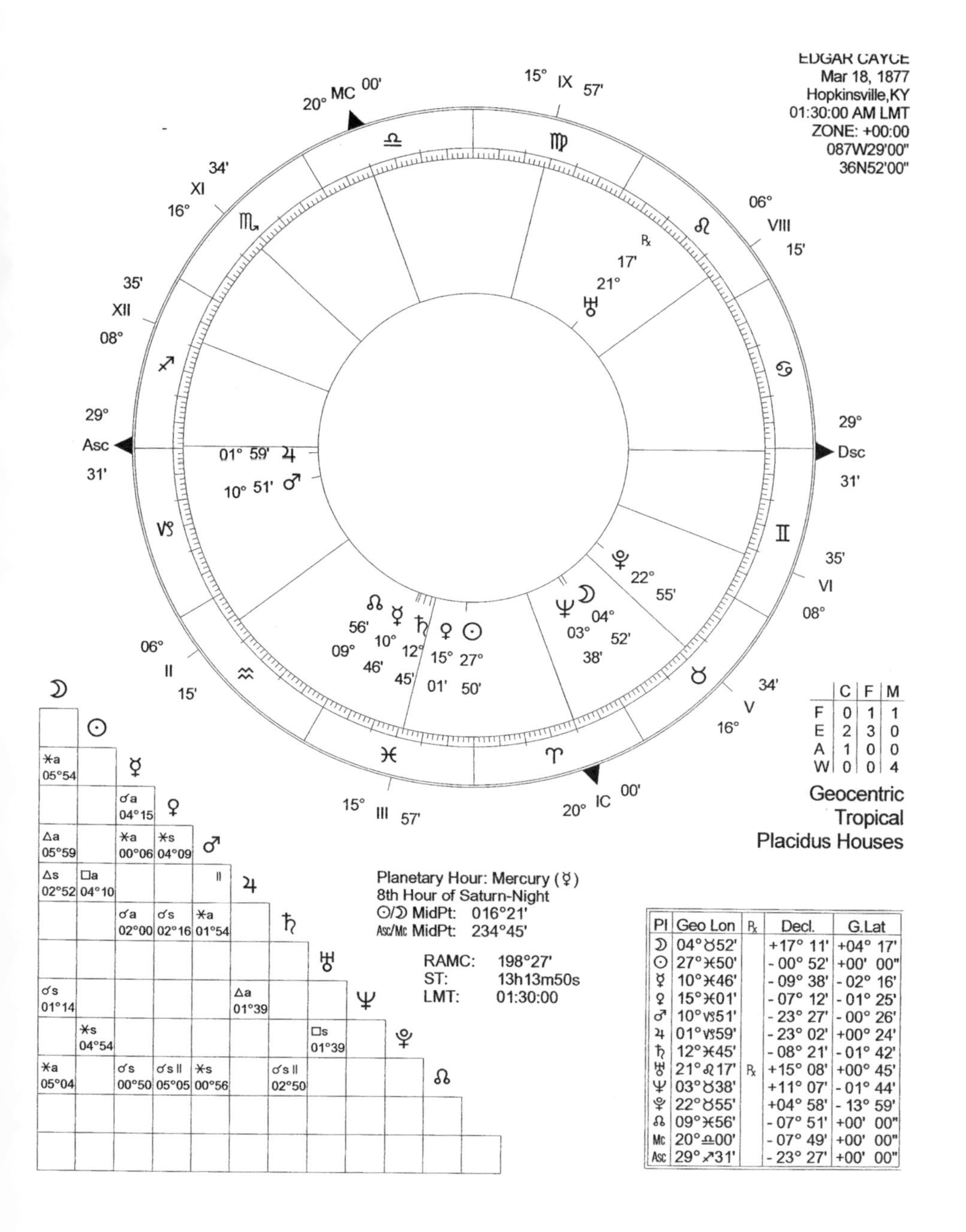

	C	F	M
F	0	1	1
E	2	3	0
A	1	0	0
W	0	0	4

Pl	Geo Lon	℞	Decl.	G.Lat
☽	04°♉52'		+17° 11'	+04° 17'
☉	27°♓50'		- 00° 52'	+00' 00"
☿	10°♓46'		- 09° 38'	- 02° 16'
♀	15°♓01'		- 07° 12'	- 01° 25'
♂	10°♑51'		- 23° 27'	- 00° 26'
♃	01°♑59'		- 23° 02'	+00° 24'
♄	12°♓45'		- 08° 21'	- 01° 42'
♅	21°♌17'	℞	+15° 08'	+00° 45'
♆	03°♉38'		+11° 07'	- 01° 44'
♇	22°♉55'		+04° 58'	- 13° 59'
☊	09°♓56'		- 07° 51'	+00' 00"
Mc	20°♎00'		- 07° 49'	+00' 00"
Asc	29°♐31'		- 23° 27'	+00' 00"

Birth / Event Data

____
Place of birth/event (city, state, county)

____
Date of birth/event

____
Time of birth/event (exact time, i.e. birth certificate)

Client Data

Edgar Cayce
First and last name

____
Mailing address

____
City, state, country, zip code

____
Telephone no. and fax no.

____
E-mail address

MEDIUMSHIP POTENTIAL – MARKERS ASPECTS

(All aspects score 10 points each, unless otherwise indicated)

CONJUNCTIONS

- ____ Neptune – Pluto (25 pts)
- ____ Saturn – Uranus
- ____ Venus –Pluto (25 pts)
- ____ Jupiter - Saturn

TRINES

- ____ Neptune – Moon
- X Jupiter – Neptune(25 pts)
- ____ Uranus – Moon
- ____ Mercury – Uranus
- ____ Saturn – Neptune
- ____ Mercury – Mars (25 pts)

SEXTILES

- ____ Jupiter – Pluto
- ____ Uranus – Pluto (25 pts)

SQUARES

- ____ Pluto – Moon (25 pts)
- ____ Venus – Neptune (25 pts)
- ____ Saturn – Neptune
- ____ Saturn – Moon
- ____ Saturn – Mars
- ____ Venus – Jupiter

OPPOSITIONS

- ____ Uranus – Neptune
- ____ Sun - Jupiter

LONGITUDINAL PROXIMITY

- X Jupiter – Mars (25 pts)

PARALLELS

- ____ Sun – Mercury
- ____ Neptune – Pluto (25 pts)
- ____ Moon – Mercury
- X Uranus – Moon
- ____ Saturn – Sun (25 pts)
- ____ Jupiter – Uranus
- ____ Saturn – Neptune (25 pts)
- X Mercury – Venus (25 pts)
- ____ Neptune – Mars (25 pts)
- X Jupiter – Mars (25 pts)
- ____ Mercury – Neptune (25 pts)
- X Saturn – Mercury (25 pts)
- ____ Sun – Jupiter (25 pts)

CONTRAPARALLELS

- ____ Moon – Mercury (25 pts)
- ____ Uranus – Moon
- ____ Uranus – Neptune(25 pts)
- ____ Neptune – Mars (25 pts)
- ____ Sun – Saturn
- ____ Saturn – Uranus (25 pts)
- ____ Mercury – Uranus (25 pts)
- ____ Sun – Jupiter
- ____ Pluto – Moon (25 pts)
- ____ Uranus - Pluto

HIDEK

- ____ Mercury
- ____ Venus
- X Mars

PROXIMITY ELEVATIONS

- ____ Neptune – Mars (parallel)
- ____ Venus – Uranus (parallel)
- ____ Venus – Mars (parallel)
- ____ Pluto – Mercury (parallel)
- ____ Sun – Uranus (parallel)
- ____ Jupiter – Uranus (parallel)
- ____ Saturn – Mars (parallel)
- ____ Mercury – Mars (parallel)

ECLIPSES

- ____ Neptune - Mars
- ____ Any Pluto eclipse
- X Any Venus eclipse(25 pts)

GRAND ELEVATIONS

- ____ + Moon
- ____ + Mars
- ____ – Sun
- ____ – Uranus
- ____ + Mercury (25 pts)
- ____ + Uranus
- X – Mercury
- ____ – Neptune (25 pts)

	GRAND TOTAL	SCALE
____	Below Average	0 - 30
____	Average	31 – 60
____	Above Average	61 - 100
____	Superior	101 - 140
180	Outstanding	141 - 180
____	Delphi Class	181+

EILEEN GARRETT

Eileen Garrett was the most respected and gifted medium of the twentieth century. Her overall contributions to the field of spiritualism and mediumship are incalculable. She had the rare distinction of being both a medium and a psychic researcher. She recognized the need for a scientific and open-minded investigation of paranormal phenomena. In addition to these fields, she was an accomplished lecturer, publisher, and author.

She was born in 1893 in County Meath, Ireland. From the beginning, here life was riddled with tragedy. Her parents both committed suicide shortly after her birth and she was then adopted by her aunt and uncle. Psychic experiences were a part of Eileen Garrett's life from the moment she saw an infant for the first time. She sensed and saw auras around people, animals and even plants. In addition, she saw various energy forms that filled her world. She said that she imaginary playmates, whom she called "the children". She claims that their appearance was a normal part of her life and that she did not have to go into a trance or meditative state in order to see them.

One day, while quite young, she saw her favorite aunt, who lived about twenty miles away, walking up the path carrying a baby. As the aunt approached, she said to young Eileen, "I am going away now and I must take the baby with me." Eileen quickly ran into the house to relate this to her adoptive aunt, who immediately punished her for making up stories. The following day she learned that her aunt Leone had died in childbirth, along with the baby. This unfortunate introduction to death had a profound impact on Eileen. She had many questions concerning birth, death, and the energy forms that she saw on a daily basis. No one in her life cared to discuss them with her and most of the people around her were somewhat resistant to her inquiries. As a means of protest, and in response to some undeserved punishment, she drowned some ducklings of which her aunt was very proud. She recalls, "The little dead bodies were quiet, but a strange movement was occurring all about them. A gray, smoke-like substance rose up from each small form. This nebulous, fluid stuff wove and curled as it rose in winding spiral curves, and I saw it take new shape as it moved out and away from the quiet forms." Thus she became aware, at a young age, that there was more to life than the physical form, and that this "more" separated itself from the body at the time of death.

Mrs. Garrett married three times during her life. Her first marriage ended in divorce and her second marriage ended when her husband died in World War I. Her young life was marred by illness, loss, and death. Despite all this unhappiness and tragedy, she was obviously being prepared for her major role in life: that of a sensitive. One day, during a table rapping session, she became drowsy and started falling asleep. When she awakened, she discovered that dead relatives of others in the room and had communicated through her. In spite of her husband's warnings never to attend such meetings again, she sought the advice of one Mr. Huhnli who took it upon himself to guide Eileen in her understanding of what was happening to her. At one such meeting, she was entranced by an Asian called Uvani who expressed his interest in helping prove survival.

Mrs. Garrett's mediumship had finally come to the surface, but fear, ill health, and the break-up of her marriage delayed its development. Despite this delay, she eventually came to meet J. Hewat McKenzie, founder of the British College of Psychic Science. It was under his careful guidance, at the College, that her mediumship blossomed. Mr. McKenzie and his wife, Barbara, were keenly aware of the need the medimship to expand well beyond that of messages from the spirits. They recognized that mediumship could provide a tool whereby the investigator could delve into the various dimensions and levels of perception and consciousness. Mr. McKenzie was probably the most powerful influence upon Eileen Garrett, as well as her attitudes concerning the process of communication. She continued studying and developing her mediumship at the College until Hewat McKenzie's death in 1929.

Mrs. Garrett moved to the United States and made some valuable connections with many noted scientists and parapsychologists. She subjected herself to intense physiological and psychological experimentation, hoping that such testing might shed some light upon the process of mediumship and psychism. She traveled to and from the States, searching, studying, and experimenting. While she was in France during the Second World War she had an epiphany. She had a wholly spontaneous and supernatural flash of intuitive knowledge of external origin. She knew that she would become a sensitive of great importance. Eileen Garrett's greatest achievement was the founding the Parapsychology Foundation, in 1951. Her honesty and acumen for business affairs helped make this one of today's most respected foundations of its type.

Eileen Garrett had four trance communicators, Uvani, a fourteenth century Arab soldier, was her control in mediumship. Abdul Latif, a seveneenth Persian physician, dealt primarily with healing. Tahotah and Ramah were her guides on philosophic and spritual matters. One of Eileen Garretts's memorable communications, as a medium, was the case of the R101. In the Encyclopedia of Psychic Science Nandor Fodor chronicled the session: "In a sitting at the National Laboratory of Psychical Research on October 7, 1930, two days after the explosion of the R101, Flight Lieutenant H.C. Irwin, Captain of the airship, suddenly entranced Mrs. Garrett, announced his presence and gave the listeners to a highly technical account of how the airship crashed. The narrative was taken down in shorthand and a copy was submitted to the Air Ministry. According to the opinion of experts, a number of observations in the message tallied in every detail with what was afterwards found in the course of the official inquiry."

Despite the wealth of information and evidence of survival which came through Eileen Garrett, she was never quite convinced that her mediumship stemmed from a separate source. This attitude probably helped to make her one of the greatest and most accurate mediums of the 20th century. Let's take a look at her birth chart and examine the astrological markers for her gift.

Mrs. Garrett's mediumship potential score was 230. She had eight Delphi marker aspects for this gift. She also has the wonderful fortune to have the top three markers for mediumship/psychic ability in all the sky: 1) Moon Mercury parallel, 2) positive grand elevation of Mercury, 3) positive grand elevation of the Moon. These elevations are the strongest associations to mediumship and psychic ability that I have ever measured. The

Moon Mercury contraparallel is such a strong predictor for advanced spiritual potential that it is found in a veritable Who's Who of highly evolved spiritual and psychic savants. The same is true for the positive grand elevation of Mercury but to a slightly lesser extent. Indeed, high levels of Mercury activity in a chart are intimately associated with elevated spiritual potential. Curiously, the ancients associated the planet Mercury with the power that connected man with the realm of Spirit. Perhaps, they were a great deal more aware of man's connection to the Universe than we are today.

THE TOP TEN ASTROLOGICAL MARKERS FOR MEDIUMSHIP POTENTIAL

1. MOON MERCURY CONTRAPARALLEL
2. POSITIVE GRAND ELEVATION OF MERCURY
3. URANUS PLUTO SEXTILE
4. ANY VENUS ECLIPSE
5. HIDEK VENUS
6. NEPTUNE MARS CONTRAPARALLEL
7. SATURN NEPTUNE PARALLEL
8. JUPITER MARS LONGITUDINAL PROXIMITY ELEVATON
9. VENUS NEPTUNE SQUARE
10. NEGATIVE GRAND ELEVATION OF NEPTUNE

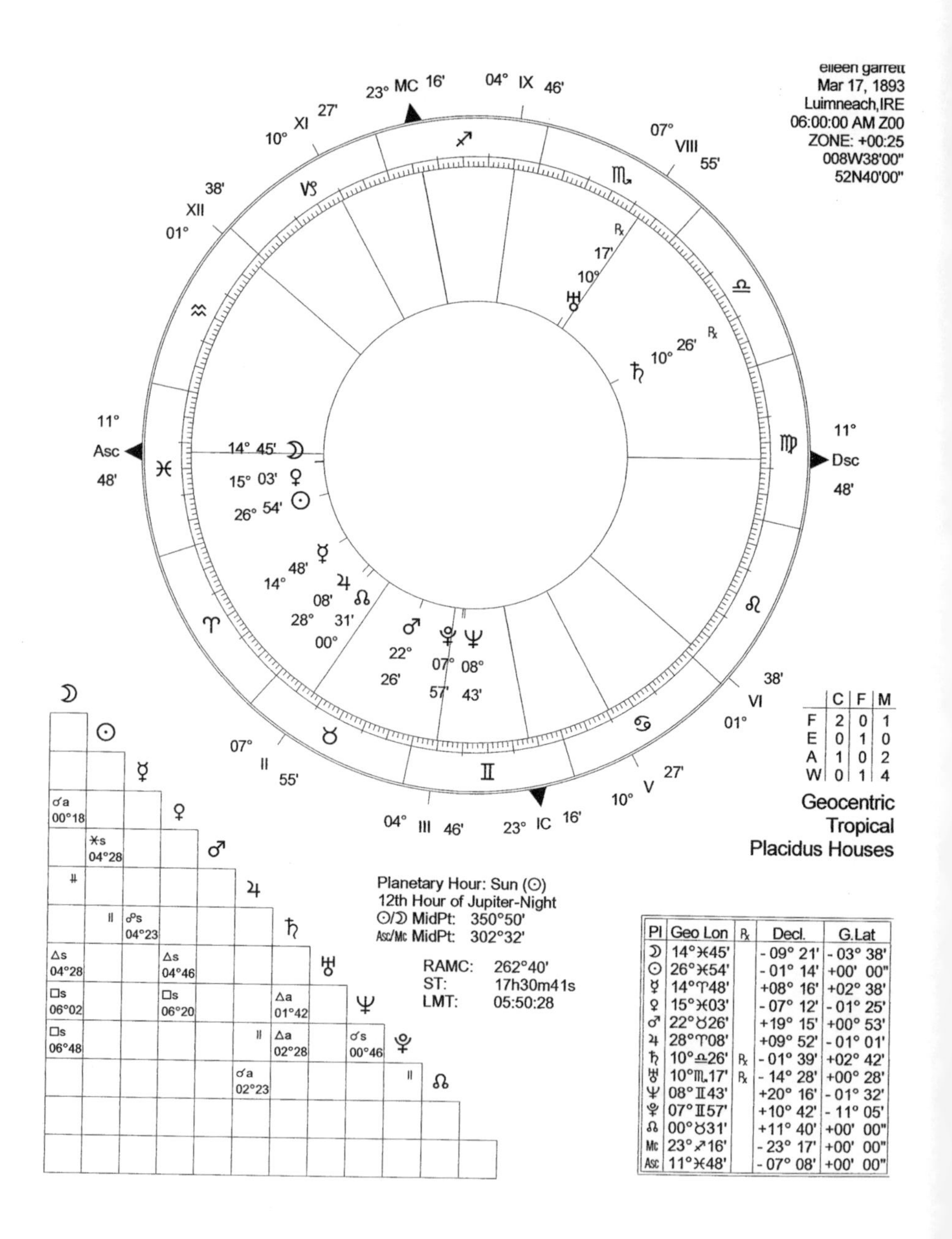

	C	F	M
F	2	0	1
E	0	1	0
A	1	0	2
W	0	1	4

Pl	Geo Lon	℞	Decl.	G.Lat
☽	14°♓45'		- 09° 21'	- 03° 38'
☉	26°♓54'		- 01° 14'	+00' 00"
☿	14°♈48'		+08° 16'	+02° 38'
♀	15°♓03'		- 07° 12'	- 01° 25'
♂	22°♉26'		+19° 15'	+00° 53'
♃	28°♈08'		+09° 52'	- 01° 01'
♄	10°♎26'	℞	- 01° 39'	+02° 42'
♅	10°♏17'	℞	- 14° 28'	+00° 28'
♆	08°♊43'		+20° 16'	- 01° 32'
♇	07°♊57'		+10° 42'	- 11° 05'
☊	00°♉31'		+11° 40'	+00' 00"
Mc	23°♐16'		- 23° 17'	+00' 00"
Asc	11°♓48'		- 07° 08'	+00' 00"

Birth / Event Data

Place of birth/event (city, state, county)

Date of birth/event

Time of birth/event (exact time, i.e. birth certificate)

Client Data

Eileen Garrett
First and last name

Mailing address

City, state, country, zip code

Telephone no. and fax no.

E-mail address

MEDIUMSHIP POTENTIAL – MARKERS ASPECTS

(All aspects score 10 points each, unless otherwise indicated)

CONJUNCTIONS

- X Neptune – Pluto (25 pts)
- ---- Saturn – Uranus
- ---- Venus –Pluto (25 pts)
- ---- Jupiter - Saturn

TRINES

- ---- Neptune – Moon
- ---- Jupiter – Neptune(25 pts)
- X Uranus – Moon
- ---- Mercury – Uranus
- X Saturn – Neptune
- ---- Mercury – Mars (25 pts)

SEXTILES

- ---- Jupiter – Pluto
- ---- Uranus – Pluto (25 pts)

SQUARES

- X Pluto – Moon (25 pts)
- ---- Venus – Neptune (25 pts)
- ---- Saturn – Neptune
- ---- Saturn – Moon
- ---- Saturn – Mars
- ---- Venus – Jupiter

OPPOSITIONS

- ---- Uranus – Neptune
- ---- Sun - Jupiter

LONGITUDINAL PROXIMITY

- ---- Jupiter – Mars (25 pts)

PARALLELS

- ---- Sun – Mercury
- ---- Neptune – Pluto (25 pts)
- ---- Moon – Mercury
- ---- Uranus – Moon
- X Saturn – Sun (25 pts)
- ---- Jupiter – Uranus
- ---- Saturn – Neptune (25 pts)
- ---- Mercury – Venus (25 pts)
- X Neptune – Mars (25 pts)
- ---- Jupiter – Mars (25 pts)
- ---- Mercury – Neptune (25 pts)
- ---- Saturn – Mercury (25 pts)
- ---- Sun – Jupiter (25 pts)

CONTRAPARALLELS

- X Moon – Mercury (25 pts)
- ---- Uranus – Moon
- ---- Uranus – Neptune(25 pts)
- ---- Neptune – Mars (25 pts)
- ---- Sun – Saturn
- ---- Saturn – Uranus (25 pts)
- ---- Mercury – Uranus (25 pts)
- ---- Sun – Jupiter
- X Pluto – Moon (25 pts)
- ---- Uranus - Pluto

HIDEK

- ---- Mercury
- ---- Venus
- ---- Mars

PROXIMITY ELEVATIONS

- ---- Neptune – Mars(parallel)
- ---- Venus – Uranus (parallel)
- ---- Venus – Mars (parallel)
- ---- Pluto – Mercury (parallel)
- ---- Sun – Uranus (parallel)
- ---- Jupiter – Uranus(parallel)
- ---- Saturn – Mars (parallel)
- ---- Mercury – Mars (parallel)

ECLIPSES

- ---- Neptune - Mars
- ---- Any Pluto eclipse
- X Any Venus eclipse(25 pts)

GRAND ELEVATIONS

- X + Moon
- ---- + Mars
- ---- – Sun
- ---- – Uranus
- X + Mercury (25 pts)
- ---- + Uranus
- ---- – Mercury
- ---- – Neptune (25 pts)

	GRAND TOTAL	SCALE
----	Below Average	0 - 30
----	Average	31 – 60
----	Above Average	61 - 100
----	Superior	101 - 140
----	Outstanding	141 - 180
230	Delphi Class	181+

TIME, SPACE, AND THE PARANORMAL

Gerard Croiset was a remarkably gifted Dutch psychic. He is best known for his psychic detective work but he is also famous for an experiment which he devised known as the "chair test". In this test, he would try to describe in advance the person who would sit in a randomly chosen chair at an upcoming public event without knowing either the nature of the event or its location. In one experiment, Croiset said that the person who would sit in the chair selected would be a man five foot nine inches tall, who brushed his black hair straight back, had a gold tooth in his lower jaw, a scar on his big toe, who worked in both science and industry, and sometimes got his lab coat stained by a greenish chemical. Two weeks later the meeting took place (in Denver, Colorado) and the person who sat down in the chair concerned was a man who fit Croiset's description in every respect except one. Instead of being five foot nine, he was five foot nine and three-quarters.[1] Croiset performed the chair test over a period of 25 years with a number of notable successes. Newtonian physics with its cause and effect ordering principles of the known universe does not allow for the rational occurrence of even one successful prediction of this sort. The fact that Croiset successfully demonstrated the efficacy in his experiments seems to point to the existence of a larger operating principle in the universe which allows man a usable, predictable, and stable "window" into the hidden patterns of space-time.

Is there an order to the events that occur within the universe that may be used to explain the existence of paranormal phenomena? In other words, is there an undiscovered natural law that allows for a rational explanation of such seemingly irrational events? In the previous chapters on astrological markers for paranormal phenomena, we saw repeated instances where individuals born with heightened abilities also tend to have a high degree of potential for manifesting spiritual power in their natal charts. If we use a bit of inverse logic in applying this data, I theorize that there may be an astrological way to gain valuable insight into the inner mechanics of the paranormal.

Astrology has been used successfully for thousands of years in making predictions regarding a host of paranormal phenomena. To date however, there is no uniform system within the teachings of astrology that would allow one to pick a day at random and make predictions as to whether a specific type of paranormal would take place on that date and to then further state what level of overall significance that event would be given to the populace at large. Simply stated, how does one answer the question: ***What is the*** likelihood that a large scale sighting of the Virgin Mary will occur in San Francisco ***on June 6, 2009 at 9:00 am?*** I believe that I can now provide an intelligent answer to this question as well as questions of this sort that would apply to all the major areas of spiritual phenomena such as healing experiences, mystical sightings and miracles, psychic predictions, and mediumistic encounters.

In tackling this problem, I applied the principle of inverse logic and treated the date in question as a birthdate for an individual and then calculated that person's inherent latent potential for mystical ability. As a sighting of the Virgin Mary would likely be considered a mystical experience, the ability in question would be mystical potential. Applying this logic, one could then conceivably take any date, place, or time and calculate the level of probability that a distinct type of spiritual event would take place within those parameters. A date, place and time that give a mystical potential score of 195 would by definition be far more likely to give birth to a large-scale mystical event than a nativity which yields a score of 40. Furthermore, if the theory holds, one could conceivably look back in time and cross check any number of famous paranormal events that have accurate related temporal parameters to examine what level of probability those events were likely to occur. For instance, the Great Fire of London was predicted by a large number of psychics and astrologers. Presumably the event could be foreseen within a psychic or mystical experience by anyone sufficiently gifted with such talents. Does the commencement of the terrible holocaust that consumed London correspond with a high mystical or psychic potential score? If an event has a high paranormal score attached to its nativity, is it more easily perceived across space-time by those who are highly sensitive, thereby creating a kind of temporal-spatial window? In order to answer these questions, we will need to examine a number of unequivocably notable events and calculate their potential scores. Since we have already mentioned the Great Fire of London, let's use that event as our first hypothetical case.

In the mid 1660s the citizens of London witnessed the greatest conflagration ever to hit that city since the plague. The Great Fire of London is reputed to have startedon September 2, 1666 at 1:00am. The astrological chart for that date has been examined countless time by scores of histories most eminent astrologers, but none have measured the chart's paranormal potential. Nostradamus predicted the exact year for the event and named it precisely in Century II Quartrain 51: *The blood of the just shall be required of London, burned by fire in thrice twenty and six, The ancient Dame shall fall from her high place, and many of the same sect shall fall.*

Nostradamus was known to have witnessed his visions in a specially prepared bowl of water while seated upon a brass tripod. Did this event emit such a loud paranormal signal across the space-time band that a large number of sensitives could perceive it?

Given his well-known spiritual proclivities, Nostradamus was also a Delphi level psychic. Was he better able to discern exact dates for the event than other savants? The mystical potential score for the "natal chart" of the Great Fire of London is 150, a score which places the event squarely in the outstanding range of probability for the occurrence or perception of a mystical event according to our theory!

GREAT FIRE OF LONDON (MYSTICAL MARKERS)

Moon Venus conjunction, Sun Mars sextile, Saturn Moon square, Moon Venus parallel, Moon Mercury parallel, Venus Mercury parallel, Jupiter Moon parallel, Saturn Neptune parallel, Pluto Mars contraparallel, Moon grand elevation, Mercury +grand elevation, and Neptune -grand elevation.

If one were trolling mystically through space time looking for outstanding events, an event with a signal score of 150 would surely catch one's "eye", especially if that event were one as monumental as the Great Fire! I do not believe that this association happened by chance. I believe that space-time is riddled with a series of preexistent temporal-spatial windows that are associated with their own specific astrological markers. If one correctly interprets and anticipates these markers and then focuses their nascent spiritual abilities on the dates that are attached to "windows" with high paranormal scores, one could conceivably develop a method of anticipating any number of such events. However, for the system to work, we must first establish that there is indeed a body of evidence to support the assertion that a significant number of predicted events have been associated with high probability scores for metaphysical potential.

I have examined more than 100 paranormal events and then determined their potential scores. More than 85% of the time, these events are associated with higher than average paranormal potential scores and in many cases, the scores for the most conspicuous events are in the Outstanding to Delphi range. Let's examine a sampling of these events so that the reader may view these fascinating associations.

It is perhaps most fitting that we begin this examination with a prediction made famous by the Prince of Seers; Nostradamus. The Seer's most successful prediction concerned the death of King Henry II. In Century I Quatrain 35, published in 1555, Nostradamus wrote:

The young Lion shall overcome the old
On a warlike field in single combat,
He will pierce his eyes in a cage of gold,
One of two breakings, then he shall die
a cruel death.

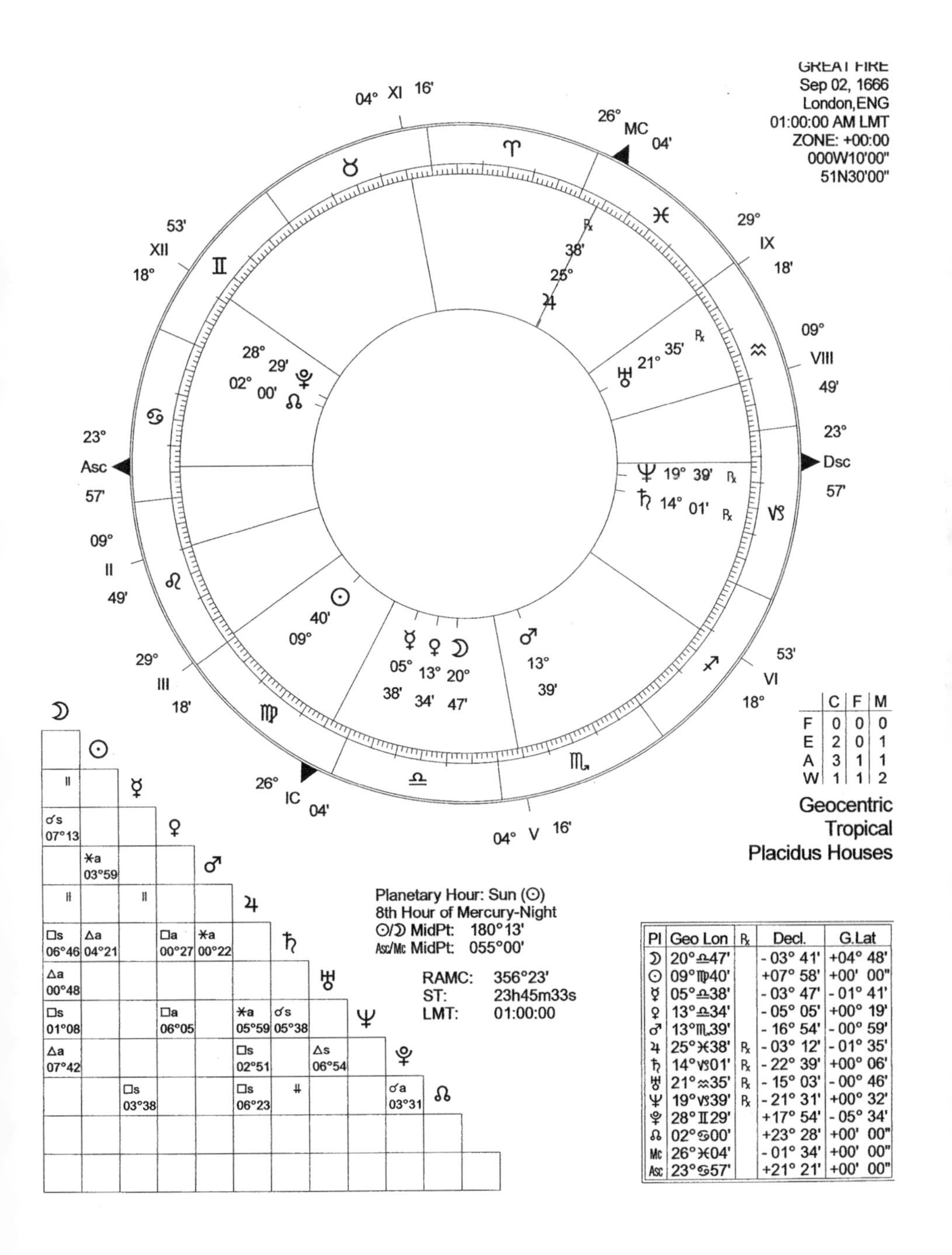

	C	F	M
F	0	0	0
E	2	0	1
A	3	1	1
W	1	1	2

	☽	☉	☿	♀	♂	♃	♄	♅	♆	♇	☊
☉											
☿	∥										
♀	☌s 07°13										
♂		⚹a 03°59									
♃	∥		∥								
♄	□s 06°46	△a 04°21		□a 00°27	⚹a 00°22						
♅	△a 00°48										
♆	□s 01°08			□a 06°05		⚹a 05°59	☌s 05°38				
♇	△a 07°42					□s 02°51		△s 06°54			
☊			□s 03°38			□s 06°23	⋕			☌a 03°31	

Pl	Geo Lon	℞	Decl.	G.Lat
☽	20°♎47'		- 03° 41'	+04° 48'
☉	09°♍40'		+07° 58'	+00' 00"
☿	05°♎38'		- 03° 47'	- 01° 41'
♀	13°♎34'		- 05° 05'	+00° 19'
♂	13°♏39'		- 16° 54'	- 00° 59'
♃	25°♓38'	℞	- 03° 12'	- 01° 35'
♄	14°♑01'	℞	- 22° 39'	+00° 06'
♅	21°♒35'	℞	- 15° 03'	- 00° 46'
♆	19°♑39'	℞	- 21° 31'	+00° 32'
♇	28°♊29'		+17° 54'	- 05° 34'
☊	02°♋00'		+23° 28'	+00' 00"
Mc	26°♓04'		- 01° 34'	+00' 00"
Asc	23°♋57'		+21° 21'	+00' 00"

At the immediate time that this verse was published, many skeptics thought its author was mad. However, in the summer of 1559, all but the most ardent skeptics changed their minds as Nostradamus' peculiar verse took on new life on a jousting field outside Paris. On Wednesday June 28, 1559, Henry II of France took place in a jousting match. It was a single combat that took place as part of a three-day tournament that was being held in honor of the joint betrothals of the king's sister Elizabeth and his daughter Marguerite to, respectively, Philip II of Spain and the Duke of Savoy. On the third day of the tournament, the King jousted with the 33-year-old commander of his Scottish guards, a man known as Coryes, or more commonly, Montgomery. The king used a lion as his personal emblem although, for him to do so was not in accordance with the laws of heraldry. The comander bore a Norman name and seems to have been born in France but his ancestors were reputed to have been natives of Scotland, a country of which the heraldic symbol was (and still is) a lion rampant. Montgomery's lance splintered, one portion inflicted a slight wound in the King's throat, while the main part of the head of the lance slipped through the golden bars of the cage-like visor that covered the King's face and entered one of his eyes. The monarch's eye became brutally infected and at least a part of the lance penetrated his brain. After 10 days of overwhelming pain and suffering, the King's agonized screams were ended by a merciful death.[2]

Was Nostradamus' most famous prediction revealed to him through a ***temporal window?*** If we again apply the principle which we explored with the Great Fire example the answer may be a resounding yes! The death of a King and its ensuing chaos would certainly qualify as a large-scale event that affects vast numbers of people. However, a prescient viewing of intricate details of the event four years prior to its occurrence would take some talent and ingenuity indeed! The chances of precognitively viewing this event would be greatly enhanced by the presence of a strong paranormal signal which would effectively mark its presence in space-time as a significant event. According to my research, such a signal definitely existed on that day in 1559.

No less than seven Delphi level mystical marker were in aspect over Paris on June 28, 1559. They were the Saturn Mars opposition, Jupiter Mercury trine, Sun Pluto trine, Mercury Venus parallel, Saturn Neptune parallel, Neptune Mercury parallel, and the Mercury Uranus contraparallel. Two additional non-delphi markers were also present: The Sun Pluto contraparallel and an extreme declination enhancement of Mars! The total mystical potential for that date was 195 marking it clearly as a delphi level event! A delphi level signal is the largest paranormal signal in existence and the higher the score, the larger the signal. I believe that through some technique still unknown to modern scholars, Nostradamus was able to scry the future in search of strong paranormal signals and their associated events. Perhaps he gleaned the technique from his studies of the occult or through contact with Arab mystics during his wanderings. In any case, I believe that the presence of such a strong association of delphi markers with a famous prediction made by a world-class see is powerful evidence that temporal windows might well be a reality.

The temporal window for the initial shots of the First World War should be a large delphi level aperture if indeed the theory of space- time dilation around important events is to hold any credence. Around AD 346 one of the most extraordinary books of prophecy, the Liber Vaticinationem Quodam Instinctumentis, was born. Written by an unknown scholar, it is the only known prophetic book to provide exact dates. This provides chillingly exact dates and descriptions of the assassination of Archduke Ferdinand on June 28, 1914. The main text is written in Latin and the manuscript divides history into a series of overlapping periods. Each of these periods is called a norma, Latin for a "rule, precept, model, or pattern." The normae cover fixed periods or windows of time, usually 60 or 144 years, and the prophecies allocated to them are exceptionally precise. This book was rigorously suppressed by theVatican, and appears to have only survived in one or two manuscript copies. One copy found its way into the huge collection of esoteric books and manuscripts amassed by the Nazis during World War II, and was stored in a warehouse in Poznan in Poland. Norma 63:5 reads:

> "*For the first a noble is twice attacked*
> *In the streets of Illyria and dies.*
> *The wolf lifts up its eyes to the moon,*
> *And the Eastern Empire loses its head.*"

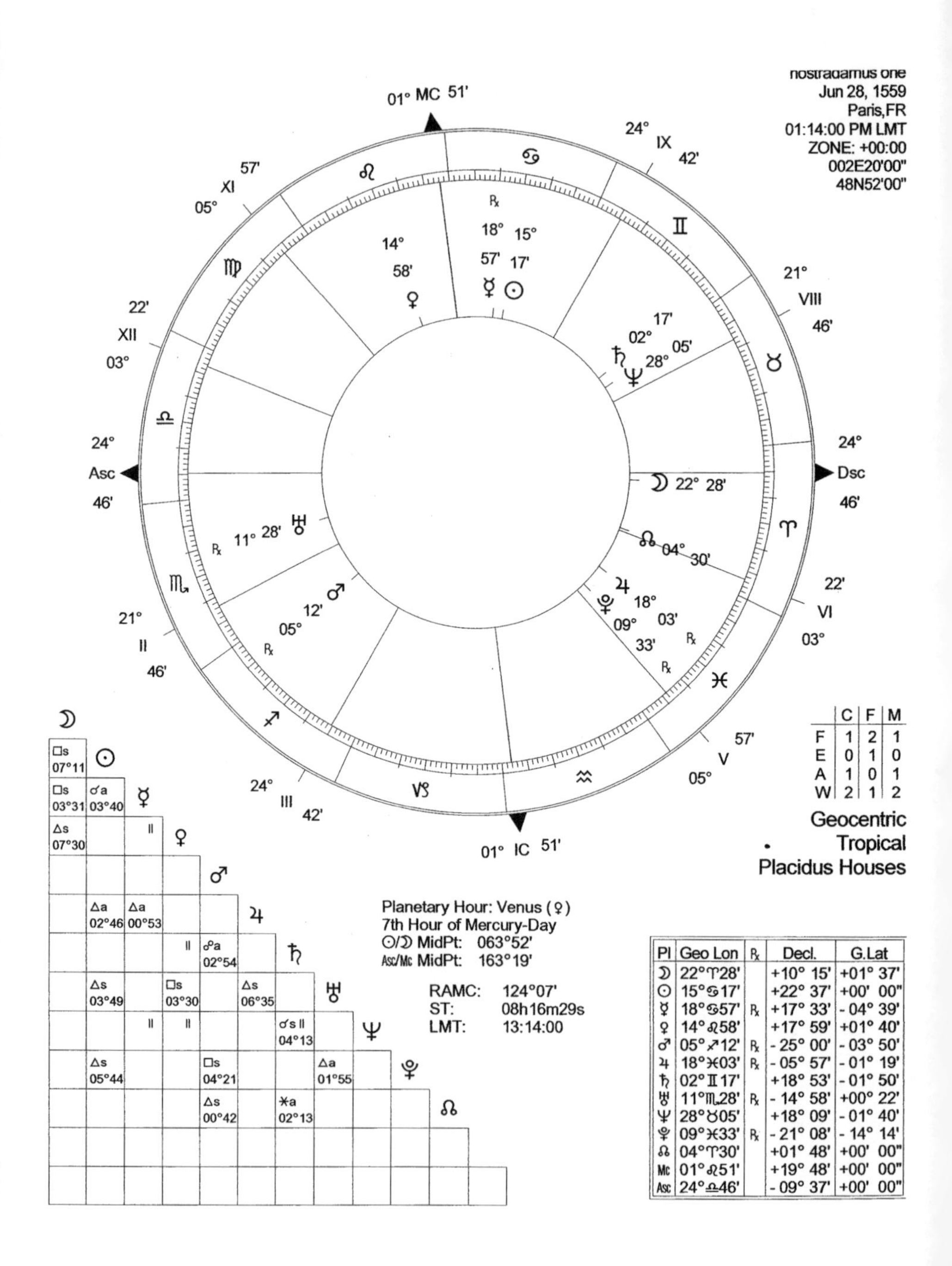

Pl	Geo Lon	℞	Decl.	G.Lat
☽	22°♈28'		+10° 15'	+01° 37'
☉	15°♋17'		+22° 37'	+00' 00"
☿	18°♋57'	℞	+17° 33'	- 04° 39'
♀	14°♌58'		+17° 59'	+01° 40'
♂	05°♐12'	℞	- 25° 00'	- 03° 50'
♃	18°♓03'	℞	- 05° 57'	- 01° 19'
♄	02°♊17'		+18° 53'	- 01° 50'
♅	11°♏28'	℞	- 14° 58'	+00° 22'
♆	28°♉05'		+18° 09'	- 01° 40'
♇	09°♓33'	℞	- 21° 08'	- 14° 14'
☊	04°♈30'		+01° 48'	+00' 00"
Mc	01°♌51'		+19° 48'	+00' 00"
Asc	24°♎46'		- 09° 37'	+00' 00"

The Austrian Archduke Ferdinand was twice attacked on June 28, 1914. There were two separate attempts to kill Ferdinand on that day. The wolf refers to Germany and the moon refers to refers to the crescent moon of Islam and Germany's coming alliance with Turkey. Russia (the Eastern empire) was drawn into the war and in 1917 deposed its Tsar ("loses its head"). This remarkable book gives exact dates for all of the above events! It further explains that certain events open the door (window?!) for other events and indeed makes their occurrence more likely. Nostradamus also predicted this event with similar accuracy. Does this event have a delphi level paranormal signal. The answer is a resounding yes! The mystical score for June 28, 1914 Sarajevo is 215, a Delphi level score of the highest order!

THE ASSASSINATION OF ARCHDUKE FERDINAND-MYSTICAL MARKERS

Jupiter Saturn trine, Sun Moon sextile, Saturn Neptune parallel, Sun Saturn parallel, Neptune Mercury parallel, Mercury Venus parallel, Neptune Pluto parallel, Mercury Uranus contraparallel, Mercury Neptune eclipse, Mars eclipse, +grand elevation of Mercury.

Thus far, my theory regarding temporal spatial windows seems to have passed its first few tests when applied to the preceding events. Let us now examine a variety of different types of large scale events which were foreseen by psychics and check their natal paranormal scores. All of the events that I present are actual events.

Tecumseh was one of the greatest Native American chiefs of all time. He was also widely respected as a medicine man and shaman who could make prediction regarding space-time that defied all rational thinking. Twenty years before the event, he predicted that a great earthquake would strike the New Madrid area of Missouri and that its power would cause the animals to leave their homes and the very earth itself to open up. He also gave a date for the coming conflagration, December 16,1811. On that date in 1811, the largest earthquake in North American history struck New Madrid. Fortunately, the area was not heavily populated and the loss of life was small in comparison to what might have been if such a quake were to strike the area today. Curiously, several days prior to the quake, scores of animals were seen leaving the forests. A number were noted to have drowned in the Missouri river in their haste to vacate the area, exactly as Tecumseh foretold. The paranormal score for this date was 200 once again Delphi range.

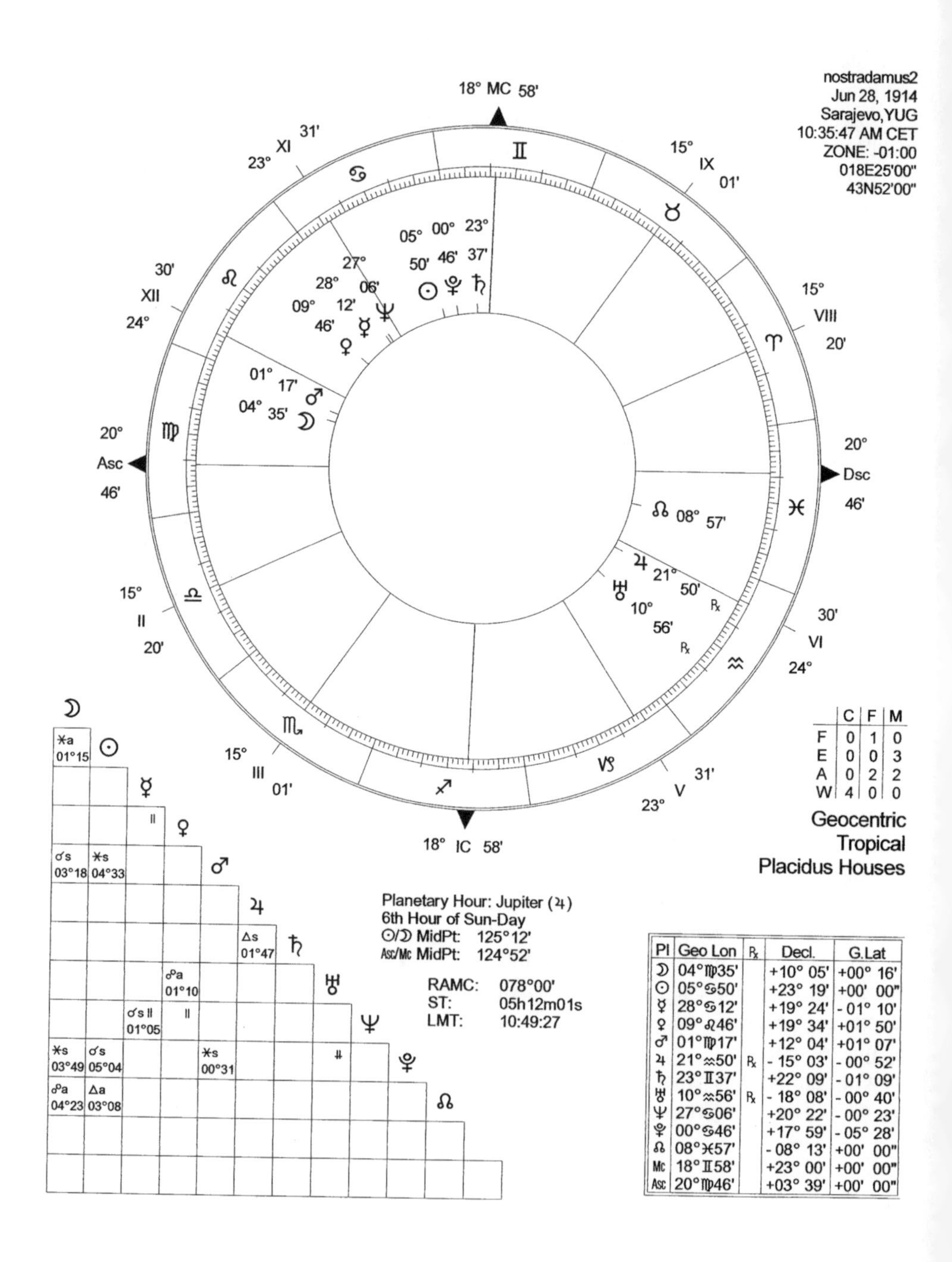

	C	F	M
F	0	1	0
E	0	0	3
A	0	2	2
W	4	0	0

Pl	Geo Lon	℞	Decl.	G.Lat
☽	04°♍35'		+10° 05'	+00° 16'
☉	05°♋50'		+23° 19'	+00' 00"
☿	28°♋12'		+19° 24'	- 01° 10'
♀	09°♌46'		+19° 34'	+01° 50'
♂	01°♍17'		+12° 04'	+01° 07'
♃	21°♒50'	℞	- 15° 03'	- 00° 52'
♄	23°♊37'		+22° 09'	- 01° 09'
♅	10°♒56'	℞	- 18° 08'	- 00° 40'
♆	27°♋06'		+20° 22'	- 00° 23'
♇	00°♋46'		+17° 59'	- 05° 28'
☊	08°♓57'		- 08° 13'	+00' 00"
Mc	18°♊58'		+23° 00'	+00' 00"
Asc	20°♍46'		+03° 39'	+00' 00"

NEW MADRID EARTHQUAKE-MYSTICAL MARKERS

Moon Venus conjunction, Sun Mars sextile, Pluto Moon parallel, Pluto Uranus parallel, Sun Mercury parallel, Mercury Venus parallel, Saturn Neptune parallel, Jupiter Saturn contraparallel, Jupiter Saturn contraparallel, Jupiter Mercury contraparallel, Jupiter Neptune contraparallel, Sun Jupiter contraparallel, Venus exdek, -grand elevation of the Sun, -grand elevation of Neptune.

Remember that less than 2% of all dates tested are likely to have a delphi level potential score and the fact that a very high percentage of exceptionally meaningful dates have this level of potential is astounding! Did Tecumseh peer through a temporal window and foresee this great earthquake? According to our theory, this fact appears likely. I believe that the high number of delphi markers which were in aspect on that day further aided Tecumseh's prescient viewing of this disaster.

One of the most famous predictions of all time also concerns one of the most profoundly disturbing American tragedies of modern times. On a drizzly morning at St. Matthew's Cathedral in Washington D.C., Jeanne Dixon stood reverently before the statue of the Virgin Mary. She then experienced something that was to haunt her for more than ten years. In her own words she stated:, "Suddenly the White House appeared before me in dazzling brightness. Coming out of the haze, the numerals 1-9-6-0 formed above the roof. An ominous dark cloud appeared, covering the numbers, and dripped slowly onto the White House. Then I looked down and saw a young man, tall and blue-eyed, crowned with a shock of thick brown hair, quietly standing in front of the main door.

I was still staring at him when a voice came of nowhere, telling me softly that this young man, a Democrat, to be seated as President in 1960, would be assassinated while in office. The vision faded into the wall-into the distance as softly as it had come, but it stayed with me until that day in Dallas when it was fulfilled." That day in Dallas came 11 years later with the assassination of President John F. Kennedy. Ironically, his funeral mass was said in the very church in which Jeanne Dixon had had her vision.[3]

This vision was reported worldwide in scores of newspapers and magazines and it probably was one of Dixon's most precise and accurate premonitions. Dixon was a very devoutly religious woman and this vision in particular fits remarkably well into a chilling description of a mystical experience. Did Jeanne Dixon experience a momentary opening of a temporal window into the future during a moment of religious contemplation? When one examines the date of November 22, 1963 using modern astrology, one finds that there were no less than six delphi markers for a profound mystical experience in aspect over Dallas! In addition, there were four non-delphi mystical markers in aspect over Dallas at that time. The total mystical potential for the assassination of John F. Kennedy on November 22, 1963 in Dallas was 165, a score that places the mystical potential of that date clearly in the outstanding range. Indeed, hundreds of mystics and psychics predicted John Kennedy's assassination. Is it sheer coincidence that this event occurred on a date that

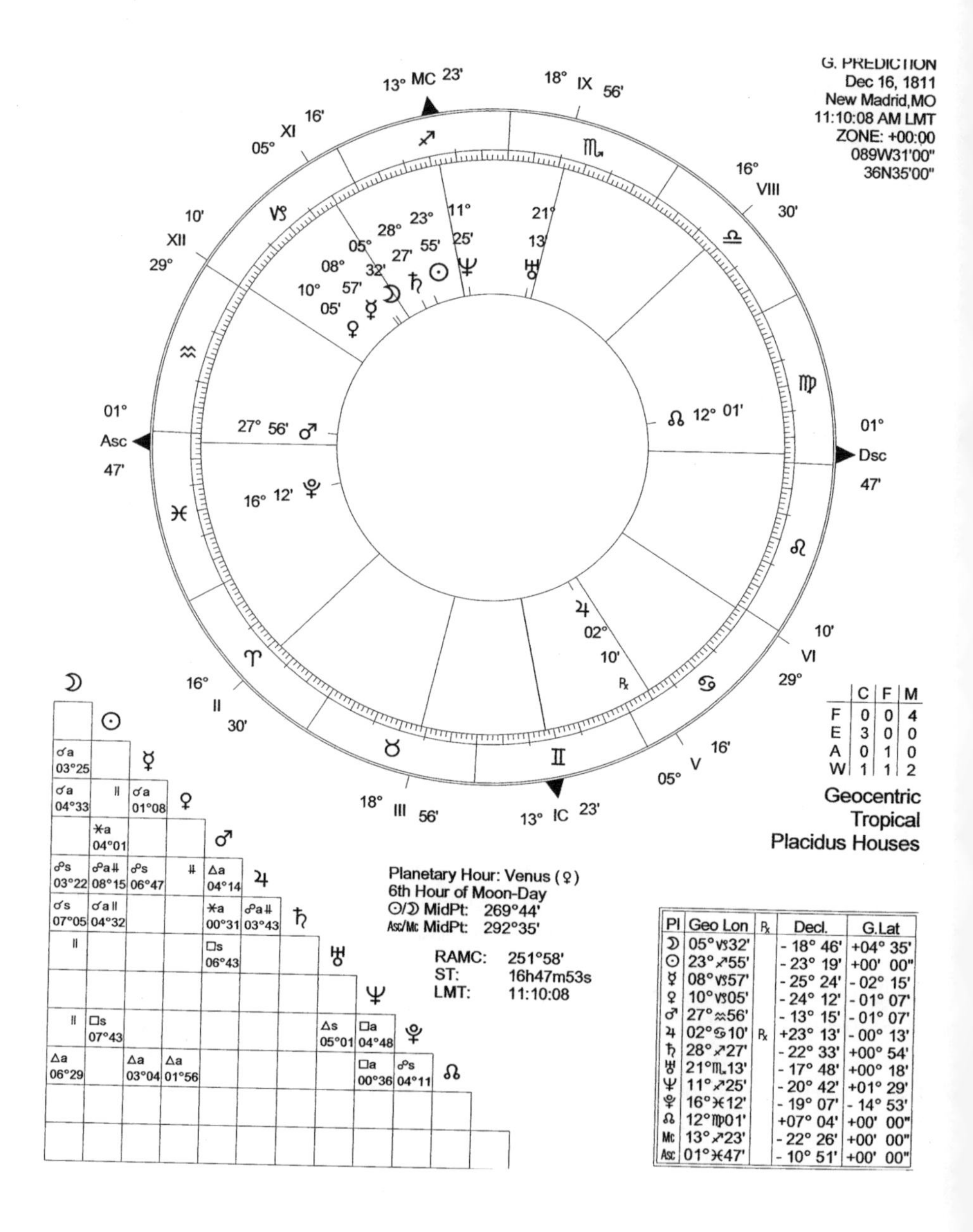

	C	F	M
F	0	0	4
E	3	0	0
A	0	1	0
W	1	1	2

Pl	Geo Lon	℞	Decl.	G.Lat
☽	05°♑32'		- 18° 46'	+04° 35'
☉	23°♐55'		- 23° 19'	+00' 00"
☿	08°♑57'		- 25° 24'	- 02° 15'
♀	10°♑05'		- 24° 12'	- 01° 07'
♂	27°♒56'		- 13° 15'	- 01° 07'
♃	02°♋10'	℞	+23° 13'	- 00° 13'
♄	28°♐27'		- 22° 33'	+00° 54'
♅	21°♏13'		- 17° 48'	+00° 18'
♆	11°♐25'		- 20° 42'	+01° 29'
♇	16°♓12'		- 19° 07'	- 14° 53'
☊	12°♍01'		+07° 04'	+00' 00"
Mc	13°♐23'		- 22° 26'	+00' 00"
Asc	01°♓47'		- 10° 51'	+00' 00"

holds outstanding mystical potential and that it was prophesied with startling accuracy by one of America's most talented seers? I don't think so.

Kennedy Assassination-
Mystical Potential Score for Dallas Texas:
November 22, 1963

Jupiter Mercury trine, Saturn Neptune square, Saturn Venus sextile, Mercury Venus parallel, Saturn Neptune parallel, Sun Pluto contraparallel, Hidek Mercury, Exdek Mars, Mars Venus eclipse, Venus eclipse.

During the three weeks over Christmas 1996, 450,000 people went to view the wall of a black glass building in south Florida where a two story high image of the Virgin Mary had appeared. The rainbow-colored image on the outside of the Seminole Finance building in Clearwater, Florida is about 50 feet wide and 35 feet tall, and stretches across nine panes of glass. According to police spokesman Wayne Shelor, "People are making shrines, bringing gifts, candles, flowers, and statues. The sick, the disabled and the curious came in droves. They were coming 500 at a time but it was not a carnival atmosphere." Later, the rainbow-colored image recovered from an attack by vandals. In June 1997 someone threw an unknown liquid on the shape, staining it. But following two days of heavy thunderstorms, the blemishes disappeared, and the image looked again as it did in December. When we calculate the paranormal potential for this time period, especially for the period that encompassed the height of the phenomenon, we again find a near Delphi score of 175.

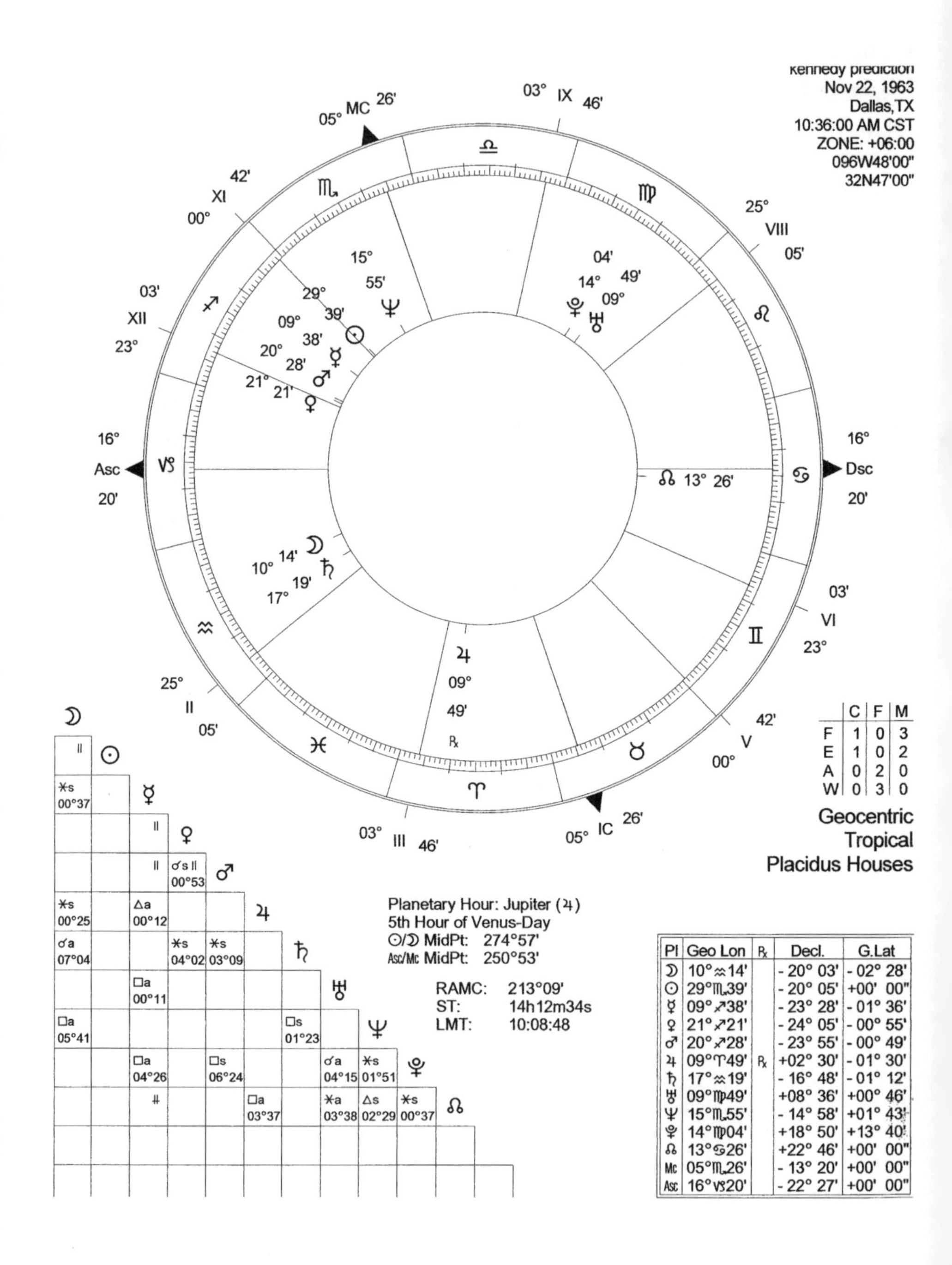
Kennedy prediction
Nov 22, 1963
Dallas,TX
10:36:00 AM CST
ZONE: +06:00
096W48'00"
32N47'00"
05° MC 26'
03° IX 46'
00° XI 42'
25° VIII 05'
23° XII 03'
16° Asc 20'
16° Dsc 20'
23° VI 03'
25° II 05'
00° V 42'
03° III 46'
05° IC 26'
☊ 13° 26'
Geocentric
Tropical
Placidus Houses
C F M
F 1 0 3
E 1 0 2
A 0 2 0
W 0 3 0
Planetary Hour: Jupiter (♃)
5th Hour of Venus-Day
☉/☽ MidPt: 274°57'
Asc/Mc MidPt: 250°53'
RAMC: 213°09'
ST: 14h12m34s
LMT: 10:08:48
Pl Geo Lon ℞ Decl. G.Lat
☽ 10°♒14' -20° 03' -02° 28'
☉ 29°♏39' -20° 05' +00' 00"
☿ 09°♐38' -23° 28' -01° 36'
♀ 21°♐21' -24° 05' -00° 55'
♂ 20°♐28' -23° 55' -00° 49'
♃ 09°♈49' ℞ +02° 30' -01° 30'
♄ 17°♒19' -16° 48' -01° 12'
♅ 09°♍49' +08° 36' +00° 46'
♆ 15°♏55' -14° 58' +01° 43'
♇ 14°♍04' +18° 50' +13° 40'
☊ 13°♋26' +22° 46' +00' 00"
Mc 05°♏26' -13° 20' +00' 00"
Asc 16°♑20' -22° 27' +00' 00"

CLEARWATER FLORIDA
VIRGIN MARY SIGHTING

Dec. 26, 1996 Mystical Markers

Saturn Mars opposition, Uranus Mars trine, Mercury Venus parallel, Sun Mercury parallel, Neptune Mercury parallel, Saturn Mars contraparallel, hidek Venus, Sun Mercury eclipse, +grand elevation of Uranus, +grand elevation of Mercury.

On Thursday September 21, 1995, a phenomenal news story swept the world of an extraordinary miracle of milk-drinking Hindu statues. Never before in history has a simultaneous miracle occurred on a global scale. Television, radio and newspaper eagerly covered this unique phenomenon and even skeptical journalists held their milk-filled spoons to the gods and watched, humbled as the milk disappeared. The media coverage was extensive. Although scientists and experts created theories of "capillary absorption" and "mass hysteria," the overwhelming evidence and conclusion was that an unexplainable miracle had occurred.

It all began at dawn in a temple on the outskirts of Delhi, India when milk offered to a statue of Ganesh just vanished into thin air. Word spread so quickly throughout India that soon thousands were offering milk to the gods and watching in amazement as it disappeared. Life in India was brought to a virtual standstill as people rushed to temples to see for themselves the milk drinking gods. Traffic in Delhi was halted as police struggled to control crowds which gathered outside hundreds of temples with jugs and saucepans of milk for the marble statues of Ganesh, the Hindu God of Removing Obstacles. India was in pandemonium. The Government shut down for several hours, and trading ground to a halt on stock markets in Bombay and New Dehli as millions in homes and temples around the country offered milk to the gods. Very soon, the news spread to Hindu communities in Singapore, Hong Kong, Nepal, Thailand, Dubai, the United Kingdom, the USA, and Canada. Reports were flooding in from all over the world. In the United Kingdom, Hindus reported miracles taking place in temples and homes around the country. At the Vishwa Temple in Southall, London, 10,000 people in 24 hours witnessed the 40cm high statue of the bull Nandi and a bronze statue of the cobra Shash Naag drinking milk from cups and spoons.

This phenomenon is a striking example of an outstanding supernatural event with an associated high paranormal score. When I checked the potential scores for the various cities that were affected by this event, they ranged from 165-205, clearly placing them in the outstanding to delphi level of potential. Once again we see an association between a large temporal window and a powerful paranormal event.

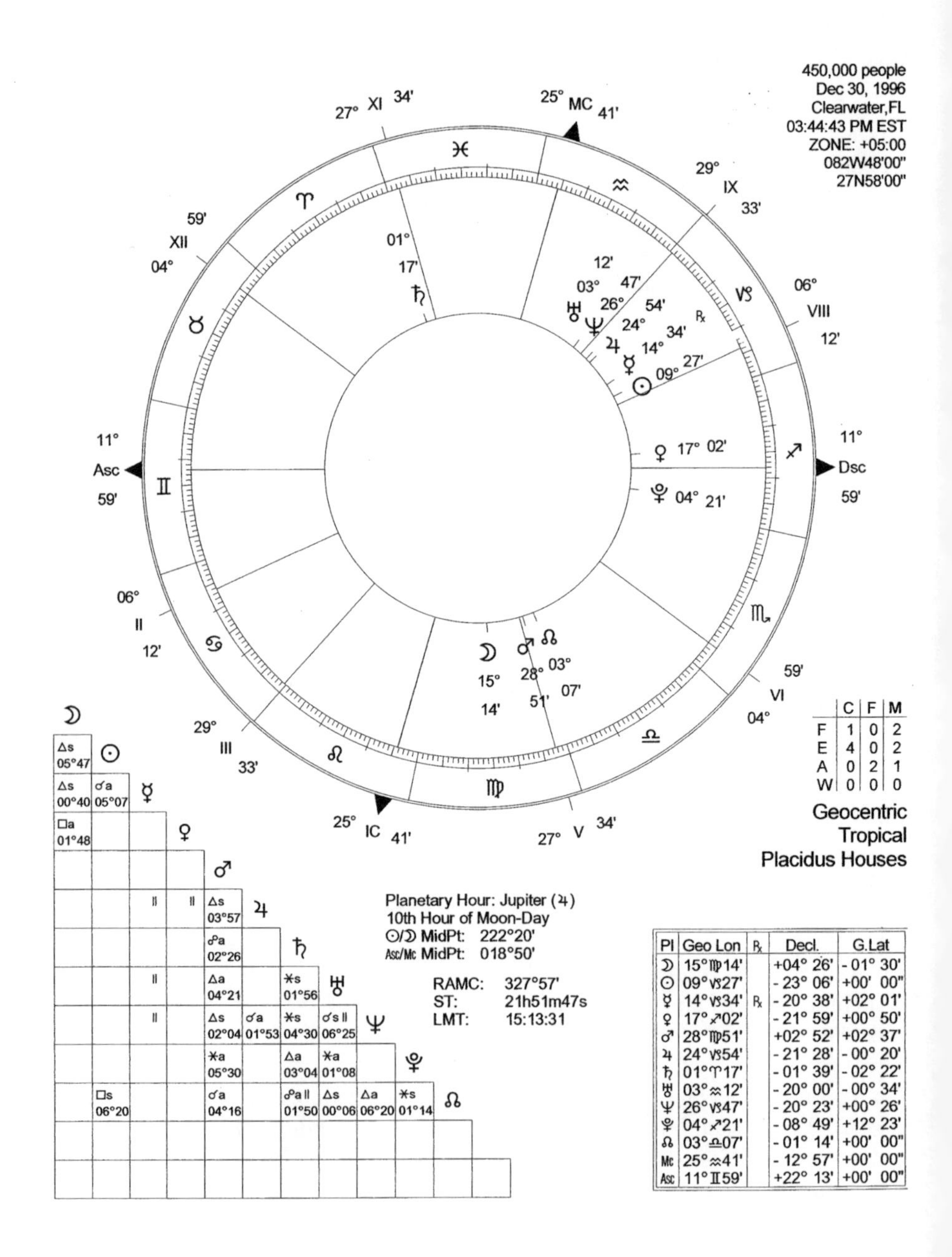
450,000 people
Dec 30, 1996
Clearwater,FL
03:44:43 PM EST
ZONE: +05:00
082W48'00"
27N58'00"
Asc 11° 59'
Dsc 11° 59'
MC 25° 41'
IC 25° 41'
Planetary Hour: Jupiter (♃)
10th Hour of Moon-Day
☉/☽ MidPt: 222°20'
Asc/Mc MidPt: 018°50'
RAMC: 327°57'
ST: 21h51m47s
LMT: 15:13:31
Geocentric
Tropical
Placidus Houses
C F M
F 1 0 2
E 4 0 2
A 0 2 1
W 0 0 0
Pl Geo Lon ℞ Decl. G.Lat
☽ 15°♍14' +04° 26' -01° 30'
☉ 09°♑27' -23° 06' +00' 00"
☿ 14°♑34' ℞ -20° 38' +02° 01'
♀ 17°♐02' -21° 59' +00° 50'
♂ 28°♍51' +02° 52' +02° 37'
♃ 24°♑54' -21° 28' -00° 20'
♄ 01°♈17' -01° 39' -02° 22'
♅ 03°♒12' -20° 00' -00° 34'
♆ 26°♑47' -20° 23' +00° 26'
♇ 04°♐21' -08° 49' +12° 23'
☊ 03°♎07' -01° 14' +00' 00"
Mc 25°♒41' -12° 57' +00' 00"
Asc 11°♊59' +22° 13' +00' 00"

WORLDWIDE HINDU MIRACLE-MYSTICAL MARKERS—190

DELHI, INDIA—9/21/1995———11:57AM

Sun Venus conjunction, Sun Saturn opposition, Jupiter Venus sextile, Moon Mercury contraparallel, Sun Venus parallel, Sun eclipse, Sun Venus eclipse, Venus eclipse, +grand elevation of the planet Uranus.

On the morning of Tuesday July 11, 1977, a small man with white hair and twinkling eyes turned up at the offices of the Seattle Post-Intelligencer. He offered to predict Thursday's headline, an offer no newspaper editor could surely resist. He gave his name only as Roge. He was 52 years old and he stated that he was an ex-newsman from Salinas, California who had come to town to attend a conference. He sealed his prediction in five envelopes. When Editor Stephen Green opened the envelopes on that Thursday morning, in Roge's presence, he found written "Massive Power Blackout hits New York City Area." Incredibly, this was exactly the same as the headline which appeared on the front page of the July 13, 1977 headline! Did Roge peer thru a temporal window which revealed to him in advance the startling revelation that he gave to Green on Tuesday! This case was documented by the Editor and published in ***Fortean Times*** magazine. Not surprisingly, the paranormal potential for that day was well into the superior range 120! Once again, we see that on the day a great prophecy was fulfilled, a large temporal window with its accompanying high paranormal score was manifest.

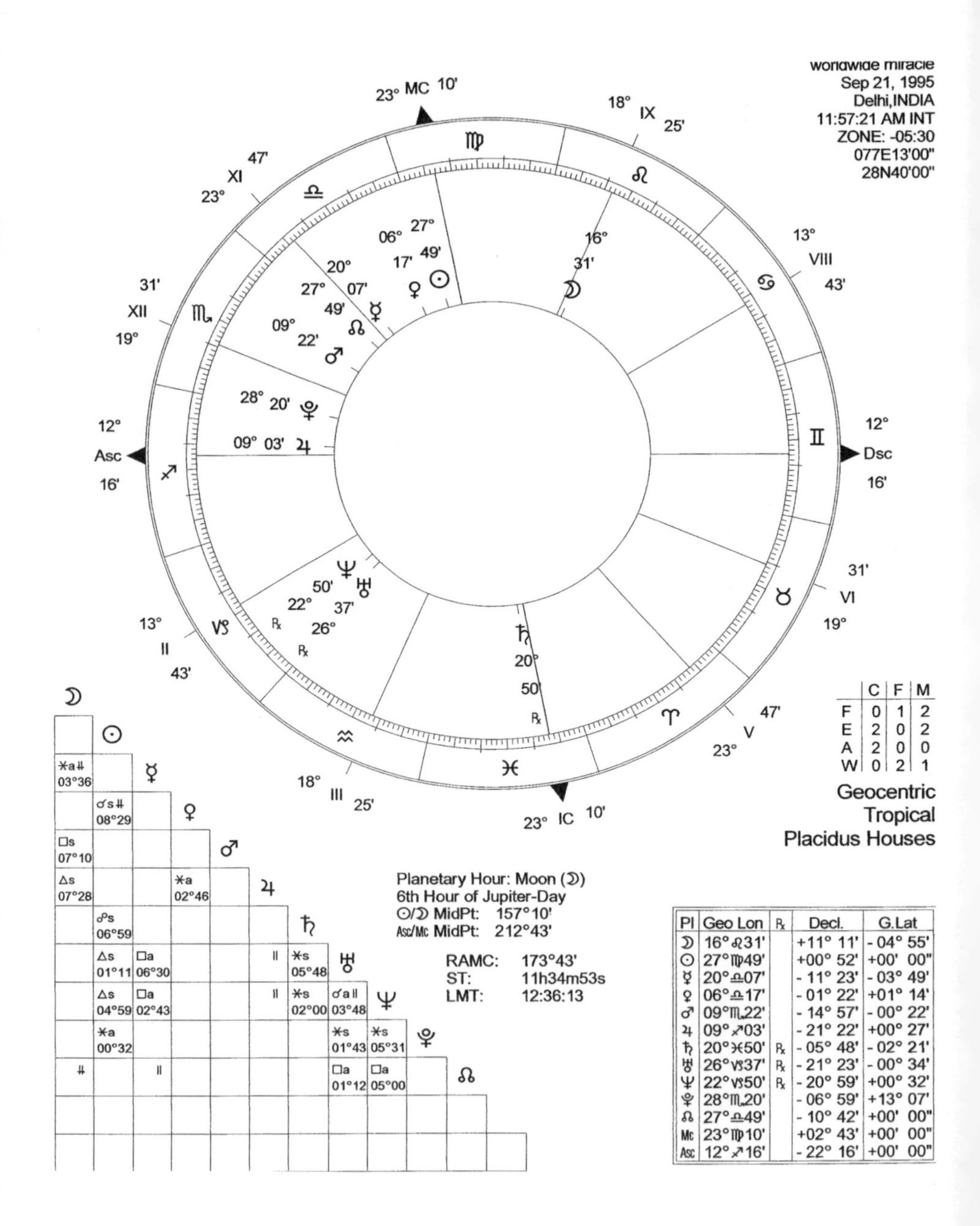
worldwide miracle
Sep 21, 1995
Delhi,INDIA
11:57:21 AM INT
ZONE: -05:30
077E13'00"
28N40'00"
Geocentric
Tropical
Placidus Houses
Planetary Hour: Moon (☽)
6th Hour of Jupiter-Day
☉/☽ MidPt: 157°10'
Asc/Mc MidPt: 212°43'
RAMC: 173°43'
ST: 11h34m53s
LMT: 12:36:13
Pl | Geo Lon | Rx | Decl. | G.Lat
☽ | 16°♌31' | | +11° 11' | - 04° 55'
☉ | 27°♍49' | | +00° 52' | +00' 00"
☿ | 20°♎07' | | - 11° 23' | - 03° 49'
♀ | 06°♎17' | | - 01° 22' | +01° 14'
♂ | 09°♏22' | | - 14° 57' | - 00° 22'
♃ | 09°♐03' | | - 21° 22' | +00° 27'
♄ | 20°♓50' | Rx | - 05° 48' | - 02° 21'
♅ | 26°♑37' | Rx | - 21° 23' | - 00° 34'
♆ | 22°♑50' | Rx | - 20° 59' | +00° 32'
♇ | 28°♏20' | | - 06° 59' | +13° 07'
☊ | 27°♎49' | | - 10° 42' | +00' 00"
Mc | 23°♍10' | | +02° 43' | +00' 00"
Asc | 12°♐16' | | - 22° 16' | +00' 00"
C F M
F 0 1 2
E 2 0 2
A 2 0 0
W 0 2 1

NEW YORK CITY BLACKOUT-
PSYCHIC MARKERS—120

Jupiter Moon conjunction, Mercury Venus sextile, Sun Mars sextile, Moon Venus parallel, Moon Mercury parallel, Mercury Mars parallel, Sun Mercury parallel, Mercury Venus parallel, +grand elevation of Mercury.

A very similar story occurred on March 20, 1977 when 18 year old Duke University student Lee Fried wrote some predictions on a card, put them in a wax-sealed envelope, and had it locked in the office of university president Terry Sanford. On March 28th, with live television coverage, the envelope was opened. Here is how Lee shaped up: Boeing 747s crash, 583 dead. (On March 27, 2 Boeings crashed at Tenerife. The Guinness Book of Records gives the death toll at 582!) He predicted that North Carolina University would lose the championship basketball game to Marquette, 68-58. The actual score was 67-59! How had he been so accurate about events one week into the future?! The temporal window for March 27, 1977 was in the superior range and Lee was well known for his prowess as a clairvoyant. Did he too see the future through this temporal aperture? An explanation that uses coincidence or chance as its foundation beginsto flounder under the weight of the evidence to the contrary.

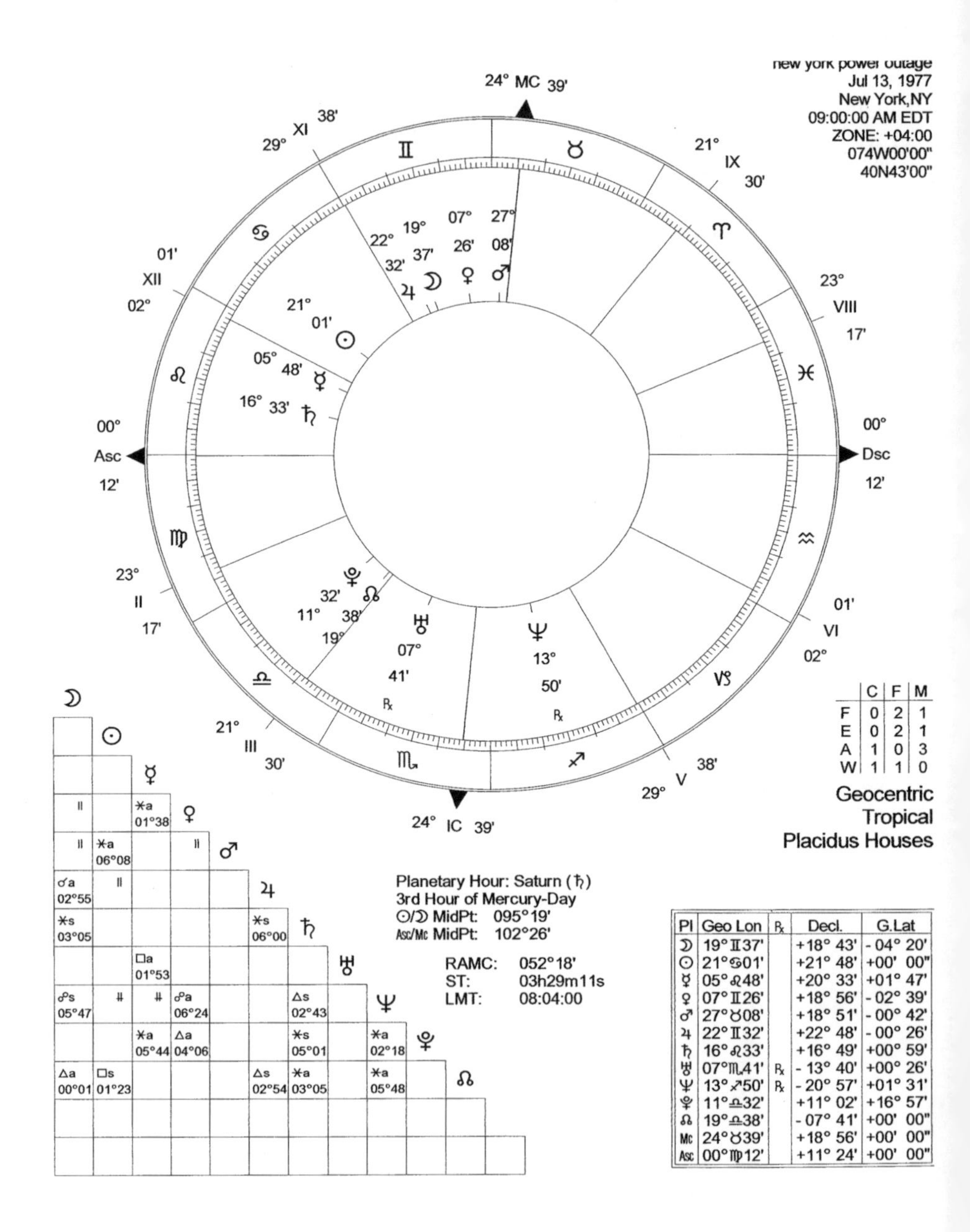

	C	F	M
F	0	2	1
E	0	2	1
A	1	0	3
W	1	1	0

Pl	Geo Lon	℞	Decl.	G.Lat
☽	19°♊37'		+18° 43'	- 04° 20'
☉	21°♋01'		+21° 48'	+00' 00"
☿	05°♌48'		+20° 33'	+01° 47'
♀	07°♊26'		+18° 56'	- 02° 39'
♂	27°♉08'		+18° 51'	- 00° 42'
♃	22°♊32'		+22° 48'	- 00° 26'
♄	16°♌33'		+16° 49'	+00° 59'
♅	07°♏41'	℞	- 13° 40'	+00° 26'
♆	13°♐50'	℞	- 20° 57'	+01° 31'
♇	11°♎32'		+11° 02'	+16° 57'
☊	19°♎38'		- 07° 41'	+00' 00"
Mc	24°♉39'		+18° 56'	+00' 00"
Asc	00°♍12'		+11° 24'	+00' 00"

TENERIFE SPAIN AIR CRASH PSYCHIC MARKERS

March 27,1977

Saturn Pluto sextile, Pluto Moon square, Moon Venus parallel, Jupiter Moon parallel, Jupiter Saturn parallel, Jupiter Neptune contraparallel, Pluto Mars contraparallel Total Score-100 superior range......

The last example of a great spiritual event that took place on a date with a high paranormal score is perhaps one of the most famous miracles of all time. On February 11, 1858, a young girl named Bernadette Soubourios experienced a vision of the Virgin Mary at a small grotto in the town of Lourdes, France. The Mother blessed the water of grotto and said that it was to become the home of a great healing temple. Since that time, millions of seekers have made the pilgrimage to Lourdes and its healing waters have evoked cures of many types for over one hundred years. The Vatican has ratified many of these cures as genuine and authentic examples of miracles! This day illustrates two of the principles which I discovered in this research. On February 11,1858, the mystical potential of Lourdes was 160, clearly placing it in the outstanding range for the development of paranormal events. Bernadette Soubourious, the young girl who was led to the grotto by the Mother, was born on a date which gave her a mystical potential of 245- Delphi range! Her complete biography and natal data are included in the chapter on Mystics.

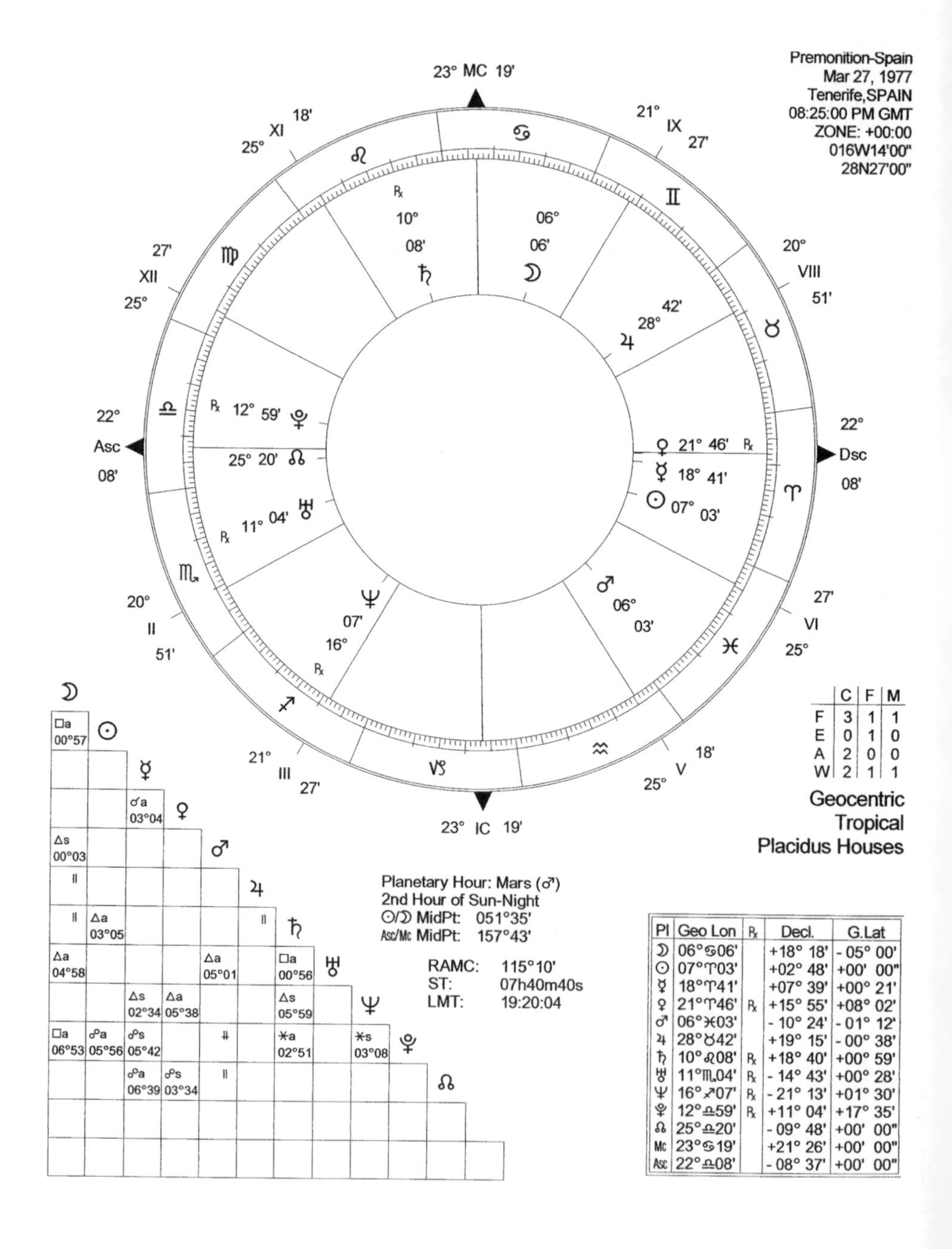

	C	F	M
F	3	1	1
E	0	1	0
A	2	0	0
W	2	1	1

Pl	Geo Lon	℞	Decl.	G.Lat
☽	06°♋06'		+18° 18'	- 05° 00'
☉	07°♈03'		+02° 48'	+00' 00"
☿	18°♈41'		+07° 39'	+00° 21'
♀	21°♈46'	℞	+15° 55'	+08° 02'
♂	06°♓03'		- 10° 24'	- 01° 12'
♃	28°♉42'		+19° 15'	- 00° 38'
♄	10°♌08'	℞	+18° 40'	+00° 59'
♅	11°♏04'	℞	- 14° 43'	+00° 28'
♆	16°♐07'	℞	- 21° 13'	+01° 30'
♇	12°♎59'	℞	+11° 04'	+17° 35'
☊	25°♎20'		- 09° 48'	+00' 00"
Mc	23°♋19'		+21° 26'	+00' 00"
Asc	22°♎08'		- 08° 37'	+00' 00"

LOURDES FRANCE- 2/11/1858
MYSTICAL POTENTIAL (160)

Sun Venus conjunction, Saturn Neptune trine, Moon Neptune sextile, Neptune Pluto parallel, Moon exdek, Sun Venus eclipse, Venus eclipse, Sun eclipse, Mercury Uranus contraparallel, +grand elevation of Uranus.

Thus far we have seen ten examples of the extraordinary pairing of dates which manifest high astrological paranormal potential matched with equally extraordinary paranormal events. In my research, I have documented hundreds of these pairings. If temporal windows can be opened clairvoyantly and used to predict events that have yet to manifest in the present time stream, would it be possible to duplicate this feat utilizing the laws of physics? As incredulous as it may sound, it is possible that one man was able to achieve just such a feat! Even more incredibly, the man was a priest!

In a February 1999 article, ***Fate*** magazine published a story reported by Austrian journalist Peter Krassa in his book *Das Schicksal is Vorherbestimmt (Your Fate is Predetermined)*. According to Krassa, Father Alfredo Pellegrino Ernetti, an Italian monk who lived on the island of San Giorgio in the Gulf of Venice from 1926 to 1996, developed a machine called the Chronovisor. Ernetti was the world's leading expert in the art of prepolyphony, an archaic music form composed from around 1400 B.C. to 1000 A.D., and for several years he occupied the Chair of Prepolyphony at the Conservatorio di Musico Benedetto Marcello on San Giorgio. Father Ernetti was consumed with an intensely passionate love for this artform and he became obsessed with the notion of finding out what the Roman opera, Thyestes sounded like when played on the original musical instruments of its time. Thyestes premiered in Rome in 169 B.C. This opera was of particular interest to Ernetti because its appearance had caused a furor in Rome among the upper classes who condemned it for its revolutionary ideas. The composer, Quintus Ennius Calaber, died shortly thereafter of mysterious causes. A few excerpts of his musical score survived and were mentioned in later decades by at least three poets of the ancient world. As unlikely as it may sound, according to Krassa, the Italian monk approached a number of eminent scientists with an unusual proposition:

Would they help him build a time machine that could access these audio-visual musical performances now lost in time?

Ernetti's theory was brilliant. He wanted to build a device which would tap into the energy fields that surround all life in the universe and which he believed also stored all knowledge of every event in time and space. Not only was Ernetti possessed of an incredible passion for his music, he also had a highly compelling and magnetic personality. He persuaded 12 scientists to help him develop and assemble his Chronovisor. According to Krassa, these scientists included Werner Von Braun and Enrico Fermi, two of the most famous and brilliant scientists in the world! The scientists contributed their expertise to the Chronovisor project from time to time from the 1950s through the 1990s. The prototype of the Chronovisor is said to have been completed by the 1970s.

News was leaked about the Chronovisor in 1972 and in a story in Rome's Domenica del Corriere, Ernetti explained that the Chronovisor could be used to extract information from any part of history. He explained that the sound of music naturally broke down in such a way that they became atom-like "particles" that were eventually bundled into a specific type of energy field. Retrieving the lost music he said, involved accessing the quanta of energy contained within these fields and gathering the atom-like particles. Then through a special process which he had discovered with the help of Von Braun and Fermi, he had actually learned to reassemble these particles into their original forms, much like recovering the data from an erased computer disk. However, Ernetti added that the reconstructions not only contained the audio information that he was looking for but the visual portion as well!

Ernetti and a number of other eminent scientists claimed that they had seen and heard events from the past in a series of successful experiments using the device. Baird T. Spaulding, an American scientist who claimed to have been present at several of these viewings, gave excited and vivid descriptions of the "telecasts" which he witnessed via the Chronovisor. He also reported the he watched a "live" performance of Thyestes from ancient Rome with Father Ernetti! Spaulding explained that the Chronovisor could be tuned into any place or time period that the inventors wanted to view and that they were busily gathering information about many of the most famous events in history. The Roman Catholic Church soon became aware of Father Ernetti's work and he was called to Rome for an audience. The Church took the position that it could not tolerate the existence of a device that might contradict its version of events from history and therefore weaken its power over parishioners. Krassa believes that the Vatican forbade Ernetti, on pain of ex-communication, to say no more, or to do more work with his machine. The Chronovisor was then disassembled into five pieces and scattered in caves around the island of San Giorgio. Krassa's attempts to track down any of the scientists who were allegedly involved with Ernetti have led to dead ends. The scientists have had nothing to say about the research or they have died mysteriously. Father Ernetti died mysteriously of unknown causes in 1996.

The amazing events of this story are true according to Krassa. If Father Ernetti's work led to the discovery of a method of viewing events across time and space, then he may have been the first person to have mechanized the process of manipulating temporal windows utilizing the laws of physics. It is somewhat of an odd testament to the theory that it would be validated by world-class scientists such as Von Braun and Fermi and a clergyman in the person of Father Ernetti. If the movements of time and space can be charted, as the work of the Ernetti group seems to imply, then astrology may be one tool through which these movements may be predicted. Unfortunately, the world has been denied access to the staggering potential of the Chronovisor. Perhaps one day, when more enlightened minds rule the outer world, major advances in science which threaten to shed new light on vistas of human experience, which are now shrouded in obscurity may once again be shared with the masses.

A very important project that resulted from my use of modern astrological techniques is the development of a software package entitled Signs 2.0. Among many of its advanced features, Signs 2.0 will enable the user to enter information regarding any date, time, or place and then generate a profile that details the paranormal potential of that astrological chart. In this way, the size of the temporal aperture which surrounds any time or place can be at least indirectly ascertained. This information would be very useful in any number of psychic and spiritual endeavors, in particular, the prediction of future events. When combined with the appropriate meditation and spiritual practices, this information would allow the average person to take advantage of the information contained within the silent movements of the stars which portend events yet unseen. Time, space, and the paranormal may well be linked in an as yet poorly understood primeval dance that those gifted with highly developed spiritual gifts may well have witnessed for countless centuries.

How does one explain the association of these marker aspects with the above events? What obscure principle could ostensibly be at work that would allow the physics of this reaction to take place? I have developed a theory that is in part based on new research findings in the field of quantum physics that may shed some light, so to speak, on this quandary. In the next chapter, I will explore in greater detail what I believe to be the mechanics of the formation of temporal mirrors.

---

[1] Sunrise Magazine, August/September 1998. "Fate or Free Will?", David Pratt; Theosophical University Press.)

[2] Death of a Lion; p. 16-17: Nostradamus- Prophecies Fulfilled and Predictions for the Millennium and Beyond. Francis X. King- St. Martins Press, 1994.

[3] The Moderns; p.130-131, The Supernatural: Signs of Things to Come; Angus Hall: The Danbury Press Aldus Books Limited. London 1975.

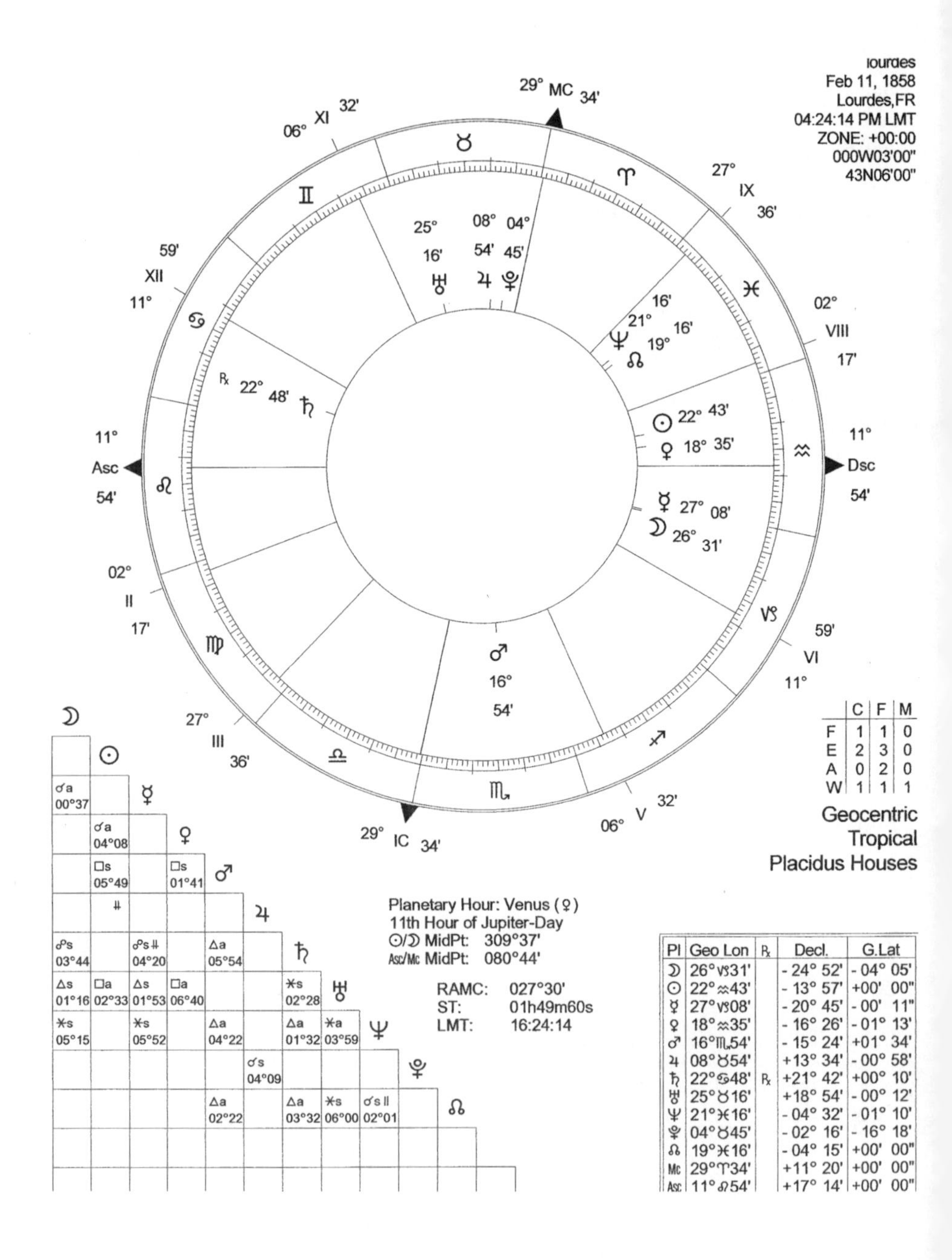

	☽	☉	☿	♀	♂	♃	♄	♅	♆	♇
☉										
☿	☌a 00°37									
♀		☌a 04°08								
♂		□s 05°49		□s 01°41						
♃		∥								
♄	☍s 03°44		☍s ∦ 04°20		△a 05°54					
♅	△s 01°16	□a 02°33	△s 01°53	□a 06°40			✶s 02°28			
♆	✶s 05°15		✶s 05°52		△a 04°22		△a 01°32	✶a 03°59		
♇						☌s 04°09				
☊					△a 02°22		△a 03°32	✶s 06°00	☌s ∥ 02°01	

	C	F	M
F	1	1	0
E	2	3	0
A	0	2	0
W	1	1	1

Pl	Geo Lon	℞	Decl.	G.Lat
☽	26°♑31'		- 24° 52'	- 04° 05'
☉	22°♒43'		- 13° 57'	+00' 00"
☿	27°♑08'		- 20° 45'	- 00' 11"
♀	18°♒35'		- 16° 26'	- 01° 13'
♂	16°♏54'		- 15° 24'	+01° 34'
♃	08°♉54'		+13° 34'	- 00° 58'
♄	22°♋48'	℞	+21° 42'	+00° 10'
♅	25°♉16'		+18° 54'	- 00° 12'
♆	21°♓16'		- 04° 32'	- 01° 10'
♇	04°♉45'		- 02° 16'	- 16° 18'
☊	19°♓16'		- 04° 15'	+00' 00"
Mc	29°♈34'		+11° 20'	+00' 00"
Asc	11°♌54'		+17° 14'	+00' 00"

TOWARD A GENERAL THEORY OF ASTROLOGY AND THE PARANORMAL

Mankind has for centuries attempted to discern the mysteries of the sky and the heavens in order to determine his place among the Creator's design. This design has eluded all but the greatest scientists and thinkers because we tend to view reality in terms that fit our desire for order. If this order is only implicit or arbitrary, how can the Creator reveal to us his true plan for our reality given our slavish ties to that which we so lovingly create. There are some aspects of the paranormal that are easily understood in terms of the new physics and holomorphic reality patterns. This new understanding is largely the work of the eminent scientist Rupert Sheldrake. How can we model a new understanding of the reality of the paranormal considering the miracles that we have witnessed throughout the course of history?

I believe that a combination of holomorphic patterning, temporal mirrors, and astrological marker activity may in part begin to explain the workings of the fabric of space and how it interacts with the microcosmic world. The art of prophecy allows us to witness the future consequences of choices that we make in the present. Echoing the beliefs of twentieth-century physicists, ancient prophets viewed time and the course of our history as a path that may be traveled in two directions, reverse as well as forward. They recognized that their visions merely portrayed possibilities for a given point in time, rather than events that would occur with certainty, and each possibility was based upon conditions present at the time of the prophecy. As conditions changed, the outcome of each prophecy would reflect that change. A prophet's vision of war, for example, could be viewed as a future to be expected only if the social, political, and military circumstances at the time of the prophecy were to continue unimpeded.

This then leaves us the tantalizing possibility that creation is already complete and that our movement within it is much like our decision making process in looking at movie or listening to a record. We can choose which selections we play, how long we listen, and under what circumstances. We can even choose to destroy the album or tape, but the recorded data is still trapped within the form and may be restored under the right circumstances. This implies that a higher implicate order controls the living of our lives and that our main function is the development and shaping of the indwelling divine will.

Prophetic insight into distant possibilities often reminds us of an analogy to parallel roads, paths of possibility that run into our future as well as our past. Occasionally, the courses of the roads appear to bend, bringing each path very close to its neighbor. It is at these points that ancient prophets believed the veils between the worlds became very thin. The thinner the veils, the easier it became to choose new courses for the future, by jumping from one point to the other. Herein lies the operative word, choice. By picking the operative points, everyday people can then intelligently determine the best path for their lives.

Modern scientists give careful consideration to such possibilities and they have even created names for the events themselves, as well as the places where the worlds are connected. Through the language of time waves, quantum outcomes, and choice points, prophecies such as those of Isaiah, Nostradamus, and Edgar Cayce take on powerful new meanings. Rather than being forecasts of events expected one day in our future, they are glimpses into the consequences of choices made in the present. Such descriptions often bring to mind the image of a great cosmic computer simulation that can intelligently allow us to view the consequences of our actions. Quantum principles allow for the possibility that time is the result of a collection of malleable and diverse outcomes determined by the choice of the observer rather than a fixed and predetermined force. Through years of research, I have isolated planetary marker aspect sets that reflect varying degrees of relative probability for an event rather than a degree of fixed certainty. A level of Delphi probability for an event would tend to give a higher rate of return for the prophet than a date giving only an average score. This is not to say that a day with an average score will always be completely bereft of a meaningful return on your prophetic investment, rather it implies that the universe tends to make choices which are dependent on a set of laws and principles that we are only now becoming scantly aware.

A psychic construct that I call a temporal mirror acts much like a choice point for the movement of time and space. When the planets align along certain marker patterns over time, a temporal mirror is formed and on the microcosmic scale, specific events and behaviors become more likely. Again these events are not completely fated or destined, just significantly more likely during the phase of the temporal mirror. This is a powerful observation in light of recent research. Since time may well travel forward and reverse, we may well have the ability to affect this flow consciously. Is it possible that our thoughts and actions may have some influence on the movement of the planets themselves! In other words, do our collective thoughts and actions direct the path that the stars and planets take thru the sky? Do we affect the direction of our own futures by thinking along certain predetermined lines and as a result, cause the stars to follow certain prepositied paths? How then may we use this knowledge to help us become better astrologers and prophets?

Astrology teaches that each planet is given a designated sphere of influence according to its nature. In reading a chart, we often refer to the planetary influences as a way of sorting the nature of the personality that we are examining. What if we reversed the process and allowed an individual personality to examine the nature of the heavens for clues to its nature? What if each pattern of planetary and stellar movement revealed a secret language which when deciphered correctly, revealed the hidden meaning of the path of an event or nativity?

In a working general theory of astrology and the paranormal, the unconscious thoughts and actions of collections of individuals create at some level the events that we call miraculous. Since our very thoughts and behaviors may at some level influence the movement of the heavens, these movements then are reflected back to us through a series of temporal mirrors that are representative of set patterns of planetary markers. These marker patterns, which I have begun to identify through research and computer models, seem to point to the presence of consistent intelligent interaction between the cosmos and mankind. When the marker pattern for healing potential is present in a high degree, a greater number of healings tend to occur. When violent marker patterns proliferate, violent events erupt on the microcosmic level. Two computer programs that I have completed, **Signs: "The Spiritual Sky" and Signs: "The Inner Sky"** calculate and display spiritual planetary marker aspects and emotional planetary marker aspects respectively. The correlation between human events and predicted computer models for the astrological parameters provided by the programs is uncanny.

Now that we can ponder our place within the cosmos as intelligent, creative beings, we must begin to understand the power of the indwelling spirit that has driven us to this point in our evolution. It is no longer enough to state the obvious and pontificate on the marvels of the brain and of our use of only fractional percentages of its capacity. In the light of astrology and astrophysics, this argument ironically begs an even bigger question. If we are currently aware of less than ten percent of reality and if we are currently using only a similar percentage of our mental capacity, where is the rest of reality and why is it hidden from us. Why is our mental capacity so limited? I believe that the answer to this question lies in the mystery of multiple realities and temporal mirrors.

Consider the premise that we exist in a multiplicity of forms scattered throughout a vast multiverse of possible existences. Our reality would then be dictated to us by our growing awareness of this fact. Perhaps only ten percent of our brain capacity is required to perceive and interact with the miniscule portion of space-time that we accept as reality. Shifting our collective consciousness toward an active exploration of probable futures and events might allow us to open up that last frontier that has until this time remained hidden from our view. Perhaps our ancient prophets, seers, and mystics have already anticipated this need and have begun to show us the way. Now, as the modern age of seers, we must follow the trail that they have laid so bravely before us.

WEBSITE: WWW.MODERNASTROLOGY.COM

MITCHELL E. GIBSON MD 2600 E. SOUTHERN AVENUE SUITE C-2 TEMPE AZ 85282

PHONE 480-838-4300 FAX-480-838-4200 EMAIL: MITCHELLGIBSON@WORLDNET.ATT.NET

APPLICATIONS

ASTROLOGICAL MARKERS OF MYSTICAL ABILITY

Mysticism may be defined as the attempt of man to attain the ultimate reality of things and enjoy communion with the Creator. Mysticism maintains the possibility of intercourse with God, not by means of revelation, or the ordinary religious channels, but by dint of introspection, culminating in the feeling that the individual partakes of the divine nature. The name mysticism cannot be applied to any particular system of religious or spiritual study. Religion teaches submission of the will and the ethical harmonies of life while mysticism strives after the realization of a direct union with God himself. The mystic desires to be as close to God as possible, if not indeed part of the Divine Essence Itself. This fact is a sharp contrast to the obeisance of the ordinary religious devotee who seeks only to walk in God's way and to obey His will.

The mystic differs greatly from the psychic in that the primary impetus for their experiences derive from a union with the Creator. Psychics identify the source of their power in a personal, often mental persona while mystics readily attribute their energies to the Divine. The art of Mysticism may be said to have originated from the East, where it probably derived from kindred philosophic concepts. The Sufis of Persia may be said to be a link between the more austere Indian mystics and those of Europe. Sufism first arose in the ninth century among the Persian Mohammedans, probably as a protest against the severe monotheism of their religion. In Sufism, the concept of God begins to take on a more tangible, approachable construct.

Some writers believed that religious truth is external to the mind but this view is fundamentally opposed by the mystic. The mystic places every confidence in human reason, and it is essential that it should have the unity of the human mind with the divine as its main tenet. The higher faculties of human reason and perception are central to the mystics ability to progress along the Path to Divinity. Some mystics are quite practical in their approach to the knowledge of God while some prefer the scholastic approach. Monasteries and spiritual temples have become the main centers for mystical development and experience. Contemplation and withdrawal from the material world are seen as necessary refinements for the mind on its Path to the Divine. Through this withdrawal, the faculty of mystical or divine intuition may be developed and enhanced. Mystics believe that all people possess this faculty in one degree or another and proper development of this intuition is a prerequisite for further attainment. Once the mystic perceives that there is no distinction between the spirit and the Divine, they believe that the mind then escapes the limitations of the personality and finite reason. The human ego then evolves into the divine ego, the next incarnation of mental awareness or understanding. The divine ego remains intimately tied to the human ego throughout the remainder of the aspirants life, but it defines and directs the human experience and its ties to the Divine for the duration of that incarnation. Some believe that once developed, the divine ego is a permanent fixture within the spirit. All future incarnations of that spirit are then marked by the presence of a heightened awareness and sensitivity to the presence of God and to techniques by which the mind may seek direct communion with Him. It is the presence of this divine ego that marks the mystic as a separate and distinct entity from all other spiritual aspirants. Through the divine ego, the mystic cements his relationship with the Creator and physical manifestations of this union are the hall mark of mystical attainment.

The divine ego allows the mystic to experience the physical and mental presence of God without the dissolution of personality that the otherwise human ego would encounter. Through the aegis of the divine ego, the mystic may enter samadhi, a meditative state that allows him to speak with and commune directly with the Creator on a variety of levels. The seven successive levels of samadhi lead to higher levels of communion with the Creator. The highest level of samadhi is said to lead to dissolution of even the divine ego and ultimate reemergence of the spirit into the infinite Light of the Creator. Most mystics avoid frequent visits to the uppermost levels of samadhi for this very reason. However, at the end of human life, all true and highly evolved mystics seek this level of attainment as a respite from human existence.

The results of your mystical potential reading will hopefully open up a new pathway within your being that will ultimately lead to a more productive, fulfilling, and exciting life. If you have high potential, develop it, train it, use it. It is a greater gift than you could ever imagine. Even if you explore it to your fullest and best potential within this lifetime, rest assured that you have only scratched the surface. The following explanations accompany the different levels of mystical potential as delineated by your birth chart. These explanations are meant to serve as a guide to the latent power of each level. Remember, each is an embodiment of the light. What you do with it is entirely up to you.

0-30 Below average- Everyone has mystical potential to some degree. This is true in large part because we are all connected to the Creator by birth. Logic ruled by ego tells us that we are dust destined to return to the earth and live no more. Spirit tells us that nothing could be further from the truth. Below average mystical potential defines the beginning state of spiritual awareness in the young soul. Lack of awareness of and ignorance regarding spiritual matters tends to be the general rule here. However, some older souls will accept this type of potential life score in order to address more pressing issues in a given incarnation i.e.; health, family karma, direct mandates from the Creator etc. To some extent, this is unavoidable and eventually we will all have to face spiritual darkness before we can see the full measure of the Light. Sometimes, ignorance of the Light and the true Nature of Creation can be powerful motivators for a soul to pursue the mysteries of Life. Obviously this environment is a poor one for initiating spiritual studies or vigils. It is likely to present obstacles and hindrances that can only slow or even impede the growth of the aspirant.

31-60 Average Mystical potential of this level defines a large percentage of the known population. Many people desire closer Communion with the Creator and this environment allows a surprising degree of this potential. Though it is not the same in intensity and intimacy of the higher spheres of potential, this potential range is not without its benefits. Mystical experiences tend to be time-consuming and overwhelming to a degree and birth within this realm allows the soul to con tinue a normal life with family and friends and still continue to maintain pursuit of the Ultimate; albeit at a lower degree of intensity. At this level, the spirit is just starting to become aware of its true potential and it is only dimly aware of the energies that are available to it at the higher levels of potential and Creation.

61-100 Above Average This level of potential signals the burgeoning availability of the true potential of Spirit. Sometimes, this environment allows the soul to experience brief glimpses of Divinity in prayer, meditation, and even dreams. However, these glimpses are often tempered with mind numbing logic "bombs" that dive in and smother the essence of the experience before it can be processed by the curious mind. A similar process happens when the soul attempts to plan activities within this environment. Excuses, delays, rationalizations, and outright procrastination tend to relieve the soul of any potential new experience before it can fully form. There is enough energy and force here however that the soul will continue pursue this elusive yet powerful experience far beyond the realms of logic and reason. This is the beginning of Form in the truest sense. At this level, the universe tends to let the soul know that the mind does not rule the created world as absolutely as it would have one believe. The mind begins to perceive the ineffable presence of God as a part of its own being.

101-140 Superior The prevailing patterns of mystical potential in this realm are dominated by the growing tide of spiritual forces that wage war on the five primary senses. These senses are the cradle in which our humanity is born. However, as our higher nature emerges, these senses must be set aside to be replaced by the superior forces of the Intellect. This level of awareness is the first real stage of spiritual realization for the Soul. The Soul to this point has toyed with the concept of God and higher reality, but now, the reality begins to assert itself in a bold new way. Intuitive flashes, spontaneous miracles, lucid dreams, inexplicable spiritual experiences begin to occur more frequently at this stage. As the mind cannot easily persuade the Soul to ignore all of these experiences, it tends to give way to the next highest level of its function, Intellect. Intellect is the most primary function of the Divine ego. The Divine ego is the higher analogue of the human ego but it tends to function at a faster, more intuitive, and more profoundly Conscious way than its lesser evolved ancestor. The function of Intellect is to allow the mind of the Soul, via the Divine ego, to accept and process spiritual experiences. As the human ego tends to attack and dissemble these nuggets of reality, this function is necessary for the further evolution of the Soul. The universe oscillates in its ability to express these functions on the physical level. This environment tends to allow Communion with this aspect of the Divine Mind.

141- 180 Outstanding This level of potential allows expression of the Divine ego and higher Intellectual functions. As the energy potential of this environment rises, spiritual experiences tend to become longer and more intense. They also tend to forcefully overwhelm the primary senses and the individual is literally held hostage by his own evolution. This process tends to allow rapid evolution of the Soul though often at the expense of job, family, and contact with the outer world. The frequency, power, and intensity of this environment are not easily handled by lower stage Intellect and Divine ego development. As a result of the continuing pressure of the prevailing spiritual forces of this level a new state emerges, Beingness. Beingness occurs primarily on the unconscious level but the instances in which it allows itself to manifest on the Conscious level are truly life-transforming. At this level of spiritual development, the soul becomes aware of the multiplicity of its existence. The soul may manifest bilocation experiences, healings, out-of-body experiences and many similar states within its physical world in order to more fully explore the reality of its new awareness. Quantum physics has proven that reality exists not only on a three dimensional level but on at least ten levels of reality. Coincidentally, mystics have maintained that the soul has at least ten different levels of physical expression. Beingness dictates that the growing Divine Ego experience all the different levels of its reality while in physical form. The macrocosmic universe can also express Beingness during this transit. These environments tend to lend themselves to outstanding miraculous events.

181+ Delphi Class

The state of direct continuous awareness of one's existence within and connection to the mind of the Creator is called Consciousness. The universe rhythmically generates time periods that allow all living beings to commune with the Creator more easily. These time periods are remarkable in that they allow the aspirant the best possible experiential episodes of Communion. Many of the highest and most profound miracles and supernatural events known to man have occurred during these periods. Nature creates these periods in accordance with the aegis of the higher spiritual tidal forces. These forces move the planets themselves as well as the microcosm of the indwelling spirit. The spirit of Man when under the influence of this temporal period is exalted. Unfortunately, most people are unaware of the potential or presence of these forces and as a result, they will squander the grandeur of the period. However, the aware and awakened soul who now knows of the existence of these periods, will commune directly with these ambient forces while they are bathing the very fabric of his being. People born under this environment have extraordinarily profound potential that is unlimited by any human sense of restraint. Consciousness is the next level of development for the Divine ego. At this level, the mind is immersed in its truest state without the illusion of separateness. Delphi class temporal environments tend to facilitate this level of awareness.

FAMOUS MYSTICS

AMMACHI	210
SYBIL LEEK	315
JOAN OF ARC	240
AUDREY SANTO	245
SAI BABA	370
SHAIK MUHAMMAD AL-CASNAZANI	130
PADRE PIO	175
EMMANUEL SWEDENBORG	205
SRI RAMAKRISHNA	215
SAINT THERESE OF LISIEUX	245

RESOURCES

Mystical transit periods lend themselves to pilgrimages, meditation, healings, and communion with the deepest levels of the supernatural. The best way to take advantage of these transits is to plan a deep meditation or ritual aimed at a specific purpose. Any purpose will be fostered by the higher energies of these periods so be careful what you pray for! Listed below are some pilgrimage sites and useful ideas for places to visit or hold rituals or vigils during high-energy transit periods.

Denali National Park- The word Denali means the "High One" and refers to on of the most sacred sites on the North American continent. This park is home to the 20,320 foot tall Mt. McKinley. Athabascan natives believe the mountain is home to Sa, the sun shaman, master of life itself, and legends of magic and mystery on the mountainside go back hundreds of years. Modern mystics believe the site acts as a transmitter of cosmic force. The park is 120 miles south of Fairbanks and 240 miles north of Anchorage.

Second Mesa- Every inch of the three plateaus that make up the Hopi Reservation is considered sacred, and tourists must exercise great care when visiting the area. The Second Mesa is where most public activities take place. The town of Mishongnovi is where one of the most important Hopi ceremonies, the Snake Dance, takes place. It is held in August of odd-numbered years. Corn Rock, a sacred shrine, is also located in the town. In even-numbered years, the Snake Dance is held at the village of Shungopavi.

Oriabi is considered the longest inhabited spot in North America. It is sacred to the Hopi and no photography or drawing is allowed. The Hopi are considered direct descendants of the mysterious Anasazi race. The Hopi Mesas are located in Northern Arizona and can be reached by Hwy 264 or by Hwy 87 from Winslow.

Sedona, Arizona- This is one of the most spiritual pilgrimage spots in all of the United States. Bell Rock, Cathedral Rock, Oak Creek, Boynton Canyon, and a host of other sites in this breathtakingly beautiful area are well known for their mystical properties. Boynton Canyon is sacred to the Yavapai and they believe that the First Woman was born there in a cave. Now the Great Mother is old and stooped over but she still resides in the canyon. Cathedral Rock is a Sedona psychic vortex spot is over 1000 feet high. Nearby Airport Mesa is so charged with electricity that people's hair stands on end. People relaxing or meditating in this area report feeling strange forces and receiving otherworldly communications. Locals say the contrast between the area's bright red rocks and deep blue skies evoke alchemical images of uniting fire and water in the quest for spiritual personal perfection.

Manitou Springs, Colorado- The word Manitou is Algonquin for "Great Spirit". The name refers to the magical power Indians believed resided in these waters. They worshipped the site and left offerings of blankets, beads, weapons, food, and carvings. Modern mystics make pilgrimages here to partake of the spiritual energy, which is said to rejuvenate the mind and the body. The springs are at the foot of Pike's Peak.

The Pyramids of Giza, Egypt- These magnificent creations are among the most awe-inspiring of all human structures. They are more than 6000 years old and their builders are unknown. Their proportions interest those who place mystical interpretations on mathematical relationships and scale models will preserve food and cure many ills. This is a must see pilgrimage spot.

Other great pilgrimage sites; Fatima, Portugal, Medjogorje, Yugoslavia, Villarica Paraguay, Pune India, Prophet's Town (Tippecanoe Indiana).

GENERAL PSYCHIC ABILITY

General psychic potential is part of the genetic and spiritual heritage of all mankind. As much as skeptics and left-brain servants would like to deny them, psychic and spiritual ability remain as an undeniable legacy of our indwelling spirit. Saints, mystics, mediums, palm readers, clairvoyants, shamans, and healers have been with us since the beginning of recorded history. Why do we deny this crucial aspect of our heritage? In some cultures, spiritual development of a certain magnitude is a prerequisite to serious political or social advancement. Ironically in our society, the leaders of the most famous and powerful companies often test at the highest level of psychic and intuitive potential. Corporate and political magnates are well known for their propensity for enlisting the services of psychic, astrologers, and spiritualists in divining the future, assessing the movements of their opponents, and in running many aspects of their daily lives. If you could assess on the degree of your own psychic and spiritual potential just from examining your birth data, you might discover that you were in possession of a psionic powerhouse that could work for you in ways that you could scarcely imagine. Discovery and training of this ability might well be the first step in liberating yourself from a repetitive cycle of financial disappointment, unfulfilling relationship, spiritual emptiness, and a sense of powerlessness in life. John Bosco discovered that he had prophetic or precognitive dreams when he was a boy. One small episode from his early life revealed the potential of his psychic ability. When he was a student, he dreamed that he was reading his next day's Latin dictation. He woke and wrote out the passage that he had dreamed. Because an earlier similar dream had been correct, he took what seemed to him the practical course of handing it in (without comment) as his Latin dictation at the end of the next day's class. The passage was entirely correct but startled his teacher, who had run out of class time and dictated only half the passage that the boy had written in its entirety. The boy chose to pass the rest his life in poverty, begging, doing charitable works, and meditating. He was later canonized and he is now known as Saint John Bosco. The point I wanted to make in this story is that this child thought nothing of his gift, until it was pointed out to him by his teachers that he was indeed very, very special. History is replete with hundreds of examples of people who have this type of gift and never fully realize their potential.

Emmanuel Swedenborg was well into the latter half of his life before he discovered his psychic gifts. One of the most famous anecdotes that illustrates his extraordinary potential concerns a widow who was dunned for an expensive silver service. She was sure her husband had paid the bill but could not find the receipt. In desperation she turned to Swedenborg because of his psychic reputation and asked him to locate it. After three days he visited her to say that her husband's spirit had told him where the receipt was: pulling out the left drawer of an upstairs bureau would uncover a board that in turn could be pulled out to reveal a secret drawer holding corresponding containing the receipt. The widow declared that she knew nothing of any such drawer, but she and her guests naturally went upstairs with Swedenborg, went through the prescribed operations, and found the drawer, the receipt, and other correspondence within it. Swedenborg was a great mystic, psychic and medium like St. John Bosco, but he was also a man of the world. He was one of the greatest scientists of his time, an assessor for the Swedish bureau of mines, a lobbyist, a researcher, and a lecturer on economics and science. He denied his own psychic proclivities until experiences such as the one above forced him to reckon with them.

The results of your psychic potential reading will hopefully open up a new pathway within your being that will ultimately lead to a more productive, fulfilling, and exciting life. If you have high potential, develop it, train it, use it. It is a greater gift than you could ever know until you let yourself explore it to the fullest. The following explanations accompany the different levels of psychic potential as delineated by your birth chart. These explanations are meant to serve as a guide to the latent power of each level. Remember, each is an embodiment of the light. What you do with it is entirely up to you.

0-30 Below average- Much of what we do during the day relies on subliminal impressions that we receive from the physical and emotional environment. Some people operate almost exclusively on this level of perception and are actually resistant to examining the inner senses. These nativities tend to be associated with psi-blocking and left-brain analysis that tends to be very destructive to the subtle spiritual processes as they impinge upon the brain. A below average level of general psychic potential does not imply that a person has no psychic potential. Rather, it suggests that these individuals will tend to block or deny their abilities within this particular lifetime or natal period. Transit periods characterized by this level of potential are not considered to be good periods during which to engage in psychic trance work.

31-60 Average Much of our day to day experience is based on information already residing in memory-even if it seem like we're simply perceiving external events and things. In fact, recognition of any given external form- an object, a friend, a pet, is based on the activation of internal abstract categories formed over many past experiences. Comparatively speaking, the actual sensory input may be of little importance. The downside of this of course, is stereotyping, jumping to conclusions, and allowing logical deduction to dominate the mental processes. This can be a good thing as the mind needs logic to operate within the everyday world. If you pay enough attention to details, body posture, facial expressions, eye contact, can all be interpreted with a great deal of accuracy in making a logical deduction about people or situations. However, psychic perceptions can get mixed into the inferential process, and we might stumble onto some very specific information about other people which simply could not have been deduced or inferred from the known elements. This is the lot of the individual with average spiritual potential. Though they do not block their abilities outright, they will tend to allow left-brain mentation and logic to cloud many useful psychic perceptions. Transit periods characterized by this score are not considered favorable for most psychic and spiritual work. Meditation and relaxation work is very useful for freeing these individuals from their self-imposed left-brain servitude.

61-100 Above average- Perception was once thought to pre-suppose awareness; we sense only that which we have perceived consciously. Much research, however, now shows that information presented below the threshold of awareness can still influence our behavior, our feelings, our thoughts, even our dreams. If a man falls asleep while listening to the radio and has a very disturbing dream about an airplane crashing, he might be concerned that he had just experienced a nightmare. If however he had inadvertently heard about a plane crash over the radio while he slept, he had unknowingly incorporated this subliminal information into his dream state. There is now abundant experimental evidence that we indeed sense and process information even without conscious awareness. Clearly, some psychic experiences are based on subliminal perception rather than psi. It is useful to not here that some psychic perceptions are clearly influenced by subliminal perceptions. During an above average potential transit period, the forces that mediate subliminal perception are extremely active. This heightened degree of subliminal force and receptivity tends to be a great boon to the activation of true psi potential. The native whose chart displays an above average degree of psychic potential is able to sense information at the subliminal much better than the average person. This fact tends to lead to a higher percentage of accurate psychic performances and experiences when compared to the control group. This transit period is very conducive to trance work but serious psychic exploration and contemplation should be saved for more fertile transit environments.

101-140 Superior- A number of diverse studies suggest that psi tends to be associated with images rather than concepts and word, symbols and metaphors rather than with logic, with holistic and non-linear thought processes rather then sequential processing. These brain functions are linked to right-brain thinking rather than left-brain functions.

In the late 60's and 70's, neurological and psychological studies suggested that each of the cerebral hemispheres develops its own specificity. Functions of calculation, logical and mathematical analysis, and language generally seemed specific to the left hemisphere, or left-brain. Functions of pattern-recognition, overall spatial apprehension, and aesthetic appreciation were generally linked to the right hemisphere. Further studies quickly revealed a more complex picture. This organization is not however a fixed condition imposed by our genetic coding. Rather, it is a kind of self-organization and tends to form over the course of an individual's lifetime and it tends to take different paths depending on the person. Left-handed persons tend to have the reverse condition in their brain functions and the right brain serves left brain functions and vice versa. Music, artistic expression, language, and psychic function depend on the participation of numerous areas of both hemispheres. Psychic researchers insist that right-brain function is clearly superior to left-brain in the realm of psi. Many experienced and gifted psychics say that an essential success factor in psi is found in drawing their impressions of a target and not just talking. The apparent superiority of "right-brain" over "left-brain" processing means that psi may not be equally at ease with all kinds of targets. Most psychics would agree that numbers or abstract figures which have no intrinsic significance in and of themselves, are especially difficult targets. Researchers have found a way to deal with such targets. They now associate them with images which are rich in meaning and sensorially engaging, and have the subject on the associated targets instead. This technique is known as associative remote viewing and it has been used successfully in a number of psi applications.

Individuals with superior psi potential have strong right-brain functioning. This allows them not only to incorporate subliminal information into their consciousness, but it also allows for a higher level of non-linear processing that opens the door for true psi functioning. It is in this realm that the true psychic gift begins to emerge in its purest form. These environments tend to make good transits during which to meditate, perform trance work, or even begin psi explorations. Though they tend to be less effective than higher environments, the results obtained within this environment are often accurate and useful.

141- 180 Outstanding Oriental sages have always maintained that psychic abilities emerge naturally as we get in touch with the deeper aspects of self. Clinical research clearly supports the idea that psi is correlated to a detachment from the conscious "I" and its everyday concerns, and movement toward the larger self which is associated with our unconscious potentials. High order spontaneous psi often occurs during psychological crises which are sufficiently profound to pull the person out of their every day preoccupations and confront them with a vaster reality. Research also suggests that psi information is most likely to come through when the person is in relaxed mental states, or altered states of consciousness, such as dreams.

Individuals with an outstanding psychic potential rating possess a deeper association between their conscious mental functions and their deeper mental states. Traditionally, deeper psychic abilities are accessed through trance states that place the ego on "hold". The ego, with all its preoccupations with worry, agendas, planning, judgment, and analysis create a permanent and pervasive mental noise. The perception of psi information depends on our capacity to reduce this noise so that we may hear the whisperings of our higher, deeper selves which lives in the stygian unconscious. The individual with outstanding potential has a much more fluid exchange between the unconscious and conscious levels of mind. This allows for a greater capacity for true psi to emerge. The outstanding environment is an excellent environment during which to perform any type of serious psi work. Diviniation and dowsing work is especially encouraged during this time period. Clairvoyant trance work aimed at the discovery of unknown connections between conscious material and deep unconscious material is also apt to be significantly more accurate during this time period.

181+ Delphi Class- The human mind is one of the most powerful of God's creations. In the Delphi class psychic, this jewel of the universe begins to achieve its fullest flower. The latent psi potential of the soul is able to manifest only when the potential of the mind, body, and spirit are in synchrony with each. In other words, the total being must be willing and able to accept and manifest a fuller measure of its divinity. This is a tall order and many beings prefer to talk about approximating the divine rather than living it. This is true of the followers of most religions and spiritual disciplines. The Delphi level of spiritual potential is a rare state. It only occurs for a period of less than three weeks out of the average year and its higher potential states are rarer still. It is in this potential state however that the highest and most powerful abilities of the human spirit begin to bear fruit. Psychometry refers to the ability of a person to divine facts about an objects's past, or about its owner, by holding the object in her hands. During the Delphi transit, this ability is extremely heightened. Divination reaches the heights of its potential manifesta tion during this transit. This is a fantastic time to get a reading for yourself or for a loved one. It is also a superb time to practice dowsing, tarot card reading, or clairvoyant trance induction. The Delphi level psychic is gifted with a soul that is ready to move to the heights of human incarnation. Whether the native admits this fact to themselves or not, this is a reality. Some Delphi psychics need training or initiation in order to realize their outstanding potential. Many are afraid to explore the person within that they have glimpsed during dreams or intuitive explorations that Shadows them and provides the spiritual food for their deepest prayers and visions. This dichotomy of reality is the bane of the Delphi psychic's existence. Accepting the utter inferiority of the human form and its relatively primitive five local senses is a major hurdle to be cleared for the spirit at this level of reality. Fourth dimensional reality and experience is the true home of the soul at this level. Accept this as your next task and life will become much more exciting. The average or below average psychic can function at a much higher level during this transit because the ambient psychic tidal energies extant at this time will heartily support greater levels of psychic functioning. True Magick is possible during this transit.

FAMOUS PSYCHICS

ERIC HANUSSEN	175 OUTSTANDING
KELLY QUINN	145 OUTSTANDING
MARK REYMONT	155 OUTSTANDING
JEAN DIXON	165 OUTSTANDING
WILLIAM WINGFIELD	205 DELPHI
CARALYN	245 DELPHI
ALAN VAUGHN	160 OUTSTANDING
JOHANN VOGHT	300 DELPHI
FRED KIMBALL	165 OUTSTANDING
SYLVIA BROWNE	115 SUPERIOR
NOSTRADAMUS	280 DELPHI

RESOURCES:

The most exciting and useful development in psychic research is remote viewing. There are a number of resources available in Remote Viewing but by far the most useful is the home-study course offered by the Academy of Remote Viewing Through Space and Time. Mr. Gerald O'Donnell is the director and he is former professional remote viewer. He was active in the European Intelligence Community in the Mental Espionage program. Recent disclosures in the US reveal that the US government funded research into psychic espionage for more than 20 years. These remote viewing units operated within the CIA, DIA, and the Army under names such as SCANATE, SUN STREAK, GRILL FLAME, CENTER LANE, AND STAR GATE. The Army unit of "remote viewers" operated out of Fort Mead, Maryland. Mr. O'Donnell feels very strongly that on the eve of the third millennium it is his duty to teach humanity a natural gift that it has forgotten for the most part because of its over reliance on and adulation of technological gadgetry. The easiest way to order the Probable Futures Course is through their website: www.probablefuture.com

Intuitive Intelligence Applications
Attn: ONLY OPERATIONS
P.O.BOX 100
NELLYSFORD, VIRGINIA 22958
WWW.MCEAGLE.COM

Joseph McMoneagle is the best remote viewer in the world. He is available for readings and private work. He is very, very expensive and somewhat choosey as to the type of work he will accept. As the best, he can afford to be. Take a look at his website and check out his requirements.

Practice Pool Targets

The US Army's full remote viewing document is available for free download on the following webpage; www.firedocs.com/remoteviewing/answers/crvmanual/

They also include a practice page of over 300 unkmown targets that are available on the net. This site is a gold mine of practice information.

www.io.com/~scifi/RV/Practice.html

MEDIUMSHIP

The term "medium" came into widespread use in the 19th century, to designate individuals who claimed to "mediate" communications between the living and the spirits of the deceased. The wave of spiritualism which overtook America and Europe in the latter 19th century brought forth a multitude of mediums who were able to contact the spirits of the departed or to invoke physical manifestations (e.g., levitations or materializations). Most often mediums began the séance by putting themselves into a trance state. A spirit or several of them, taking turns, would come forth and speak through the medium for a certain time. Then the person would come out of the trance, usually recalling nothing of what had been said. Spirit communication was also mediated by other means, such as automatic writing, raps or tapping noises, Ouija boards, and a pointer held by the medium, but usually guided by the spirit.

Extremely talented mediums manifest an extreme dedication to scientific research and have collaborated with researchers over several decades, while accepting some pretty extreme constraints on their personal freedom. Often, their mail, their movements and personal relationships were constantly surveyed by detectives, to eliminate any chance of deception. The famous American medium Leonora Piper was one such medium. William James and Richard Hodgson concluded that Ms. Piper had repeatedly demonstrated very strong psychic talents over a number of years. Similarly, in the 1950's, Eileen Garrett a medium and a brilliant psychic showed an active interest in scientific investigations of her psi capacities. She was not only proven to be a genuine medium, but she later founded the Parapsychology Foundation, which has helped to advance scientific psi research after her passing.

Trance mediumship is in some ways related to multiple personality disorder. However, trance mediums do not display the psychopathology often seen in these patients. Scientists are intensely studying the phenomenon of multiple personality disorder in order to better understand mediumship. Channeling is similar to mediumship but its focus tends to shift toward higher entities such as angels and cosmic beings. Mediumship is a discrete spiritual ability and as such is a rare gift indeed. The score depicted on your sheet gives an approximation of the level of intensity of the gift of mediumship denoted by the natal information provided. Each of the score levels denote a different level of proficiency within this sphere. Mediumship like any other gift is best developed with constant practice and persistence. A high score denotes high potential nothing more. Michael Jordan has exceptionally high athletic ability and is the best basketball player in the history of the NBA. However, he did not make his high school basketball team. Only after prolonged practice and dedication could he develop his talents to the fullest. Such is the way of the medium. After the list of potential scores we have provided a summary of resources for further reading and development of your abilities, regardless of your potential level. Remember, even if your score is not what you hoped it would be, attempting a trance session on dates that denote higher potential scores will allow you to function at that level during that time period. For example, if your score gives you above average ability, attempting a mediumistic trance on a date that has an outstanding potential score will allow you to perform at that level much more easily at that time.

0-30 Below average- this score represents a below average degree of latent mediumship ability when compared to the control group. This score does not mean that a person with below average latent mediumship ability possesses no mediumship ability, rather that they would tend to manifest this ability at a significantly lower level of proficiency than a person with a higher potential score. Psi missing is one of the most startling discoveries of modern parapsychology. At times, certain persons persist in generating poor performances in psi tests. The accumulation of systematically poor performances can be so flagrant that it suggests something quite different than a mere lack of psi ability, it suggests that these people consistently avoid a good performance, unconsciously sabotaging their own efforts. This phenomenon is very common at the below average level of mediumship potential. Selective perception undoubtedly plays a role in our interpretation of apparently paranormal experiences. The more an individual harbors a reductionistic view of the world, the less chance mediumistic phenomena will emerge (let alone be witnessed by them); the more one is interested in interconnectedness, and open to psi experiences, the more likely the world will respond by creating such experiences.

31-60 Average- this score represents an average degree of latent astrological mediumistic ability when compared to the control group. Individuals with astrological mediumship potential scores in this range tend to manifest this ability at approximately the same frequency as the control group. We intuitively sense that psi is an expression of openness and relatedness. It involves interaction with the world, an extension beyond the isolated self; boundaries and distinction seem less fundamental than our capacity for participation and communion with others. This group represents the largest grouping of mediumistic abilities when compared to the control group. This level of potential score does allow for a reasonable mediumistic performance, however, the degree of performance delivered will be substantially below that of nativities with higher scores.

61-100 Above average- this score was measured in the top 25% of mediums and it represents an enhanced tendency toward the development of mediumistic potential. At this level, intuitive experiences begin to occur at a greater frequency than normal. Intuitive mediumship refers to a phenomenon that occurs when a person is able to perceive information from spirits or the environment. This type of mediumship is available to most people and is particularly heightened at this level of potential. This is a better than average environment for trance but higher potential dates are better suited for this work.

101-140 Superior- this score was measured in the top 10% of mediums and it represents a greatly enhanced tendency toward the development of mediumship ability potential. Individuals with scores in this range tend to report frequent spontaneous manifestations of a variety of mediumistic phenomena. At this level mental mediumship begins to display itself at an increased rate. Mental mediumship involves the relating of information through thought transference or mental telepathy. Mental telepathy is the relaying of information via thought, without using any of the five physical senses. Medium mediumship takes place within the consciousness of the medium. The results are expressed verbally and must pass through the medium's mouth. Because of its telepathis nature, mental mediumship is sometimes referred to as telepathic mediumship. In a demonstration of mental mediumship, it is the medium who hears, sees, and feels what the spirit communicators are relating. It is also the medium's function to relate the information, with minimum personal influence and predjudice.

141-180 Outstanding- this score was measured in the top 2% of mediums. Mediums with scores in this range are rare and represent the elite of the psychic and spiritual mediumship world. Many of the most talented and famous mediums of antiquity have latent mediumship ability scores that fall within this range. At this level in addition to mental mediumship and intuitive mediumistic powers, physical mediumship begins to manifest very strongly. Physical mediumship involves the manipulation and transformation of physical systems and energies. The spirit operators, in this case, are causing something to happen upon the physical plane. What actually happens can be seen and heard by others. At this level, spontaneous materializations, movement of objects, and direct voice occur quite commonly. Ectoplasm is the material that is the vector for the manifestation of these phenomenon. Ectoplasm is a physical substance that emanates from the medium's body. It varies in colour from white to gray and may extrude from bodily orifices, a psychic center, or the solar plexus. Typically, this ability is much more common in trained mediums than in the uninitiated.

181+ Delphi Class- this score is measured in less than 1% of mediums. The Delphi Class medium represents a group of individuals so special that their mediumistic abilities often become legendary, even among other mediums. Mediums at this level can develop to unbelievable levels of proficiency with training. At this level, all of the most esoteric and refined mediumistic abilities are likely to manifest given sufficient training and focus. Direct voice, wherein the Spirit operators create an ectoplasmic voice box through which they can speak physically and audibly to all present. This is often done using a small conical device, known as a trumpet. The trumpet acts very much like the medium's cabinet, in the energies are focused inside the trumpet. The trumpet is often levitated around the room. Apportations are common at this level as well. In this phenomenon, Spirit causes objects to materialize, apparently from nowhere. The apported object sometimes does and does not remain. Often, the materialized object is dematerialized back to where it came from. Stones, gems, animals, ancient relics, and even people have been known to be apported into séance rooms. Delphi level mediums are often able to accomplish the crème de la crème of physical mediumship; materialization. In materialization, the Spirit people use ectoplasm to create an image or molding of themselves. The degree and strength of the materialized form varies quite a bit. A full-form, head to toe materialization of a spirit is perhaps the most amazing phenomenon witnessed in mediumship. There are countless recorded cases where spirits have materialized fully, with full dress and facial features. Some have been as clear and solid as an earthly body. Materialized spirits have been known to walk among the sitters, talk to the sitters via direct voice, touch, hug, and kiss the sitters; allow the sitters to touch them, pass through walls, and dematerialize in full view of the sitters. A very interesting phenomenon seen during materialization is the physical link between the spirit and the medium. After a spirit materializes and walks away from the medium, there can be seen a cord of ectoplasm linking the spirit form with the medium. This ectoplasmic cord may be likened to the umbilical cord of a fetus. Through it, the spirit operator receives a supply of etheric energy matter from the medium. The spirit may be dematerialized by withdrawing the ectoplasm back into the medium's body via this cord.

FAMOUS MEDIUMS AND THEIR POTENTIAL SCORES

REVEREND OWEN	190 DELPHI LEVEL
ELIANE GUERRI	145 OUTSTANDING
MADAME DAVIA	175 OUTSTANDING
EDGAR CAYCE	195 DELPHI LEVEL
KATIE CROOKES	240 DELPHI LEVEL
EMMANUEL SWEDENBORG	205 DELPHI LEVEL
EILEEN GARRETT	230 DELPHI LEVEL
HENRY NUSSELEIN	190 DELPHI LEVEL
AULIKKI PLAAMI	160 OUTSTANDING
BRENDA CRENSHAW	185 DELPHI
ARTHUR FORD	160 OUTSTANDING
MAXINE BELL	180 DELPHI LEVEL
DAVID HOME	120 SUPERIOR

RESOURCES:

TRAINING: THE COLLEGE OF SPIRITUAL SCIENCE
NSAC
13 COTTAGE ROW
PO BOX 217
LILY DALE, NY 14752-0217
PHONE: (716)-595-2000

As one of the educational branches of the National Spiritualist Association of Churches (NSAC), the College of Spiritual Science is a non-residential college offering BA and AA degrees in Ministry and Religious Studies as well as diploma programs in Licentiate Ministry, Healing, Mediumship and Teaching.

THE MORRIS PRATT INSTITUTE
11811 Watertown Plank Road
Milwaukee, WI 53226-3340
Phone: (414) 774-2994

The Morris Pratt Institute, established in 1901, has educated some of the world's best mediums. Presenting a correspondence course in Modern Spiritualism is just a part of the Morris Pratt Institute. The school also presents a two week residential course in Pastoral Skills and Special Seminars on the aspects of Spiritualism. To enhance the study of Spiritualism, the MPI has an extensive research library in Milwaukee, open to the public.

LINKS:

TRY THESE NATIONAL WEBSITES

NATIONAL SPIRITUALIST ASSOCIATION OF CHURCHES

THE MORRIS PRATT INSTITUTE

NSAC LYCEUM Spotlight

THE SPIRITUALIST CHURCH OF REVELATION

THE NOAHS ARK SOCIETY

SPIRITUALIST'S NATIONAL UNION

FIRST SPIRITUALIST TEMPLE

PSYCHIC HEALING

Psychic healing refers to the ability to effect cures on others, using only mental means. Contemporary healers use age-old practices such as rituals, prayers or suggestion, as well as more recent approaches, such as meditation, magnetism, or laying on of hands. Many very remarkable healings have been well documented, even with severe illnesses, but we are far from understanding the cause and processes involved.

Suggestion is certainly a major facet of many healings. However, psychic healing requires that the healer draw energy from his physical body, mainly from the solar plexus in the back of the stomach and at the top of the head, where groups of nerves come together. This energy is then channeled through his/her hands and applies to the aura, or the magnetic field extending somewhat beyond the physical body of the patient. By placing his/her energy into the troubled areas of the aura, the healer displaces the diseased particles and momentarily creates a vacuum. Into this vacuum, healthy electrically charged particles rush to fill the gap in the aura. Healing often takes place whether the patient believes in psychic healing or not. It is a purely mechanical process, and its success depends on the healer's ability to draw enough of his life force into his hands to effect the healing. The degree of a particular healer's life force is a significant factor in affecting the degree of healing of which they are capable. Each healer is different and some healers go so far as to specialize in a particular type of healing. Whatever the gift, each of us has some degree of healing potential. The score depicted on your sheet gives an approximation of the level of intensity of the gift of healing denoted by the natal information provided. Each of the score levels denote a different level of proficiency within this sphere. Healing like any other gift, is best developed with constant practice and persistence. A high score denotes high healing potential, nothing more. Michael Jordan has exceptionally high athletic ability and he is the best basketball player in the history of the NBA. However, he did not make his high school basketball team. Only after prolonged practice and dedication could he develop his talents to the fullest. Such is the way of the healer. After the list of potential scores we have provided a summary of resources for further reading and development of your abilities, regardless of your potential level. Remember, even if your score is not what you hoped it would be, attempting a healing session on dates that denote higher potential scores will allow you to function at that level during that time period. For example, if your score gives you superior ability, attempting a healing session on a date that has an outstanding potential score will allow you to perform at that level much more easily at that time.

0-30 Below average-
this score represents a below average degree of latent healing ability when compared to the control group. This score does not mean that a person with below average latent healing ability possesses no healing ability, rather that they would tend to manifest this ability at a significantly lower level of proficiency than a person with a higher potential score. People with this level of proficiency tend to block their healing abilities at the conscious level and often unconsciously sabotage their efforts as well. This level of proficiency is not a good temporal period in which to undertake surgery, circle healings, healing trances, or other elective healing procedures.

31-60 Average- this score represents an average degree of latent astrological healing ability when compared to the control group. Individuals with astrological healing potential scores in this range tend to manifest this ability at approximately the same frequency as the control group. Healing is primarily an intuitive and mental process. Healers know when someone is in pain even when they are not informed as to the nature of a situation. All people possess some degree of healing ability. How we choose to use or develop it depends entirely on our personal motivation and actions. A person with an average score who is highly motivated to learn healing can become a good healer.

61-100 Above average- this score was measured in the top 25% of the healers and it represents an enhanced tendency toward the development of healing potential. At this level, the healing energies that are latent within us all begin to manifest spontaneously. Some of the world's most famous healers have potential in this range. This occurs primarily because they choose to develop their skills and abilities to the fullest. The man who knows his limitation and abilities and chooses to define them according to the divinations of his heart is truly a great being. Though this environment can often yield good healing results, a higher potential environment is recommended for serious healing work.

101-140 Superior this score was measured in the top 10% of healers and it represents a greatly enhanced tendency toward the development of healing potential. Individuals with scores in this range tend to report strong healing experiences and respond well to training. Mental healing potential develops spontaneously at this level. Faith healing and the ability to influence the growth of plants and animals is heightened in this range. Some healers tend to downplay their abilities and sometimes they refuse to apply them even when they realize that they are not the product of their imagination. Superior class healers sometimes fall into this quandary and often struggle with the validity of their own power. Once this impasse is breached, greatness of a kind may be achieved. Embracing the light of the gift is the best way to overcome this transitional block of the growth process of the spirit.

141-180 Outstanding - this score was measured in the top 2% of healers. Healers with scores in this range are rare and represent the elite of the world of spiritual healers. At this level of healing, distance healing power, psychic surgery, and life regenerating gifts begin to emerge. Some healers in this range can restore dying animals or plants after a fashion and even cause the remission of life-threatening illnesses. Advanced cancers have remitted under the aegis of healers of this magnitude. Healing is one of the gifts of the soul that develop over the lifetime of the spirit. As the spirit is enveloped by the soul, its interface is a series of nodal growth points that over time ripen and manifest as the fruits of the spiritual labors of the spiritual mind. Some of these nodal points will require a series of lifetimes in order to ripen, but some of them will manifest within a few decades of a single incarnation. This lifetime, or point of incarnation, is important to understand and assess carefully. Some individuals fail to make a full assessment of their latent spiritual gifts and abilities. Without a thorough ongoing assessment, the conscious mind tends to fall into the ennui of the illusory mental processes and the gifts of spirit are often dismissed as ephemeral aspects of a dancing dream. Healing talents in this range need to be nurtured and trained to whatever extent possible. Healing environments of this magnitude are excellent for any type of healing procedure, trance, prayer circle, distant healing, or surgical procedure.

181+ Delphi Class-

this score is measured in less than 1% of healers. The Delphi Class healer represents a group of individuals so special that their healing abilities will become legendary, even among other healers. If this nativity contains the Sun/Venus eclipse or the Moon/Mercury contraparallel, the power of the rating is essentially doubled. Healers of this magnitude are evidence of a maturing spiritual node which is in the midst of final manifestation. Souls who have matured to this level are often aware of their gifts and at some level long to develop them to some degree. This particular spiritual node is capable of creating miniature copies of itself in the form of objects which are capable of transmitting healing power independent of the healer. This occurs through the aegis of the spirits reproductive power that the healer is able to affix to an object or place. The physical body of a true Delphi Class healer is a healing relic in and of itself. This is evidenced by the hundreds of healing miracles that occur even with the severed body parts of the world's great healers. Sometimes, focusing the mind on a Delphi healer during a Delphi class healing transit and applying the resultant force to the desired object of a healing can bring miraculous results. Healing transits above the 250 range are special times and are recommended for the most serious healing work one would care to engage. These periods are rare so the usual caveats of fasting, prayer, and meditation apply doubly. Never miss an opportunity to pray for yourself and someone else during a Delphi healing transit environment.

FAMOUS HEALERS

OLGA WORRALL	190 DELPHI CLASS
GIOVANI BONI	205 DELPHI CLASS
DAVID BRAY	125 SUPERIOR
YOLANDA BETEGH	235 DELPHI CLASS
SERGE LEON ALALOUF	240 DELPHI CLASS
RASPUTIN	150 OUTSTANDING
GERARD CROISET	155 OUTSTANDING
DR. ERNESTO MONTGOMERY	185 DELPHI CLASS
ELLEN YOAKUM	260 DELPHI CLASS
KATHRYN KUHLMAN	210 DELPHI CLASS

Healing Resources
One Star in Site
PO Box 390
Oranger IN 46530

Offers three levels of training in the healing arts. All events are personally conducted by the founder of the Trinity Project, Jim Harmon. Trinity Center is a natural site in the rural countryside of Red River Valley in Texas.

The White Rose Foundation
Charisma
Frances Avenue
Maidenhead England, Berkshire
PHONE: 01628 625603
www.wrforg.co.uk

Spiritual healing centres and schools teaching healing and mediumship in Maidenhead, England, Zurich, Switzerland, and Germany

Dittons Healting Centre
C/O, Barn Close
EPSOM KT18 7HQ
England, Surrey, UK
+44(0) 1372 817778
www.altguide.com/healers

DHC is Surrey's premier healing centre and operates on the highest ethical standard of healing conduct. It is a non-profit, strictly non-denominational healing center providing reiki, spiritual healing, and training in hands on and distance healing.

Delphi University
P.O. Box 70
OLD SILVERMINE RD.
MCCAYSVILLE, GA 30555
PHONE 706-492-2772
WWW.DELPHI-CENTER.COM

Since 1974, Delphi University has been teaching and certifying students in channeling, alternative healing, and rohun psychospiritual therapy. Located in the Blue Ridge Mountains of North Georgia, Delphi was founded by Patricia Hayes. The university is divided into three separate schools: The Arthur Ford Academy, The Patricia Hayes School of Inner Sense Development, and The Rohun Institute. The school maintains a full time staff of gifted teacher, healers and counselers. Delphi combines ancient wisdom with contemporary knowledge.

Shambhala International Healing Center
814 N. OGDEN
West Hollywood, CA 90046
PHONE 213-653-2716
www. geocities.com/rainforest/5013

Shambhala is a non-profit spiritual and educational organization with healing centers in Russia and the US. The headquarters are in Los Angeles. The center offers energy healing, esoteric eastern healing, and a number of yogic healing disciplines. The center is staffed by internationally renowned healers and teachers.

Calculating Modern Astrology Charts

The ALGORITHM for the calculation of a modern astrology chart is an extension of the research that I have completed. The chart formations are new and for the most part do not represent a reiteration of old patterns that exist on previous packages. In order to complete the first phase of the production of a chart, I have divided the calculations into six separate categories; longitudinal measurements, declinational measurements, multiple planet aspects, positional elevations, summary indices, and marker aspects.

Longitudinal and declinational planetary measurements are necessary for the completion of these calculations.

1. After generating a complete list of conjunctions, trines, sextiles, squares, and oppositions, you will need to assign a positive or negative value to each aspect. The tolerances (in degrees) for the Ptolemaic aspects are as follows:

	SUN	MOON	PLANETS	ENTER	LEAVE
CONJUNCTION:	9	8	7	1	1
OPPOSITION:	9	8	7	1	1
TRINE:	7	7	6	1	1
SQUARE:	7	7	6	1	1
SEXTILE:	7	6	5	1	1

ALL NUMBERS LISTED ABOVE ARE LISTED IN DEGREES.

2. Each square listed in the chart is assigned a negative value.
3. Each opposition listed in a chart is assigned a negative value.
4. Any conjunction, trine, sextile, square and opposition involving Saturn is con sidered to be negative.
5. All conjunctions, trines, and sextiles are positive when they do not involve Saturn or Mars.

6. All conjunction, trines, and sextiles involving Mars are positive if they also involve the Sun, Jupiter, or Venus.
7. All conjunctions, trines, and sextiles involving Mars are negative if they also involve Mercury, Uranus, Neptune, Pluto, or the Moon.

Longitudinal proximity elevations are calculated by determining the planets that occur within a ten-degree orb of each other but are not already listed as being in conjunction.

a. All proximity elevations involving Saturn are negative.
b. All proximity elevations involving Mars are positive if they also involve the Sun, Jupiter or Venus.
c. All proximity elevations involving Mars are negative if they also involve Mercury, Uranus, Neptune, Pluto or the Moon.

8. The total number of aspects within the longitudes is then calculated by adding together the total number of all of the conjunctions, trines, squares, oppositions, and longitudinal proximity elevations. This number is the general planetary index or GPI for the longitudinal planetary measurements and it is included in the calculation of the total GPI for the chart.

9. The total number of positive elevations and the total number of negative elevations are tallied into separate groups. This number is the p/n ratio for the longitudinal planetary measurements and it is included in the calculation of the total p/n ratio for the chart.

Declinational Measurements

1. Parallels and contraparallels are identified using the declinational coordinates of the chart. I have adopted the orb of two degrees, thirty four minutes as the orb of reference for parallels and contraparallels. I have allowed two minutes of tolerance for these calculations; that is, up to two degrees and thirty six minutes.

Positive and negative values for declinational measurement are calculated as follows.

a. All parallels and contraparallels that involve Saturn are negative.
b. If a planet is parallel or contraparallel to another planet that is contraparallel or parallel to Saturn, all declinational aspects involving that planet are also negative. This is called the carryover effect.

SUN PARALLEL VENUS (-)

VENUS PARALLEL SATURN (-)

Normally a Sun Venus parallel is counted as a positive elevation, but since Venus is parallel to Saturn in this case, the Sun Venus parallel becomes negative.

c. All parallels and contraparallels involving Mars are positive when they involve the Sun, Jupiter, or Venus.

SUN PARALLEL MARS (+)
VENUS PARALLEL MARS (+)
JUPITER CONTRA PARALLEL MARS (+)

d. If Saturn is parallel or contraparallel to an otherwise positive Mars parallel or contraparallel, then that positive aspect becomes negative.

JUPITER PARALLEL MARS (-)
MARS CONTRAPARALLEL SATURN (-)

Normally a Jupiter Mars parallel is considered positive, but in this case since Mars is contraparallel to Saturn, the Jupiter Mars parallel becomes negative. This is the carryover effect.

e. All parallels and contraparallels involving Mars are negative when they involve Uranus, Neptune, Mercury, Pluto, and the Moon but do not include the Sun, Jupiter, or Venus.

f. If a negative parallel or contraparallel involving Mars that does not also involve Saturn is parallel or contraparallel to the Sun, Jupiter or Venus, then that negative parallel or contraparallel involving Mars be comes positive. This is called the rescue effect.

EXAMPLE:
MARS PARALLEL URANUS (+)
URANUS CONTRAPARALLEL SUN (+)

The normally negative Mars Uranus parallel is made positive by the Uranus Sun contraparallel.

g. No planetary interaction can rescue a planet parallel or contraparallel to Saturn.

2. Identify the Triangle elevations within the chart. Triangles are formed in the declinations when three planets form a parallel or contraparallel relationship to each other simultaneously.

a. All triangle elevations involving Saturn are considered to be negative.
b. All triangle elevations involving Mars are positive when they include the Sun, Jupiter, or Venus and (do not include Saturn). This is true unless the Sun, Jupiter or Venus are in the extreme declination within that chart.

Example: JUPITER, MARS, URANUS TRIANGLE (+)
UPITER (EXDEK), MARS, URANUS TRIANGLE (-)

The normal Jupiter, Mars, Uranus triangle is positive. A Jupiter placement within the Exdek position changes the value of the triangle to negative. Note, if in the above case of: JUPITER (EXDEK), MARS, URANUS TRIANGLE; THE TRIANGLE BECOMES (+) IF JUPITER IS RESCUED BY VENUS OR THE SUN.

JUPITER (EXDEK), MARS, URANUS TRIANGLE (+)
JUPITER CONTRAPARALLEL SUN (+)

c. If Saturn is parallel or contraparallel to an otherwise positive planetary triangle, that triangle becomes negative.

d. All planetary triangles involving Mars are negative when they include Uranus, Neptune, Mercury, Pluto, or the Moon but do not include the Sun, Jupiter or Venus.

e. If a planetary triangle that includes Uranus, Neptune, Mercury, Pluto or the Moon (exclusive of the Sun, Jupiter, or Venus) is parallel or contraparallel to Mars, then that triangle is negative.

f. If a planet is involved in a positive triangle, it is credited with an additional positive elevation for each positive planetary triangle.

g. If a planet is involved in a negative triangle, it is credited with an additional negative elevation for each negative triangle it is part of.

h. Each triangle elevation is tallied into the calculation of the GPI.

i. Identify the Quad elevations (four planets that form a parallel or contraparallel relationship with each other.)

   1. If the Quad involves Saturn, it is given a negative value.
   2. Quad elevations involving Mars are positive when they include the Sun, Jupiter, or Venus (and do not include Saturn).

2. All planetary quads involving Mars are negative when they include Uranus, Neptune, Mercury, Pluto, or the Moon but do not include the Sun, Jupiter or Venus.

3. If a planetary Quad that includes Uranus, Neptune, Mercury, Pluto or the Moon (exclusive of the Sun, Jupiter, or Venus) is parallel or contraparallel to Mars, then that quad is negative.

4. If a planet is involved in a positive quad, it is credited with an additional positive elevation for each positive planetary quad.

5. If a planet is involved in a negative quad, it is credited with an additional negative elevation for each negative quad.

6. Each quad elevation is tallied into the calculation of the GPI.

h. Identify the Plenary elevations in a chart, (five planets forming parallel or contraparallel relationship with each of the other planets.)

1. All Plenary elevations involving Saturn are considered to be negative.

2. All plenary elevations involving Mars are positive when they include the Sun, Jupiter, or Venus. A plenary involving the Sun, Jupiter and Venus and any other planet except Saturn is considered positive unless Jupiter or Venus within the plenary is found in the Exdek position and is not rescued.

3. All planetary plenary elevations involving Mars are negative when they include Uranus, Neptune, Mercury, Pluto, or the Moon but do not include the Sun, Jupiter or Venus.

4. If a planetary plenary includes Uranus, Neptune, Mercury, Pluto, or the Moon (exclusive of the Sun, Jupiter, or Venus) is parallel or contraparallel to Mars, then that plenary is negative.

5. If a planet is involved in a positive plenary, it is credited with an additional positive elevation for each positive plenary it is part of.

6. If a planet is involved in a negative plenary, it is credited with an additional negative elevation for each negative triangle it is part of.

7. Each plenary is tallied into the calculation of the GPI.

i. Identify the Band elevations in a chart, (six or more planets forming parallel or contraparallel relationship with each of the other planets in the band)

1. All Band elevations involving Saturn are considered to be negative.

2. All band elevations involving Mars are positive when they include the Sun, Jupiter, or Venus. The rescue rule applies here as well, that is, if the Sun, Jupiter or Venus within the band are found in the Exdek position and are not rescued, then the elevation is negative.

3. If Saturn is parallel or contraparallel to an otherwise positive planetary band elevation, that band becomes negative.

4. All planetary band elevations involving Mars are negative when they include Uranus, Neptune, Mercury, Pluto, or the Moon but do not include the Sun, Jupiter or Venus.

5. If a planetary band includes Uranus, Neptune, Mercury, Pluto, or the Moon exclusive of the Sun, Jupiter, or Venus is parallel or contraparallel to Mars, then that band is negative.

6. If a planet is involved in a positive band, it is credited with an additional positive elevation for each positive elevation for each positive band.

7. If a planet is involved in a negative band, it is credited with an additional negative elevation for each negative band.

8. Each band is tallied into the calculation of the GPI.

Identify the High declination (hidek) elevations in the chart. Hidek elevations occur when a planet if found in a declinational position between 21 degrees and 23 degrees and 30 minutes on either side of the celestial equator.)

1. Saturn in the Hidek position is negative.

2. If any planet in the hidek position is parallel or contraparallel to Saturn, the hidek elevation for that planet is negative.

3. If a Hidek planet is parallel or contraparallel or contraparallel to a planet that is parallel or contraparallel to Saturn, its value in that elevation is negative (the carryover effect).

4. If the Sun, Jupiter, or Venus are parallel or contraparallel to a Hidek planet but are not themselves parallel or contraparallel to Saturn, the value of the planet in Hidek elevation is positive.

5. If a Hidek planet is parallel or contraparallel to Mars but is not parallel or contraparallel to the Sun, Jupiter, or Venus, the value of that planet in Hidek is negative.

6. If Uranus, Neptune, Pluto, Mercury, or the Moon occur in the Hidek position and are not parallel or contraparallel to Mars or Saturn (or in the Exdek position), they are considered to have a positive value.

7. If the Sun, Jupiter, or Venus occur in the Hidek position and are not parallel or contraparallel to Saturn, they are considered to have a positive value.

8. If the Sun, Jupiter, or Venus occur in the Hidek position and are parallel or contraparallel to Mars, they are considered to have a positive value.

9. Each Hidek elevation is tallied into the calculation of the GPI.
Identify the Exdek (extreme declination) elevations in the chart. Exdek occurs when a planet is found above 23 degrees and 30 minutes on either side of the c elestial equator.

All planets in the Exdek position are negative unless they are parallel or contraparallel to the Sun, Jupiter, or Venus. In that case, the Sun, Jupiter, or Venus must not form a parallel or contraparallel aspect to Saturn, and they must not be in the Exdek position themselves.

Each Exdek elevation is tallied into the calculation of the GPI.

Identify the Proximity elevations in the chart. Proximity elevations occur when two planets are found within thirty minutes of declination to each within a parallel or contraparallel.

The positive or negative value of the elevation is not changed by proximity enhancement. Each proximity elevation is tallied into the calculation of the GPI.

The total number of elevations within the declinations (positive and negative) is tallied to be used as a part of the calculation of the GPI.

Planetary Eclipses

1. Identify all planetary eclipses. A planetary eclipse occurs when two or more planets are parallel and in conjunction to each other. Planetary eclipses are not assigned separate positive or negative values and are not included in the tally of the GPI.

2. A simple planetary eclipse occurs when two planets are parallel and in conjunction at the same time.

3. A binary eclipse occurs when three planets are parallel and in conjunction to each other at the same time.

4. A plenary eclipse occurs when four or more planets are parallel and in conjunction to each other at the same time.

Degree of Elevation

Degrees of elevation represent the total of the positive and negative activity of each planet. A planet has a positive degree of elevation and a negative degree of elevation. This number is representative of the planet's level of activity within a particular chart. A planet with only one positive interaction in a chart has a first degree positive elevation in that chart. If that planet has five negative elevations in that particular chart it has a fifth degree negative elevation in that chart. A planet with six or more elevations (positive or negative) is said to have a grand elevation within that chart.

Therefore, if a planet has four negative elevations and eight positive elevations, it may be said to have a fourth degree negative elevation and a positive grand elevation within that chart.

Planetary Indices

The planetary index is a relative value of the overall activity of a planet within a particular chart. It is calculated by adding together the total number of positive and negative elevations within a chart. Therefore, a chart with a fourth degree negative elevation of Mars and a third degree positive elevation of Mars is said to have a (-100) planetary index for Mars in that chart.

If a planet has a third degree negative elevation of Mars and a fifth degree positive elevation of Mars, that planet is said to have a (+200) planetary for Mars in that chart. (Note: Planetary eclipses are not used in the calculation of planetary indices.)

General Planetary Index

The general planetary index or GPI is found by adding the total of all the longitudinal and declinational elevations within a chart. In the longitudes, this includes the conjunctions, trines, sextiles, squares, oppositions, and longitudinal proximity elevations. In the declinations, the parallels, contraparallels, triangles, quads, plenaries, and bands are counted toward the GPI. In the positional elevations, the hidek elevations, exdek elevations, and the proximity elevations are counted toward the GPI. On the average, there are 28-30 total planetary interactions in a chart.

Positive/Negative Ratio (p/n ratio)

The p/n ratio is calculated by dividing the total number of positive planetary elevations by the total number of negative planetary elevations.

If there are 30 positive elevations in a chart and 25 negative elevations within that chart, the p/n ratio for that chart is 1.2. The average p/n ratio is around 1.16.

Temporal index

The temporal index is calculated by multiplying the GPI by the P/N and then multiplying that number by 100.

If the GPI is 28 and the P/N is 1.2, the temporal index for that chart is 3360.

Positive Karmic Index

The positive karmic index is calculated as follows:

(Sun index + Jupiter index + Venus index) X P/N

If the Sun index is 200, Jupiter index is 300), the Venus index is (-200), and the P/N is 1.2, then the positive karmic index for that chart is

200+300+ (-200) X 1.2 = 360

Negative Karmic index

The negative karmic index is calculated as follows:

(Saturn index + Mars index) divided by the P/N

If the Saturn index is (-600) and the Mars index is (-400) and the P/N is 2.3, then the negative karmic index for that chart is

(-600) + (-400) divided by 2.3 = 434.78

BIBLIOGRAPHY AND RESOURCES

Benor, D.J. (1990). Survey of spiritual healing research. Complementary Medical Research, 4. 9-33.

Berger, R.E. (1988). Psi effects without real time feedback. Journal of Parapsychology. 52, 1-27.

Berger, R.E. & Honorton, C. (1984). PsiLab II: A standardized psi-testing system., Research In Parapsychology, 1985 (85-88). Metuchen, NJ Scarecrow Press.

Berger, R.E. & Persinger, M.A. (1991). Geophysical variables and behavior: LXVII. Quieter annual geomagnetic activity and larger effect size for experimental psi(ESP) studies over six decades. Perceptual and Motor Skills 73,1219-1223.

Bierman, D.J. (1995). A free response precognition experiment via the World Wide Web. Proceedings of Presented Papers, 38th Annual Convention of the Parapsychological Association, Durham, North Carolina, pp. 38-42.

Bierman, D.J. & Wezelman, R. (1996). Anomalous correlations between mental intentionand remote traffic density with direct feedback over the Internet. Proceedings of Presented Papers, 39th Annual Convention of the Parapsychological Association, San Diego, pp. 197-204.

Bisaha, J.P. & Dunne, B.J. (1979). Multiple subject and long-distance precognitive remote viewing of geographic locations. In C. Tart, H.e. Puthoff & J.R. Targ (eds.) Mind at large (pp. 107-124). New York: Praeger.

Bigu,J. (1976): On the biophysical basis of the human 'aura'. Journal of Research on Psi Phenomena, Vol 1, 8-43.

Blackmore, S.J. (1982): Beyond the body. London: Heinemann.

Blackmore, S.J. (1984): A psychological theory of the out-of- body experience. Journal of Parapsychology, 48,201-218.

Bohm, D. (1952). Quantum theory as an indication of new order in physics. Part B. Implicate order and explicate order in physical law. Foundations of Physics, 3, 139-168.

Bohm, D. (1986). A new theory of the relationship of mind and matter. Journal of the American Society for Psychical Research,80, 113-136.

Bohm, D. (1980). Wholeness and the Implicate Order. London: Routledge & Kegan Paul. Ed.fr. (1987).

Bowles, N. & Hynds, F. (1978). Psi Search. New York: Haper & Row.

Bozzano, E. (1923). Les phenomenes de hantise au moment de la mort. Paris: Ed. De la B.P.S.

Braud, L.W. (1976). Openness vs. closedness and its relationship to psi. Research In Parasychology 1976.

Braud, L.W. (1976). Openness vs. closedness and its relationship to psi. ResearchIn Parapsychology 1976.

Braud, W. (1975). Psi conductive states. Journal of Communication, 25, 141-152.

Braud, W. (1990). Distant mental influence of rate hemolysis of human red blood cells. Journal of the American Society for Psychical Research, 84, 1-24.

Braud, W. & Schlitz,M. (1991). Conciousness interactions with remote biological systems. Subtle Energies, 2, 1-46.

Braud, W. & Schlitz, M. (1989). A methodology for the objective study of transpersonal imagery. Journal of Scientific Exploration, 3, 43-63.

Braud, W., Wood , R. & Braud, L. (1975). Free-response GESP preformance during an experimental hypnagogic state induced by visual and acoustic ganzfeld techniques. A replication and extension. Journal of the American Society for Psychical Research, 69, 105-114.

Braude, A. (1989). Radical spirits: Spiritualism and women's rights in nineteenth-century America. Boston, MA: Beacon Press.

Braude, S.E. (1979). ESP and PK: A philosophical examinaiton. Philadelphia: Temple University Press.

Braude, S.E. (1986). The limits of influence: Psychokinesis and the philosophy of science. New York: Routledge & Kegan Paul

Braude, S.E. (1991). First person plural: Multiple personality and the philosophy of mind. New York: Routledge

Broad, C.D. (1960). The Mind and its place in nature. Littlefield, Adams & Co.: New Jersey.

Broughton, R. (1991). Parapsychology: The controversial science. New York: Ballantine Books.

Broughton, R. (1982). Computer methodology: total control with a human face. In B. Shapin & L.Coly (Eds.) Parapsychology and the experimental method (pp.24-42). New York: Parapsychology Foundation.

Burdick, D. S. and Kelly, E.F. (1977/1986). Statistical methods in parapsychological research. In B.B. Wolman, L.A. Dale, G.R.Schmeidler & M. Ullman (Eds). Handbook of Parapsychology (pp.81-120). Jefferson, North Carolina: McFarland & Company.

Burt, Cyril (1961): The structure of the mind. British Journal of Statistical Psychology, 14. 145-170.

Capra, F. (1975). The Tao of Physics. Berkely: Shambhala.

Carpenter, J. C. (1975). Toward the effective utilization of enhanced weak-signal Esp effects. Unpublished paper presented at the Annual Metting of the AAAS, New York.

Casti, J. (1989). Lost paradigms. William Morrow: New York.

Chauvin, R. (1986). A PK experiment with mice. Journal of the Society for Psychical Research, 53, 348-351.

Chauvin, R & Genthon, J. P. (1965). Eine untersuchung uber die moglichkeut psychokinetscher experimetn mit uranium nad geigerzalher. Zeitschrift fur Parapsychologie and Grenzebiete der Psychologie, 8, 140-147.

Child, I. (1985). Psychology and anomalous observations: The question of ESP in dreams. American Psychologist, 40, 1219-1230.

Combs, A. & Holland, M. (1990). Synchronicity: Science, myth, and the trickster. New York: Marlowe & Co.

Costa de Beauregard, O. (1975). Quantum paradoxes and Aristotle's twofold information concept. In L. Oteri (Ed.), Quantum physics and parapsychology (pp. 91-108). New York: Parapsychology Foundation

Costa de Beauregaurd, O. (1983). Implications of relativity, quantum theory and information theories for paraparapsychology. Psychoenergetics, 5, 16-170.

Costa de Beauregaurd, O. (1985). On some frequent but controversial statements concerning the Einstein-Podolsky-Rosen Correlations. Foundations of Physics, 15, 871-887.

Costa de Beauregaurd, O. (1988). La physique moderne et les pouvoirs de l'esprit. Paris: Le Hameau.

Costa de Beauregaurd, O. (1989). Relativity and probability, classical or quantal. In M. Kafatos (Ed.), Bell's theorem, auantum theory and conceptions of the universe (pp. 117-125). Kluwer cademic Publishers.

Costa de Beauregaurd, O. (1990). Le temps deploye. Paris: Ed.du Rocher

Cox, W. (1956)/ Precognition: An analysis. Journal of the American Society for Psychical Ressearch, 50, 99-109.

D'Espagnat, B. (1979). The quantum theory and reality. Scientific American,. 128-241-245.

Dalton, K., Steinkamp, R. & Sherwood, S. (1996). A dream GESP experiment using dynamic targets and consensus vote. Proceedings of Presented Papers, 37th Annual Convention of the Parapsychological Association, San Diego, pp. 57-72.

Dean, D., Mihalasky, J., Ostrander, S. & Schroeder, L. (1974). Executive ESP. Englewood Cliffs, NJ: Prentice Hall.

Delanoy, D.L. & Sah, S. (1994). Cgnitive and physicological psi responses to remote positive and neutral emotional states. Proceedings of Presented Papers, 37th Annual Convention of Parapsychological Association, Amsterdam, pp. 128-138.

Declos, M. (1987). Le toucher interieur: En direct dune boyante. Pairs: Souffles.

De. Martino, E. (1948/1971): Le monde magique. Paris: Ed. Marabout.

Dixon, N. F. (1978). Subliminal perception and parapsychology: Points of contact. In B. Shapin & L. Coly (Eds.), Brain/Miond and parapsychology (pp.206-220). New York: Parapsychology Foundation.

Dixon, N. (1981). Preconscious processing. Chichester: John Wiley & Sons.

Don, N.S., McDonough, B.E., & Warren, C.A. (1995). Differential brain responses to targets and nontargets in a precognitive forced-choice task. Proceedings of Presented Papers, 38th Annual Convention of the Paarapsychological Association, Durham, North Carolina, USA, pp. 113-121.

Dunne, B.J. (1991). Co-operator experiments with an REG device. Princeton, NJ: Princenton University, PEAR Technical Note 91005.

Dune, B.J. (1996). Gender differences in huuman/machine anomalies. Princeton, NJ: Princeton University, PEAR Techinical Note 96001.

Dune, B.J. & Jahn, R.G. (1992). Experiments in remote human/machine interaction. Journal of Society for Scientific Exploration, 6, 311-332.

Dunne, B.J., Jahn, R.D. & Nelson, R.D. (1983). Precognitive remote perception. Princeton, NJ: Princeton University, PEAR Technical Note 83003.

Duplessis, Y. (1984). Les Couleurs visibles et non visibles. Paris: Ed du Rocher.

Duplesisis, Yvonne (1975). The pranormal perception of color. Parapsychological Monographys, No. 16. New York: Parapsycho-logy Foundation.

Dutheil, R. (1990). L'Univers superlumineus. Paris: Sand.

Duval, P. & Montredon, E. (1968). Further psi experiments with mice. Journal of Parapsychology. 9, 53-56.

Eccles, J. (1977). The human person in its two-way relationship to the brain. Research In Parapsychology, 1976. Metuchen, NJ: Scarecrow Press.

Eccles, J. (1989). Evolution of the brain: Creation of the self. New York: Routledge.

Edelman, G.M. (1992). Bright air, brilliant fire: On the matter of the mind. New York: Basic Books.

Edge, H.L., Morris, R.L.,palmer, J. & Rush, J.H. (1986). Foundations of parapsychology: Exploring the boundries of human capability. New York: Routledge & Kegan Paul.

Ehrenwald, j. (1954). Telepathy and the child-parent reltionship. Journal of the American Society for Psychical Research, 48, 43-55.

Ehrenwald, J. (1955). New dimensions of deep analysis. New York: Grune and Stratton.

Ehrenwald, J. (1977/1986a). Psi, psychotherapy and psychoanalysis. In B.B. Wolman, L.A. Dale, G.R. Schmeidler & M. Ulman (Eds). Handbook of Parapsychology (pp. 529-540). Jefferson, North Carolina: McFarland & Company.

Ehrenwald, J. (1978). The right hemisphere: Pathway to psi and creativity. In B. Shapin & L. Coly (Eds.), Brain/Mind and parapsychology (pp. 221-232). New York: Parapsychology Foundation.

Ehrenwald, J. (1978). The ESP experience: A psychiatric validation. New York: Basic Books

Einstien, A., Pololsky B., & Rosen, N. (1935). Can quantum mechanical description of physical reality be considered complete? Physical Reviews, 47-777-780.

Eisenbud, J. (1970). Psi and psychoanalysis. New York: Grune and Stratton.

Ertel, S. (1994). Testing Sheldrake's claim of morophogentic fields. In E.W. Cook & D.L. Delanoy (Eds.), Research in Parapsychology 1991. (pp. 169-192). Metuchen, NJ: Scarecrow Press.

d'Espagnat, B. (1979). The quantum theory and reality. Scientific American, 128, 241-245.

Evans, C. (1973). Parapsychology-what the questionnaire revealed. New Scientist, 57, 209.

Eysenck, H.J. (1967). Personality and extrasensory perception. Journal of the Society for Psychical Research, 44, 55-71.

Feinberg, G. (1967). Possibility of faster-than-light-particles. Physical Review, 159, 1089.

Feinberg, G. (1967). Possibility of faster-than-light-particles, Physical Review, 159, 1089.

Feinberg, G. (1975). Precognition—A memory of things future. In L. Oteri (Ed.), Quantum physics and parapsychology (pp. 54-75). New York: Parapsychology Foundation

Flammarion, C. (1923): Les maisons hantees. Paris: Lib Ernest Flammarion.

Flammarion, C. (1923): La mort et ses mysteres. Paris: hai lu.

Frank, J. (1973). Persuasion and Healing. New York: Schocken Books.

Franz, M.L.von. (1980) On divination and synchronicity. Toronto: Inner City Books.

Garrett, E.J. (1949). Adventures in the supernormal. New York: Garrett.

Garrett, E.J. (1968). Many voices: The autobiography of a medium. New York : Putnam.

Gauld, A. (1977/1986). Discarnate survival. In B.B. Wolman, L.A. Dale, G.R. Schmeidler & M. Ullman (Eds). Handbook of Parapsychology (pp. 577-630). Jerfferson, North Carolina: McFarland & Company.

Gauld, A. (1992). A history of Hypnotism. Cambridge University Press.

Gauld, A. (1983). The founders of psychical research. London: Routledge & Kegan Paul.

Giroldini, W. (1991). Eccles model of mind-brain interaction and psychokinesis: a preliminary study. Journal of Scientific Exploration, 5, 145-161.

Gissurasion, L.R. & Gunnarsson, A. (1997). An experiment with the alledged human aura. Journal of the American Society for Psychical Research, 91, 33-49.

Grad, B. (1965). Some bilogical effects of the laying on of hands: A review of experiments with animals and plants. Journal of the American Society for Psychical Research, 59, 95-127.

Grad, B. (1967). The 'laying on of hands': Implications for psychotherapy, gentling and the placebo effect. Journal of the American Society for Psychical Research, 61, 286-305.

Gurney, E., Myers, F.W.H. & Podmore, F. (1886). Phantasms of the living (2 volumes). London : Trubner.

Gurney, E. & Myers, F.W.H. (1985). Some higher aspects of Mesmerism. Proceedings of the Society for Psychical Research, 401-423.

Hall, H. (1982). Hypnosis and the immune system: A review with implications for cancer and the psychology of healing. American Journal of Clinical Hypnosis, 25, 92-103.

Hameroff, S., Kaszniak, A. & Scott, A. (1996). Toward a schience of consciousness. Cambridge, Mass: MIT Press.

Hansen, G.P., Schlitz, M.J. and Tart, C.T. (1984). Remote viewing research 1973-1982. In R. Targ & K. Harary: The mind race: Understand and Using Psychic Abilities (pp. 279-282). New York: Ballantine Books.

Haraldsson, E. et al. (1977): National survey of psychical experiences and attitudes towards the paranormal in Iceland. Research In Parapsychology 1976 (pp. 182-*186). Mjetuchen, NJ: Scarecrow Press.

Haraldsson, E., Houtkooper, J. & Hoeltje, C. (1987). The Defense Mechanism Test as predictor of ESP preformance. Journal of Parapsychlogy, 51, 76-90.

Haraldsson, E., Houtkooper, J. (1992). Effects of perceptual defensiveness, personality and belief on extrasensory perception tasks. Personality and Individual Differences, 13, 1985-1096.

Haraldsson, E., Houtkooper, J. (1995). Children claiming previous life memories: Their personality and abilities. Proceeding of Presented Papers, 38th Annual Convention of Parapsychological Association, Durham, North Carolina, USA, pp. 122-131.

Haraldsson, E. (1996). The giftedness of children who claim previous life memories. Proceeding of the 3rd EuroSSE meeting, Freiburg, Germany, pp. 48.

Harary, K., Targ, R. & White, A. (1985). An applications orientation to psi research. Research In Parapsychology 1984 (pp. 119-120). Metuchen, NJ: Scarecrow Press.

Hardy, C. (1986). L'Apres-vie a l'epreuve de la science. Paris: Editions du Rocher.

Hardy, C. (1988). La Science et les etats frontieres. Paris: Editions du Rocher.

Hardy, C. (1994). Le livre de la divination. Paris: Profrance, Maxi-Livres.

Hardy, C. (1994). Le regard cree du sens: les synergies semantiques. Troisieme Millenaire, 31, 26-29.

Hardy, C. (1995). La connaissance de l' invisible: le vecu de la transe. Paris: editions du Dauphin.

Hardy, C. (1996). Theorie des champs semantiques: dynamiques de l'interpretation et de la creation de sens. Bio-Math, 135, 21-37.

Hardy, C. (1996). Semantic fields and meaning: a bridge between mind and matter. World Futures, 48, 161-170.

Hardy, C. (1988). Networks of meaning. Westport, Conn: Greenwood.

Hervert, N. (1985). Quantum reality: Beyond the new physics. New York: doubleday.

Hebert, N. (1988). Faster than light: Superluminal loopholes in phycisd. Canada: Penquin Books.

Heisenberg, W. (1961): Physique et philosophie. Paris: Albin Michel.

Hibbard, W. & Worring, R. (1982). Psychic criminology: An operations manual for using psychics in criminal investigations. Springfield, III: Charles C Thomas.

Honorton, C. (1974). Psi-conductive states of awareness. In Mitchell, E. G. & White, J. (Eds.), Psychic exploration: A challenge for science (pp.616-639). New York: G.P. Putnam's Sons.

Honorton, C. (1975). Error some place. Journal of Communication, 25, 103-116.

Honorton, C. (1977/1986). Psi and internal attention states. In B.B. Wolman, L.A. Dale, G.R. Schmeidler & M. Ullman (Eds). Handbook of Parapsychology (pp. 435-472). Jefferson, North Carolina: McFarland & Company.

Honorton, C. (1985). Meta-analysis of psi ganzfeld research: A response to Hyman. Journal of Parapsychology, 49, 51-91.

Honorton, C. (1987). Precognition and real-time ESP performance in a computer task with an exceptional subject. Journal of Parapsychology, 51, 291-320.

Honorton, C. (1993). Summarizing research findings: Meta-analytic methods and their use in parapsychology. In L. Coly & J.D.S. McMahon (Eds.), Psi research methodology: A re-examination (pp. 90-106). New York: Parapsychology Foundation.

Honorton, C., Berger, R., Varvoglis, M., Derr, P, Schechter, E. & Ferrari, D. (1990> Psi communication in the ganzfeld: Experiments with an automated testing system and comparizon with a meta-analysis of earlier studies. Journal of Parapsychology, 54, 99-139.

Hornton, C. & Ferrari, D. (1989). Meta-analysis of forced choice precognition experiments 1935-1987. Journal of Parapsychology, 53-281-308.

Honorton, C., Ferrari, D. & Bem, D. (1992). Extraversion and ESP performance: A metanalysis and New Confirmation. Research inParapsychology 1990 (pp. 35-38). Metuchen, NJ: Scarecrow Press.

Honorton, C. & Schelcter, E. (1987). Ganzfeld target retrieval with a n automated testing system: A model for initial success. Research In Parapsychology, 1986. Metuchen, NJ: Scarecrow Press.

Honorton, C. & Tremmel, L. (1979). Psi correlates of volition: a preliminary test of Eccles "neurophysicological hypothesis" of mind-brain interaction. Research In Parapsychology, 1978 (pp. 36-38). Metuchen, NJ: Scarecrow Press.

Hyman, R. (1977). "Cold reading": How to convince strangers that you know all about them. Zetetic/Skeptical Inquirer, 1. 18-37.

Hyman, R. & Honorton, C. (1986). A joint communique: The psi ganzfeld controversy. Journal of Parapsychology, 50, 4, 315-370.

Irwin, H.J. (1985). Flight of mind: A psychological study of the out-of –body experience. Metuchen, NJ: Scarecrow Press.

Irwin, H.J. (1996). Childhood antecedents of out-of-body experiences and deja ve experiences. Journal of the American Society for Psychical Research, 90, 157-174.

Jahn, R.G. (1982). The persistent paradox of psychic phenomena: Am engineering perspective. Proceedings of the IEEE, 70, 136-170.

Jahn, R. & Dunne, B. (1985). On the quantum mechanics of consciousness, with application ot anomalous phenomena. Foundations of Physics, 16, 721-772.

Jahn, R. & Dunne, B. (1987). Margins of reality: The role orf consciousness in thphysical world. New York: Harcourt, Brace, Jovanovich.

Jahn, R., Nelson, R. & Dunne, B. (1987). Engineering anomalies research., Journal of Scientific Exploration, 1, 21-50.

James, W. (1958). The varieties of religious experience. New American Libraray. Ed.fr: L experience religieuse, Paris: Alcan

Janet, P. & Gilbert, M. (1886). Sur quelques phenomenes de somnambrlisme. Revue Philosophique, I and II.

Janin, P. (1977). Le tychoscope. Psi realite, 1, 37.

Jones, E. (1957). The Life and Work of Sigmund Freud. New York: Basic Books, Vol . 3.

Jones, S. (1984). Proceedings of a symposium on applications of anomalous phenomena. Santa Barbara, CA: Kaman Sciences Corporation.

Josephson, B.D. & Pallikari- Viras, F. (1991). Biological utilisation of quantum nonlocality. Foundations of Physics, 21, 197-207

Jung, K.G. (1977). Psychology and the occult. Bollingen series. Princeton, NJ: Princeton University Press.

Jung, K.G. & Pauli, W. (1955). The interpretation of nature and the psyche: Synchronicity and the influence of archetypal ideas on the scientific theoris of Kepler. New York: Pantheon.

Jung, K.G. (1973). Synchronicity, an acausal connecting priniciple. Bollingen series. Princeton University Press.

Jung, K.G. (1967). Metamorphoses de l'ame et ses symboles. Paris: Buchet-Chastel.

Kardec, A. (1857). Le livre des esprits. Paris: dervy Livres

Keil, Jurgen (1996). Cases of the reincarnation type: An evaluation of some indirect evidence. Proceedings of the 3rd Euro SSE meeting, Freiburgh, Germany, page 52.

Kelly, E. (1978). Converging lines of evidence on mind/brain relations. Parapsychology Foundation: Brain/Mind and Parapsychology.

Kihlstorm, J.F. (1996). Unconscious processes in social interaction. In S. Hameroff, A. Kaszniak & A. Scott (Eds) Toward a science of conscious-ness (pp. 93-104). Cambridge, Mass: MIT Press

Klimo, Jon (1987). Channeling: Investigations on receiving informaiton from paranormal sources. Tarcher: Los Angeles

Krippner, S. & Welch, P. (1992). Spiritual dimensions of healing. Irvington Publishers: New York.

Krippner, S. & Persinger, M.A. (1993). Enhance-ment of accuracy of telepathic dreams during periods of decreased geomagnetic activity: The William E experiments. Proceedings of Presented Papers, 36th Annual Convention of the Parapsychological Association, Durham, North Caroloina, USA (pp. 126-131).

Kristen, M. (1994). Fille des etolies. Paris: Ed. Du Levant.

Kristen, M. (1996). La partique des arts divin-atoires. TF! Editions.

Kuhn, T.S. (1962). The Structure of scientific revolutions. Chicago: University of Chicago. Laszlo, E. (1994): The creative universe. Edinburgh: Floris Books.

Laszlo, E. (1995): The interconnected universe. London: World Scientific Publishing.

Lawrence, T. (1993). A meta-analysis of forced choice sheep-goat studies 1947-1993. Proceedings of Presented Papers, 36th Annual Conventionof the Parapsychological Association, Durham, North Carolina, USA (pp. 75-86).

Lorimer, D. (1987). Survival? London: Routlege & Kegan Paul.

Luchadou, W. v. (1988). The model of pragmatic informtion (MPI). Research in Parapsychology 1987 (pp. 18-22). Metuchen, NJ:L Scarecrow Press.

Lyons, A. & Truzzi, M. (1991). The blue sense: Psychic detectives and crime. New York: Mysterious.

McCaffrey, A. (1974). To ride Pegasus. London: Corgi Books.

McConnell, R. (1983). An introduction to parapsychology in the context of science. Pittsbrugh, PA: McConnell.

McLenon, J. (1984). Deviant Science. Philadelphia, PA: University of Pennsylvania Press.

Maher, M.C. & Hansen, G.P. (1992). Quantitative investigation of a reported haunting using several detection techniques. Journal of the American Society for Psychical Research, 86, 347-374.

Maher, M.C. & Hansen, G.P. (1995). Quantitave investigation of a recurrent apparition. Journal of the American Society for Psychical Research, 69, 341-352.

Marks, D. & Kamman, R. (1978). Information transmission in remote viewing experiments. Nature, 272, 680-681.

Mauskopf, S.H> & McVaugh, M.R. (1980). The elusive science. Baltimore: John Hopkins University Press.

May, E.C. (1996). The American Institutes for Research Review of thc Department of Defense's STAR GATE program: A commentary. Journal of Scientific Exploration, 10, 89-108.

May, E.C., Humphrey, B.C. & Hubbard, G.S. (1980). Electronic system perturbation techniques. Final Report. Menlo Park, Ca: SRI International.

May, E.C., et al. (1990). Advances in Remote Viewing analysis. Journal of Parapsychology, 54, 193-228.

May, E.C., Utts, J.M. & Spottiswoode, S.J.P (1995). Decision Augmentation Theory: Applications to the RNG datatbase. Journal of the Society for Scientific Exploration, 9, 453-488.

Millar, B. (1978). The observational theories: A primer. European Journal of Parapsychology, 2, 304-332.

Mishlove, J. (1986). Psi development systems. Jefferson, NC: McFarland & Company.

Mishlove, J. (1986) Psionics: The practical application of psi. In B. Shapin & L. Coly (Eds.), Current trends in psi research (pp. 120-136). New York: Parapsychology Foundation.

Mishloove, J. (1993). The Roots of Consciousness. Tulsa, OK: Council Oak Books.

Monroe, R. (1971). Journeys out of the body. New York: Doubleday & Co.

Moore, L. (1977). In search of white crows: Spiritualism, parapsychology, and American culture. New York: Oxford University Press.

Moreau, C. (1976). Freud et l'occultisme. Toulouse: Ed. Privat.

Morris, R.L. (1974). The use of detectors for out of body experiences. Research In Parapsychology 1973. Metuchen, NJ: Scarecrow Press.

Morris, R.L. (1977/1986). Parapsychology, biology and anpsi. In B.B. Wolman, L.A> Dale, G.R. Schmeidler & M. Ullman (Eds). Handbook of Parapsychology (pp. 687-715). Jefferson, North Carolina: McFarland & Company.

Morris, R.L., Harary,B.,Janis, J., Hartwell, J. & Roll, W. (1978). Studies of communication during out-of –body experiences. Journal of the American Society for Psychical Research, 72, 1-21.

Murphy, G. (1945). Field theory and survival. Journal of the American Society for Psychical Research, 39, 181-209.

Murphy, G. (1977/1986). William James and psychical research. In B.B. Wolman, L.A. Dale, G.R. Schmeidler & M. Ullman (Eds). Handbook of Parapsychology (pp. 48-55). Jefferson, North Carolina: McFarland & Company.

Murphy, M. (1993). The Future of the Body. New York: Tarcher.

Myers, F.W.H. (1903). Human Personality and its survival of bodily death (2 volumes). London: Longmans, Green.

EDUCATIONAL AND RESEARCH ORGANIZATIONS

ARGENTINA

Instituo de Psicologia Paranormal
Asociacion Ibero-Americana de Parapsicologia
Salta 2015m (1137) Capital Federal
Buenos Aires

Instituto de Parapsicologia
Zabala 1930
1712 Castelar
Prov. De Buenos Aires

AUSTRALIA

Australian Institute of Parapsychological Research
P.O. Box 445
Lane Cove, NSW 2066
Australia

BRAZIL

Instituto de Pesquisas Interdisciplinares
Das Ares Fronterícas da Psicologia
Rua Vicente Jose de Almeida, 228
Jardim Cupece-Sao Paulo/SP
CEP: 04652-140

ENGLAND

Perrot-Warrick Research Unit
Dept. of Psychology
Univ. of Hertfordsire
College Lane, Hatfield AL 109AB

SMN: Scientif and Medical Network
Lesser Halings, Tilehouse Lane
Denham, Uxbridge
Middlesex UB 9 5DG

SRP: Society for Psychical Research
49 Marloes Rd
London W8 6LA

FRANCE

IMI: Institut Metapsychique International
1, place Wagram
Paris 75017

Laboratoire de Parapsychologie
UER de Mathematiques, Bureau 644
Univ. de Tolouse le Mirail
31058 Toulouse Cedex

GERMANY

Institu fur Grezebiete der Psychologie und Psychohygiene
Eichalde 12
Freiburg i.BR. D-79104

HOLLAND

Chair of Parapsychology
Univ. of Utrecht, Postbus 80125
3508 TC Utrecht

Department of Psychology
University of Amsterdam

Parapsychology Insitute
Springweg 7
3511 VH Utrecht

ITALY

Centro Italiano di Parapsicologia
Via Poggio de Mari, 16
801290 Napoli

MEXICO

Insituto Latinoamericano de Psicologia Paranormal
Apartado Postal 156
San Juan del Rio, 76800 Queretaro

PUERTO RICO

Centro de Estudios Intergrales de Puerto Rico
P.O. Box 194176
San Juan 00919-4176.

SCOTLAND

Koestler Chair of Parapsychology
Dept. of Psychology,
Univ. of Edinburgh, 7 George Sq.
Edinburgh EH8 9JZ

SWITZERLAND

Foundation Odier de Psychophysique
Route de la Capite 77
1223 Cologny (Geneve)

USA

ASPR: American Society for Psychical Research
5 W. 73rd St.
New York, NY 10023

Center for Frontier Sciences
Temple Univ. Ritter Hall 003-00
Philadelphia, AO 19122

Center for Advanced Cognitive Studies
Unvi. of Nevada
4505 Maryland Pkwy
Box 454009
Las Vegas, NV 89154

Cognitive Sciences Labortaory
330 Cowper St.
Suite 200
Palo Alto, CA 94301

Exceptional Human Experiences Network
414 Rockledge Rd.
New Bern, NC 28562

IONS: Institute of Noetic Sciences
475 Gate Five RD, Suite 300
P.O. Box 909, Sausalito CA 94966

ITP: Institute for Transpersonal Psychology
250 Oak Grove Ave
Menlo Park, CA 94025

Kairos Foundation
1187 Wilmette Ave. #174
Wilmette, IL. 60091

Office of Paranormal Investigations
P.O. Box 875
Orinda, CA 94563

PA: Parapsychological Association, Inc.
P.O. Box 797
Fairhaven, MA 02719

PF: Parapsychology Foundation
228 E. 71st St
New York, NY 10021

PEAR: Princeton Engineering Anomalies Rs.
C131 Engineering Quad
Princeton Univ.
Princeton, NJ 08544

RRC: Rhine Research Center
402 N. Buchanan Blvd
Durham, NC 27701, USA

Rosebridge Graduate School of Integrative Psychology
1040 Oak Grove Road, Suite #103
Concord, CA 94518.

Saybrook Institute
450Pacific Ave.
San Fransicso, CA 94133

SSE: Society for Scientific Exploration
ERL 306, Stanford Univ.
Standford, CA 94305, USA

SCIENTIFIC
JOURNALS

Australian Parapsychological Review
P.O. Box 445
Lane Cove, NSW 2066
Australia

Cuadernos de Parapsicologia
Zabala 1930
1712 Castelar
Prov. De Buenos Aires

European Jounal of Parapsychology
Koestler Chair of Parapsychology
Dept. of Psychology,
Univ. of Edinburgh, 7 George Sq.
Edinburgh EH8 9JZ, Scotland

Exceptional Human Experience
414 Rockledge Rd.
New Bern, NC 28562, USA

Frontier Perspectives
Center for Frontier Sciences
Temple Univ.
Ritter Hall 003-OO
Philadelphia, PA 19122, USA

Journal of Amer. Society for Psychical Research
A.S.P.E., 5 W 73rd St.,
New York, NY 10023, USA

Journal of the Society for Psychical Research
S.P.R., 49 Maroles Rd, London,
England, W8 6LA

Journal of Scientific Exploration
ERL 306, Stanford University
Stanford, CA 94305, USA

Journal of Parapsychology
402 N. Buchanan Blvd
Durham, NC 27701 Usa
Revista Argentina de Psicologia
Paranormal
Institue fo Paranormal Psychology
Salta 2015 (1137) Capital Federal
Bueno Aires

Revista Brasileira de Parapsicologia
Rua Vicente Jose de Almeid, 228
Jardim Cupece-Sao Paulo/ SP
CEP: 04652-140

Revista Mexicana de Psicologia Paranormal.
Apartado Postal 156
San Juan del Rio, 76800 Queretaro
Mexico.

Revue Francaise de Psychotronique
UER de Mathematiques, Bureau 644
Univ. de Toulouse le Mirail
31058 Toulouse Cedex, France

Tijdschrift voor Parapsychologie
Redactie TvP
Bloemgracht 81,
1016 KH Amsterdam, Holland

Zeitschrift fur parapsychologie und
    Grenzebiete der psychologie
Eichalde 12
78 Freiburg i. BR., D-79104
Germany

Newsletters and Popular Journals:

ASPR Newsletter
    Amer.Soc. for psychical Research
    5 W. 73rd St
    New York, NY 10023, USA
Brain-Mind Bulletin
    Box 421069
    Los Angeles, CA 90042, USA
Bulletin
    Fond. Odier de Psychophysique
    Route de la Capite 77
    1223 Cologny, Geneva, Switzerland

Intuition Magazine
    P.O. Box 460773
San Francisco, CA 94146, USA
Network
    Scientific and Medical Network
    Lesser Halings, Tilehouse Lane,
    Denham, uxbridge
    Middlesex UB9 5DG, England
Noetic Sciences Review
    Institute of Noetic Sciences
    475 Gate Five RD, Suite 300
    Sausalito CA 94965, USA
PA News
    c/o Puente Publications
    P.O. Box 194176
    San Juan, Puerto Rico 00919-4176
Parapsychology Review(no longer published)
    Parapsychology Foundation
    29 W. 57th St, N.Y. 10019, USA
Science Frontieres
    8 bis rue du Chemin de Fer
    94110 Arcueil, France

The Explorer
Society for Scientific Exploration
ERL 306, Stanford Univ.
Stanford, CA 94305, USA
The Paranormal Review
Society for Psychical Research
49 Marloes Rd, Kensington
London W8 6LA, England
Thinking Allowed Videos
2560 Ninth St., Suite 123
Berkeley, CA 94710, USA

Major
Reference Books
And Series:

Advances in Parapsychological Research
McFarland & Co
Box 611
Jefferson, North Carolina 28640, USA.
Foundations of Parapsychology (1986)
Edge,H., Morris, R., Palmer, J., Rush, J.
Routledge & Kegan Paul.
New York, NY USA
Hndbook of Parapsychology (1977/1986)
B. Wolman (Ed.)
McFarland & Co
Box 611
Jefferson, North Carolina 28640, USA.
Proceedings of International Conferences
Parapsychology Foundaiton
29 W. 57th St,
New York, NY 10019, USA
Research In Parapsychology (RIP)
Scarecrow Press Inc.
C/o University Presses of America
4720 Boston Way
Lanham, Maryland 20706 USA
The Future of the Body
Michael Murphy
Tarcher/Perigree
The Putnam Publishing Co.
200 Madison Ave.
New York, NY 10016, USA

Websites

LABS AND RESEARCH CENTERS

UNIVERSIYT OF AMSTERDAM
http://www.psy.uva.nl/abnomal

UNIVERSITY OF EDINBURGH
http://www.ed.ac.uk/~ejua35/for.html
http://moebius.psy.,ed.ac.uk/kpu.html

COGNITIVE SCIENCES LAB
http://jsasoc.com/~csl/index.html

RHINE RESEARCH LAB
http://www.mindspring.com/~rhine/

UNIVERSITY OF NEVADA
http://eeyore.lv-hrc.nevada.edu/~cogno/para1.html

PRINCETON ENGIN. ANOMALIES RESEARCH
http://www.princeton.edu/~rdnelson/pear.html

ASSOCIATIONS AND INFORMATION RESOURCES

SCIENTIFIC AND MEDICAL NETWORK
http://www.cis.plym.ac.uk/SciMedNet/home.htmnl

EXCEPTIONAL HUMAN EXPERIENCES
http://www4.coastalnet.com/ehenet

INFORMATION ABOUT PARPASYCHOLOGY
http://www.tcm.phy.cam.ac.uk/~bdj10/psi.html

PARAPSYCHOLOGICAL ASSOCIATION
http://www.world.std.com/~parapsyc

SOCIETY FOR PSYCHICAL RESEARCH
http://moebius.psy.ed.ac.uk/spr.html

PREMONITIONS REGISTRY
http://yaaron.clever.net/precog/precog.html

INTUITION NETWORK
http://www.ih.com/Intuition

THINKING ALLOWED
http://www.thinking-allowed.com

Index

A

Akashic Records 132
Ammachi 108
Archduke Ferdinand 145
ashram 8, 10
astrological marker 44, 165
Astrology 3, 4, 5, 7, 21, 29, 43, 87, 112
Atlantis 132

B

band elevation 39
Bernard Grad 70

C

clairvoyance 19
conjunction 19, 35, 40, 49, 83, 99, 141, 149, 155
consciousness 21, 25, 128, 136, 167, 178, 183, 206
contraparallel 38, 62, 77, 141, 144, 147, 151, 155, 188, 192, 193, 194, 195
Creator 18, 103, 165, 169, 170, 171, 172

D

D-Day 76
Delphi Class healer 76, 188
Delphi marker 136
divine ego 104, 170
Divine Mind 172
DNA 27
Dr. Mitchell E. Gibson 3, 4, 12
dreamtime 24
Dusec 13, 14

E

earthquake 147
ectoplasm 184
Ed Dames 20
Edgar Cayce 4, 11, 65, 66, 122, 132, 166

Eileen Garrett 12, 20, 119, 122, 135, 136, 181
Einstein 3, 24, 54, 203
elevation 38, 41, 62, 109, 141, 149, 155, 193, 194, 195, 197, 198
ELF 24
Emmanuel Swedenborg 121, 175
ESP 18, 19, 21, 200, 202, 205, 207, 208
Evangeline Adams 43

G

general psychic ability 21, 43
Gerard Croiset 11, 20, 140
Gladys Osborne Leonard 128
grand elevation of Mercury 84, 116, 132, 136, 153, 157
Great Fire of London 141

H

healer 49, 69, 70, 72, 76, 80, 83, 90, 93, 186, 188
high declination 39

I

Indira Devi 8, 11

J

Jean Dixon 56
Joan of Arc 4, 115, 116
John F. Kennedy 58, 132, 149
Joseph McMoneagle 58, 180
Jupiter 192, 193, 194, 195, 196, 199
Jupiter Mars parallel 127, 129, 132, 193

K

Kathryn Kuhlman 91, 93

L

left-brain 175, 176, 177
Lourdes 121, 159

M

marker aspects 44, 50, 54, 66, 72, 80, 90, 99, 121, 127, 128, 129, 163, 167, 191
Mars 141, 144, 149, 157, 193, 195, 196, 199
materialization 120, 184
medical school 11, 14, 16
mediums 5, 28, 119, 121, 124, 128, 136, 175, 181, 182, 183

mediumship 21, 119, 121, 124, 127, 128, 129, 132, 135, 136, 181, 184, 189
mental telepathy 183
Michael Jordan 181, 186
Moon 30, 31, 77, 136
Moon Mercury 84, 141, 155
Morris Pratt Institute 185
mystic 53, 87, 103, 109, 169, 170, 175
mystical marker 104, 144
mystical potential 104, 106, 112, 141, 149, 159, 170
mysticism 103, 124, 169

N

Neptune 33, 93, 141, 142, 144, 147, 149, 151, 153, 159, 161
New Madrid 147
Nostradamus 4, 11, 49, 50, 53, 141, 142, 144, 147, 163

O

Olga Worrall 4, 11, 83
Ontario Hydro 19
opposition 35, 144, 155, 191

P

p/n ratio 192, 198
parallel 24, 53, 80, 129, 132, 136, 141, 144, 149
paranormal 4, 5, 12, 23, 62, 71, 77, 80, 90, 96, 99, 135, 140, 141, 142, 144, 151, 153, 155, 159, 161, 163, 165, 166, 182, 207, 210
Paul Tesla 7
Pentagon 21
perception 24, 25, 103, 136, 141, 169, 176, 177, 178, 182, 203, 205
Peter Hurkos 62, 65, 66
planet 28, 30, 33, 37, 40, 99, 102, 137, 155, 166, 191, 192, 197, 198
Pluto 33, 35, 77, 80, 129, 144, 159, 161
prediction 30, 58, 77, 140, 142, 144, 147, 155
Princess Diana 77
probability 23, 24, 141, 142, 166, 203
prophecies 50, 65, 132, 145, 166
psi 18, 19, 21, 23, 24, 25, 27, 119, 176, 181, 201
psi genes 23, 27
psychiatrist 4, 17
psychic 4, 11, 18, 19, 21, 23, 24, 26, 27, 43, 44, 50, 53, 54, 62, 65, 66, 69, 70, 72, 103, 112, 119, 120, 128, 135, 137, 140, 141, 166, 169, 174, 175, 176, 177, 179, 183, 186, 209
psychic potential 43, 44, 54, 141, 176

Q

quad 39, 109, 194, 195
quantum physics 163

R

Rasputin 4, 87
resources 179, 182, 186
right-brain 177, 178
RNA 27

S

saint 11, 115
samadhi 104, 170
Saturn 191, 193, 195, 196, 199
Sedona, Arizona 174
Serge Leon Alalouf 80
sextile 35, 141, 147, 151, 159, 191
Signs 2, 3, 4, 5, 11, 12, 27, 28, 162, 163, 167
Signs 2.0 162
Spirit 26, 119, 128, 137, 170, 174, 181, 183
spiritual 4, 5, 9, 18, 26, 35, 41, 43, 44, 53, 66, 69, 72, 103, 104, 109, 116, 119, 137, 140, 142, 163, 167, 169, 170, 172, 174, 175, 189, 200
spiritualism 119, 120, 135, 181
square 35, 77, 151, 191
Sri Matajhi 8, 11
Stanford Research Institute 54
Sufism 103, 169
SUN 102
Sun 29, 30, 32, 35, 77, 99, 141, 149, 192, 194, 195
sun 49
Sybil Leek 112

T

temporal window 144, 149, 153, 157
trine 35, 53, 80, 144, 153, 191

U

Uranus 33, 39, 77, 99, 192, 194, 195, 196
Uri Geller 53

V

Venus 32, 53, 77, 80, 99, 141, 147, 151, 157, 188, 193, 199
Vietnam 25, 61, 62
Virgin Mary 96, 121, 140, 141, 159

W

Werner Von Braun 161
World War I 50, 135
World War II 76, 77, 132, 145